CHART of the N.W. COAST of AMERICA, and N.E. COAST of ASIA. Explored by Capt. Cook and Capt. Clerke, in the Years 1778 & 1779.

ALASKA

A Golden Past, A Rich Future

Harbor Seal.

Squirrel Grass in Interior Alaska.
Ernst Schneider, photographer; courtesy of Alaska Division of Tourism.

The publisher thanks the Alaska Division of Economic Development and the Alaska Division of Tourism for their sponsorship of this publication. Specifically, the publisher thanks William Paulick and Mary Pignalberi for their unwavering enthusiasm and support.

The publisher gratefully acknowledges the efforts and contributions made in the preparation of this publication by the following individuals and organizations: the staff of the Alaska Division of Economic Development and of the Alaska Division of Tourism; Alaska Department of Commerce and Economic Development; Governor's Office, State of Alaska; Anchorage Museum of History and Art; Tundra Times; R. J. Hayes; and innumerable other groups and individuals whose help, cooperation and guidance made this project possible.

Alaska: A Golden Past, A Rich Future
Copyright 1995 by Wyndham Publications Incorporated
Printed in the United States of America

ALL RIGHTS RESERVED. No part of this book may be used or reproduced in any manner whatsoever without written permission, except in the case of brief quotations embodied in critical articles or reviews. For information, mail your request to : Wyndham Publications Incorporated, P.O. Box 45, Kirkland, Washington, 98083-0045. All information contained in this publication is accurate to the best knowledge of the publisher.

Library of Congress Catalog Card Number: 94-062215
Library of Congress Cataloging Information:
    Alaska: A Golden Past, A Rich Future
    Authors: Mike Miller
            Jeff Richardson
            Sean Reid
            Scott Foster
            Corinne Murray

Editor: Nancy Leichner
Design: Hines Design
Proofreader: Kim Sutherland
Wyndham Publications Incorporated
Vice President: Kim A. Halverson

First Edition
Includes Bibliography, Index
ISBN: 0-9634100-3-2

"How high is up?" Nalukataq blanket tossing in Pt. Barrow offers splendid recreation and teaches perfect control.
Anchorage Museum of History and Art.

Table of Contents

PART ONE

CHAPTER ONE
Alyeska — The Great Land *by Mike Miller* 8

CHAPTER TWO
The Golden Past *by Jeff Richardson* 24

CHAPTER THREE
Getting From Here to There *by Mike Miller* 40

CHAPTER FOUR
Host to the World *by Jeff Richardson* 56

CHAPTER FIVE
Communication Networks *by Scott Foster* 72

CHAPTER SIX
Entrepreneurial Spirit *by Sean Reid* 88

CHAPTER SEVEN
Challenges in the Great Outdoors *by Mike Miller* 104

CHAPTER EIGHT
Bright Minds and Strong Ideas *by Sean Reid* 118

CHAPTER NINE
Harvesting the Ocean *by Mike Miller* 134

CHAPTER TEN
Alyeska — Its Great People *by Scott Foster* 152

CHAPTER ELEVEN
The Rich Future *by Jeff Richardson* 166

LEFT: *Fourth Avenue traffic in Anchorage.*

Glory of Russia Point on St. Matthew Island.

PART TWO

Governmental and Community Organizations 180

Networks. 190

Raw Materials and Production 216

Seafood Industry 240

Business and Professional Service 250

Quality of Life 272

Building Alaska 278

Marketplace, Accommodations, Tours and Journeys 296

BIBLIOGRAPHY 312
PARTNERS IN ALASKA INDEX 314
INDEX 317

LEFT: *Sea lions.*

Introduction

Alaska is not only the largest of the 50 states — more than half a million square miles in area — it is also a land of amazing diversity and startling contrasts, as rich in history as it is in natural resources and scenic wonders.

This book is intended to offer an overview of the past, the present, and the potential of Alaska, in an eclectic mix of chapters by various authors, covering almost every aspect of life in what has come to be known as The Great Land.

Alaska's central location and ease of access, combined with unparalleled scenery, modern transportation, comfortable facilities, and almost unlimited recreational opportunities, have made it a favorite destination for millions of visitors from all over the globe. It has become a prime site for national and international conventions — and is rapidly gaining a reputation as one of the best places in today's world in which to do business.

In addition to a radio, TV, and communications network incorporating the most sophisticated technology available, Alaska boasts two other major assets as well: a skilled, educated, motivated workforce; and government entities interested in working in partnership with business and industry at every level, from local to international.

In this book, you will be introduced to some of the major corporate players in the Alaska economy, and learn more about the resources, residents, and exciting prospects for growth and development of this unique environment.

Alaska. It's big, it's beautiful, it has a future as golden as its past — and right now, it's the place to play, work, and live.

We welcome you.

Turnagain Arm, Cook Inlet.
R.J. Hayes, photographer.

PART ONE

ALYESKA: The Great Land

by Mike Miller

Mount McKinley from the Reflection Pond in Denali National Park and Preserve.
Bob Richey, photographer.

Chapter One

The name says it all. Alaska, from the Aleut word Alyeska, means "the Great Land." Great it is. In land mass, it is one-fifth the size of the continental U.S. If a map of Alaska is placed over the rest of the nation, the 49th state stretches from Minnesota and the Dakotas in northern mid-America to Florida and California in the southeast and southwest.

Also for the collector of superlatives: The continent's highest mountain rises here. Mt. McKinley, which Alaskans call Denali, climbs to a height of 20,320 feet. Alaska has more coastline (6,640 miles) than all the coastal "lower 48" states combined. The state contains more than 100,000 glaciers, a pair of which (Malaspina and Bering on the Gulf of Alaska coast) are the two biggest in North America.

To make such hugeness comprehensible, Alaskans generally break their state into five smaller regions:

• **Southeast Alaska**, the coastal panhandle of lush forested islands and mainland. It extends southeasterly from the main body of Alaska toward British Columbia, Canada and Washington state.

• **Southcentral Alaska**, a place of mountains, inlets, peninsulas and waterways. It is Alaska's most populous region. Its hub is Anchorage, Alaska's largest city.

• **The Interior**, a vast region surrounding Fairbanks, containing sky-piercing mountains, sub-Arctic tundra, and long, major, meandering rivers including the storied Yukon.

• **The Far North**, a rich but challenging land whose northern shore is lapped by waters of the Arctic Ocean.

• **Southwest Alaska**, a panoramic spectacle that ranges from gentle grasslands on the Aleutian Islands to smoldering volcanoes.

SOUTHEAST ALASKA

Curious thing about this part of Alaska, outside of the established cities, the look of Southeast Alaska has changed little from the late 1800s when naturalist John Muir came sailing this way by steamer. "To the lover of pure wildness, Alaska is one of the most wonderful countries in the world," he noted in his book *Travels in Alaska*. "Day after day, we seemed to float in true fairyland, each succeeding view more and more beautiful."

Historic cabins near Talkeetna, Alaska.
R.J. Hayes, photographer.

Alaskans have created a "Marine Highway" system of large, frequent passenger and auto ferries that connect with roads at Bellingham, Washington, Prince Rupert, B.C., Haines, and Skagway.

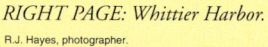
RIGHT PAGE: Whittier Harbor.
R.J. Hayes, photographer.

Now, a century later, an estimated 300,000-plus visitors sail each year on cruiseships or ferries past the same thick-forested islands. They view many of the same magnificent glaciers and they marvel, as Muir did, at whales in the water and bears on shore and at lofty mountain goats high on mountain cliffs. They, too, return to their homes convinced that this is, truly, one of earth's most treasured locales.

Southeast Alaska residents happily share this view. They reside along the little sliver of mainland and among the one thousand islands that make up the Alexander Archipelago. Their region stretches some five hundred miles from the Native community of Yakutat in the north to the Canadian border at Dixon Entrance. Mostly they make their livings from fishing, government, timber, tourism and, in recent years, from mining. Some twenty percent of Southeast's residents are Tlingit, Haida, or Tsimshian Indians; many of them choosing to live in ancestral villages such as Angoon, Hoonah, Kake, Klawock, Metlakatla, Saxman, Yakutat and others.

Alaska's state capital, Juneau, is in this region, as well as the fishing and timber community of Ketchikan (called "Alaska's First City" because it is the first city you come to as you sail up the coast); Wrangell, also active in fishing and wood products; Petersburg, called "Little Norway" because of its Scandinavian heritage; Sitka, which was the headquarters of Russian America until the Alaska

Purchase in 1867; Haines, with a rich and highly acclaimed heritage of Indian arts and crafts; and historic Skagway where visitors can re-live the Klondike Gold Rush of 1898.

No traditional highways connect these communities. Instead, Alaskans have created a "Marine Highway" system of large, frequently scheduled passenger and auto ferries that connect with main highways at Bellingham, Washington, Prince Rupert, B.C., Haines, and Skagway. Air travel, from small "bush" aircraft to large jets, is also scheduled daily and easy to arrange.

An Eskimo "umiak" (skin boat) is silhouetted by the Arctic sun.

CHAPTER ONE: ALYESKA: THE GREAT LAND

Petersburg Slough.

SOUTHCENTRAL ALASKA

In Southcentral Alaska, a traveler can visit Houston and Honolulu (on the Alaska Railroad); plus other places like Seward, Homer, Valdez, and Anchorage — especially Anchorage.

Literally half the people of Alaska live in or around Anchorage and they love it. This is Alaska's "big city" with the largest malls, the most (and most varied) restaurants, the largest corporate presence, and the greatest number of roads and highways.

Anchorage International Airport, one of the busiest in the nation, hosts jets every day from Asia, Europe, Hawaii, and the U.S., not to mention big and little planes from Alaska points like Juneau, Fairbanks, Prudhoe Bay, the Aleutian Islands and the Pribilofs in the middle of the Bering Sea. From Anchorage, one can take the Alaska

CHAPTER ONE: ALYESKA: THE GREAT LAND

Railroad southbound to Seward and Whittier or travel north past Houston and Honolulu en route to Denali National Park and Fairbanks.

For all its bigness, Anchorage is Alaskan to the core. The World Championship Open Sled Dog Race is staged here every February during the state's biggest winter whoop-it-up, the Anchorage Fur Rendezvous. The Iditarod sled dog classic, "the Last Great Race on Earth," starts here en route to Nome each March. In summer and winter, Anchorage residents and their visitors revel in the mountains, forests, shores, and waters of adjacent Chugach State Park, one of America's largest.

East of Anchorage, on Prince William Sound, lies Valdez at the southern end of the 800-mile Trans Alaska Pipeline. Sometimes called the "Switzerland of Alaska," the city and its environs is notable for its piercing, spectacular mountains and glaciers.

South of Anchorage one can drive beside the shores of Cook Inlet to the Kenai Peninsula, acclaimed for its world-class fresh and salt water angling, its federal moose refuge, its oil producing and refining facilities (the Kenai being, in fact, the birthplace of Alaska's petroleum industry). Also enjoyable are the region's recreational opportunities in and around communities like Kenai, Kalifonsky, Ninilchik, Clam Gulch, Homer, and — at the head of Resurrection Bay and Kenai Fjords National Park — Seward.

To the north of Anchorage there is Eagle River where many Anchoragites reside; Palmer and Wasilla in the agriculturally-rich Matanuska Valley; as well as Talkeetna, Big Lake, and, the popular Denali National Park and Preserve, where southcentral Alaska blends into the Interior.

The picturesque Immaculate Conception Church is located in the downtown area of Fairbanks, Alaska.

LEFT: *Hikers enjoy the forest trails that abound in Southeast Alaska, like this one near Wrangell.*

Bull walrus on Round Island, Alaska.

CHAPTER ONE: ALYESKA: THE GREAT LAND

Petersburg Harbor in Southeast Alaska.

THE INTERIOR

You are standing at the sternwheel riverboat's rail, staring down at a wooded island to which your ship is moored. You are surrounded by scores of other travelers, everyone waiting in excited anticipation. Something dramatic, you have been told, is about to happen — and it does!

From out of the woods comes an Alaska sled dog team and driver, bounding along the sandy shore like they were racing on midwinter ice. The parka-clad musher behind the sled is Mary Shields, the first woman to compete in the famed Iditarod sled dog race. Soon she will bring her team to a halt and, with the aid of a wireless microphone, she will tell passengers on board about the thrills and chills of sled dog racing, and also about Athabascan Indian village

LEFT: *Mount McKinley, Denali National Park and Preserve, is found in the Interior region of Alaska.*
R.J. Hayes, photographer.

The Fur Rendezvous is held every February in Anchorage. The festivities include an ice sculpture exhibition.

CHAPTER ONE: ALYESKA: THE GREAT LAND

culture which they will shortly witness first-hand after they disembark for a visit.

The river is the Tanana, a subsidiary of the mighty Yukon. The sternwheeler is the immensely popular riverboat Discovery. The locale is in Interior Alaska, just a short distance from Fairbanks, which serves as hub city and trading center for this region.

Immense and fascinating country this, bounded by the Canadian Yukon Territory to the east, by the Arctic to the north, and by the arc of the Alaska Range to the south. It extends westerly almost to the shore of the Bering Sea. It is a region of rolling hills and sub-Arctic tundra, of snow-capped mountains and wild rivers. Gold and coal mining is still a way of life here, as is homestead agriculture and a subsistence lifestyle, especially among Athabascan Natives. Important as well are trading and transportation, petroleum production, research and education through the University of Alaska's first campus at Fairbanks and, of course, tourism enterprises such as the riverboat Discovery.

The Interior is accessible in almost any way — by jet from Anchorage and the "lower 48" states, by road, or on the train from Anchorage by way of Denali National Park and Preserve. However travelers get there, for business or for pleasure, they will find the Alaska spirit alive, well, and thriving.

THE FAR NORTH
This is truly a magical part of Alaska. Most of it lies north of the Arctic Circle, a vast tundra land of Eskimo peoples living a lifestyle that merges many of the trappings of the twentieth century with age-old traditions such as hunting for caribou, bear and other creatures of the land and of venturing out in oomiaks to seek the bowhead whale of the Arctic Ocean.

It is also a frontier for outdoor recreation; a place of hikes and river floats and campouts in areas where the visitor may not see another human being for days. Alaska's remote Little Diomede Island, in the middle of the Bering Strait, sits just two miles from Big Diomede, part of Russia.

The region is the site of North America's greatest known oil basin. Prudhoe Bay and other nearby fields produce ten percent of the USA's petroleum. The crude is transported eight hundred miles

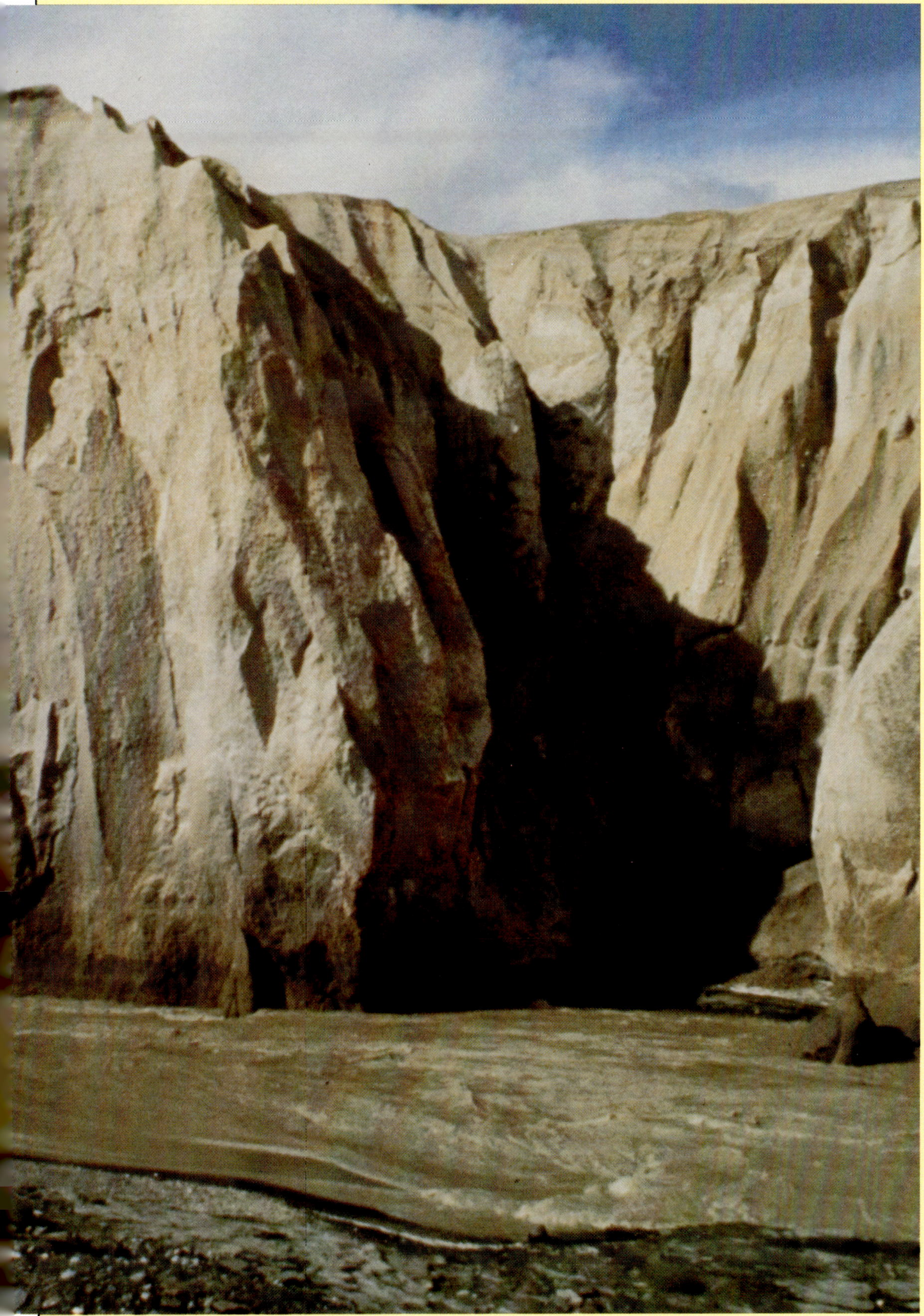

Ernst Schneider, photographer; courtesy of Alaska Division of Tourism.

At the region's extreme tip at Pt. Barrow it is a land where, beginning with sunrise on May 10th each year, the sun literally does not set for nearly three months, a fact greatly celebrated by summer visitors to the area.

The Valley of 10,000 Smokes is a beautiful and fascinating phenomenon located in Katmai National Park.

This harbor at sunset is located in Homer in the Southcentral area of Alaska.

by pipeline from a space-age living and gathering complex practically on the shores of the Arctic Ocean to Valdez, an ice-free port in southcentral Alaska's Prince William Sound.

At Pt. Barrow, the region's northernmost tip, is a land where, beginning with sunrise on May 10th each year, the sun literally does not set for nearly three months, a fact greatly celebrated by summer visitors to the area. When the sun goes down on November 18th, residents do not see it again for nearly two months.

Hub and trading centers for Far North Alaska can be found at the historic Gold Rush town of Nome, located south of the Arctic Circle on Norton Sound; the Eskimo community of Kotzebue, which lies north of the circle on Kotzebue Sound, and Barrow, the farthest north point on the continent. Access to this part of Alaska is strictly by air, except for the Dalton Highway "haul road" which stretches from a southern terminus near Fairbanks, across the Brooks Range, to Prudhoe Bay.

SOUTHWEST ALASKA

It sounds weird but Alaska contains the northernmost, westernmost, and the easternmost lands among the states of the U.S.A.: northernmost at Pt. Barrow at the very top of the North American continent; westernmost on Amatignak Island in the Aleutian Islands, which stretch toward Japan and the Russian mainland; and easternmost on Pochnoi Point on Semisopochnoi Island, also in the Aleutians. Since this and others of the farthest islands cross the 180th meridian (where west meets east), they actually reside in the globe's eastern longitudes. Ironically, the 180th meridian makes Attu Island neither the westernmost nor easternmost point in the United States, even though it is the most remote island of the Aleutians.

America's next-to-largest island can be found in Southwest Alaska; Kodiak Island comes in second only to the Big Island of Hawaii in the nation's bigness sweepstakes. If Kodiak Islanders feel slighted at their second-place status they can take comfort in the fact that America's largest land carnivore, the Kodiak bear, also calls the island home.

For visitors, the Southwest region of Alaska probably ranks as the least explored and developed of Alaska's regions. However, there are several major visitor attractions and destinations here including Kodiak (the island and the city); Katmai National Park and Preserve on the Alaska Peninsula; the Pribilof Islands way, way, way out in the middle of the Bering Sea; and Dutch Harbor/Unalaska, where a new deluxe hotel has recently opened.

The Amanita Mushroom grows on the floor of Alaskan forests.

Arctic scenes such as this one in Northern Alaska illustrate the vast and remote nature of the Alaskan wilderness.

A playful brown bear poses at McNeil River in Southwest Alaska.
Robert Angell, photographer; courtesy of Alaska Division of Tourism.

Described as "The Last Great Race," the Iditarod Trail Race starts in Anchorage and ends in Nome.

If the region is little known by most tour visitors it is certainly well-known among commercial fishers. The fishing waters off Kodiak and the Aleutians, in fact, are among the most productive in the world for salmon, crab and other bounty from the sea.

There are three ways you can visit Southwest Alaska. The most common way for both visitors and commercial travelers is by air from Anchorage. Another way to visit is by way of a few adventuresome cruiseships that venture through these waters, some of them en route to Russia. Also, the Alaska Marine Highway System's MV Tustumena schedules several Southwest sailings along portions of the chain each summer. Off-the-beaten-path travelers call it one of the most memorable trips of a lifetime.

Fact is, all of Alaska's regions are memorable, and bursting with opportunities for the visitor or the entrepreneur. Alaska, the Great Land, is a land living up to its state motto: "North to the Future!"

CHAPTER ONE: ALYESKA: THE GREAT LAND

The tundra on the North Slope is both dramatic and seemingly endless.

ALASKA:
A Golden Past

by Jeffrey Richardson

On July 13, 1938, Howard Hughes stopped in Fairbanks during his record around-the-world flight. He arrived in New York the next day, setting a record that held until after World War II.

Chapter Two

What do Wyatt Earp, Will Rogers, Ingrid Bergman, and Richard Nixon all have in common?

Alaska.

A land of complex and fascinating history, and historical paradox. One of the most remote places on earth, and one of the most cosmopolitan. A land where many have come and relatively few have stayed. A land that even now looks empty to the untutored eye, but which actually has been peopled for a millennia by diverse peoples, endowed with distinctive cultures and a shared genius for survival.

THE FIRST ALASKANS

The rich lore of the First Alaskans places their arrival here far back in a misty time full of divine mystery. Archeologists and anthropologists attribute the arrival of the first humans in Alaska to a gradual migration from Asia over a stretch of high ground where the Bering Straits now mark the boundary between the Bering and Chukchi Seas. Human occupation in Alaska has been dated as far back as 12,000 years. It should be noted that modern research has yet to achieve unanimous consent on the migration scenario. Arrival theories notwithstanding, there is no disagreement about the eventual dispersal of these hardy peoples across the vast landscape of Alaska according to patterns still very much in evidence today.

In southeast Alaska, the Tlingits, Haidas and Tsimshians built their large towns, complex societies and rich material cultures around the abundance of the deeply forested coastline, sometimes feuding and sometimes trading with the Eyak Indians of Prince William Sound, as well as various Indian groups. Further west, the Aleuts, masters of the stormy seas where they pursued their livelihood as marine mammal hunters, held sway. Their influence gave way to the Yupik Eskimos of the western coast of Alaska. Further north, above the Arctic Circle, the whaling communities of the Inupiaq Eskimos still ring the coast all the way to the Canadian border. Occupying a huge expanse of Alaska's interior river country, including the fabled Yukon and stretching all the way to Alaska's southcentral coast, lived the bands and villages of many Athabascan

Mining at Pedro Creek, circa 1915.
Huey, photographer; courtesy of Anchorage Museum of History and Art.

> Archeologists and anthropologists attribute the arrival of the first humans in Alaska to a gradual migration from Asia over a stretch of high ground where the Bering Straits now mark the boundary between the Bering and Chukchi Seas.

RIGHT PAGE: The old gold mine in Chatanika, which is near Fairbanks, is now a successful restaurant and tourist attraction.
Ernst Schneider, photographer; courtesy of Alaska Division of Tourism.

World War II spent cartridges scattered on the shore on an Aleutian Island.

Indian groups. Comprised of numerous dialects, the Athabascan were, and remain, master hunters of moose and other woodland animals.

THE EXPLORERS

There were some territorial conflicts between these groups, yet nothing compared to the clash that erupted with the arrival of a new wave of would-be Alaskans: the fur traders of the Russian Empire. Even though their tenure in Alaska only lasted 126 years, beginning in 1741 with the voyage of Vitus Bering and ending with the purchase of Alaska by the United States, the mark they left on the history of the future state was indelible. Although the interest of the court at St. Petersburg waxed and waned through the years, Russian settlement was driven far more by the fur frenzy than by grand colonial design, or royal diplomacy. Mercantile men like Baranof and Shelikof not only ran the affairs of commerce, especially the pursuit of lush sea otter pelts, they also represented the moral and municipal authority of European civilization in the wilderness. They presided over the establishment of Kodiak, Kenai, Sitka, as well as other settlements and outposts, as far north as Nulato on the Yukon River and as far south as the short-lived stockade at Fort Ross in California.

Sadly, the Russian *promyshlenniki* exploited not only otter, seals, sea lions and other furbearing animals, they also exploited the Native people they encountered with a brutality that bordered on enslavement. Some efforts were made by Russian Orthodox Church officials to halt the violence, but they had their own ideas about what was best for the indigenous peoples, and court officials were largely indifferent to their pleas.

Although the Russians ultimately gained a colonial toehold in Alaska, other European powers prowled Alaskan waters to search for their own commercial opportunities, to keep tabs on czarist expansionism and to conduct scientific research. Indeed, some of Alaska's more exotic place names bear witness to the passing of French, Spanish and English navigators, conjuring images of lands far distant from these northern latitudes. Juan Perez, a Spanish ensign, discovered and named the Queen Charlotte Islands in British Columbia in 1774. The following year, Lieutenant

A Dall sheep ewe makes its home in Denali National Park.

An unitized Cardwell Mobile Rig in South Barrow, 1951.
Anchorage Museum of History and Art.

CHAPTER TWO: ALASKA: THE GOLDEN PAST

Crow Creek Mine in Alyeska, Alaska.

Bodega y Quadra pushed further north, bestowing names like Cordova, Valdez, and Revillagigedo Island. These trips were followed by several other Spanish expeditions. Jean-Francois de Galaup, the Comte de la Perouse, carried the French flag to Alaska in 1785.

By far the best known of these seamen was Captain James Cook, the brilliant British explorer who was the first to systematically and accurately chart many Alaskan waters. In the time-honored tradition, he, too, gave names to landmarks which have become fixtures in Alaskan history and geography: Prince William Sound, Cook Inlet, Turnagain Arm, Prince of Wales Island and Bristol Bay, to name a few.

The great Russian bear, which eventually retreated, left a mixed legacy in Alaska. From Sitka to New Stuyahok, the distinctive domes of Russian Orthodox churches look down on congregations dating from the Russian occupation and experiencing a renaissance, of sorts. Some folk dances and cuisine survive in several communities, as well. But the decades of fur slaughter sealed the doom of several bird and animal species; sea otters have only recovered relatively recently. Likewise, Native communities were decimated by disease and their traditional lifeways disrupted or destroyed.

ALASKA AND THE UNITED STATES

In light of the harsh treatment of Natives, it is ironic that when the U.S. "bought" Alaska from the Czar in 1867, it was not, per se, a real estate transaction. Though the years would long obscure the fact in the public mind, the Russian and American negotiators understood clearly that the land belonged to the original occupants by virtue of actual and long-standing use and possession. The Russians never occupied more than a fragile coastal fringe in a few areas. The Treaty of Cession and subsequent U.S. laws acknowledged the existence of this "Native title" and promised that it would be formalized at a later time. What Secretary of State William H. Seward essentially bought for $7.2 million was the opportunity for unhindered American exploitation of Alaska. The unresolved question of Native title was effectively deferred for another hundred years.

Actually, Americans moved only slowly to exercise their new

Prospectors in 1898 brave the winter snows as they ascend the summit of Chilkoot Pass.

option. Several fact-finding expeditions were initiated, both military and private. American whalers ventured further and with increasing regularity along the Arctic coast, a region rich in marine mammals. Late in the 19th century, the first commercial fish processing plants appeared in some of the forested, fog-bound inlets of southeast Alaska.

Alaska's first really defining moment under American rule sprang from the wanderings of prospectors who braved terrible privations in the form of mosquitoes, extreme summer heat, brutal winter cold, isolation and rugged terrain, essentially in search of a miracle. They picked, panned and shoveled up and down the tidewater creeks and boreal streams in search of gold. Ironically, the Russians had found the precious metal on the Kenai Peninsula in 1848, but kept it to themselves. There were important strikes both before and after Canada's huge discovery on the Klondike in 1896. But the proximity of Alaska to the Klondike brought unprecedented numbers of prospectors into the new American territory, and in 1896, Alaska was indelibly marked on the world's map when gold was found on the beaches of Nome in 1898 — a lot of gold. Daniel Libby had actually found color in 1866 but was not immediately

This is one of the last photographs taken of Will Rogers and Wiley Post at Fairbanks in August of 1935. They crashed near Pt. Barrow on August 15, 1935.

Russian ferry pilots for the American planes flown from Alaska, in 1943.

Near Illiamna Village, salmon is drying in a traditional manner.

able to return to further the search. By 1900, Nome was a rowdy city of 20,000, full of saloons and con men of all description. Nome was also the home for a time of Wyatt Earp, who came north to put memories behind him.

Other minerals have become important to Alaska's modern economy, but gold still ranks high on the list, and remains the stuff of dreams. All over Alaska, ghost towns, small hamlets and thriving cities mark the trails of Alaskan prospectors, including Silver Bay (where gold was discovered in 1874, near Sitka), Juneau (1880), Resurrection Creek (1888), Sunrise (1896), Chistochina (1898), Fairbanks (1902), Valdez Creek (1903), Ruby (1907), Iditarod (1909) and Marshall (1913), to name but a few. In some of these remote places, miners are still toiling after elusive fortunes, but their long-term importance to Alaska was the cumulative effect they had in "opening up the country," at least a little bit, and making people more aware of this remote American possession.

Still, in the minds of most, Alaska was a cold and distant place rich in natural resources, and resource extraction was what brought most people to America's north. After the big gold strikes peaked and after the rushes slowed to a trickle and the human tide was actually reversed and more flowed out than in, life settled into a relatively quiet period. For those who stayed in the largely roadless country, life was enhanced by the advent of the airplane. Newspapers the world over were filled with the exploits and record-breaking flights of aviators. It was during this period that Will Rogers and Wiley Post, embarking on an international tour in their small plane,

of persistent drumbeating on the part of territorial leaders, but Washington finally awoke to Alaska's strategic importance and the potential threat of Japanese invasion. An enormous construction campaign hacked a series of army posts out of tundra, forest and swamp. Garrisons from as few as a dozen to as many as tens of thousands of GIs were exposed to the beauty and prospects of Alaska during their tours of duty. They were also entertained by the likes of film star Ingrid Bergman and other Hollywood luminaries, even as they went about the very serious business of repulsing the Japanese invasion of the Aleutian Islands and supporting the movement of aircraft and other Lend Lease supplies to Russia.

With the end of hostilities, a lot of military personnel decided to stay, or return to start civilian life in a new land. They also added

A Tlingit woman and her son have on their traditional Potlatch dancing costumes.

made a fateful trip to Barrow that cost them their lives. Bush flying, sometimes reckless, never a sure thing, gave rise to a generation of heroes who hauled mail, mining supplies, pregnant women in mid-delivery, missionaries, sled dogs and more mundane passengers and cargo.

If gold fever gave Americans a solid beachhead in their Alaskan wilderness, a second human wave washed into the territory as the conflicts leading to World War II deepened and embroiled people all over the world, even in the most remote arenas. It took several years

The Kennecott Mine, near the Kennecott Glacier, is in Southcentral Alaska.

significantly to a growing body of territorial electorate who favored statehood over colonial status.

Although the first statehood bill had been introduced in 1916, national apathy, remoteness and other factors combined to frustrate the aspirations of residents who sought economic and political parity with their southern neighbors. Also, mining and fishing interests, controlled by outside corporations, had always fought hard against statehood, fearing higher taxes and curtailment of their prerogatives. Fisheries conflicts were especially bitter in southeast Alaska, where the fish traps employed by large commercial operators at the mouths of salmon spawning streams stirred charges that fish stocks were being decimated. While some historians and biologists today are less than certain this was true, the fish traps became a potent symbol in the fight for statehood, which was seen by many as a struggle both to throw off the yoke of federal indifference and to end the economic imperialism exercised by outside corporations, many of whom were based in Seattle and Portland. After statehood was finally attained in

Emptying a salmon trap, circa 1940.

RIGHT PAGE: *Kitch Kawk of Sitka in traditional Tlingit dancing garb, circa 1900.*

CHAPTER TWO: ALASKA: THE GOLDEN PAST

CHAPTER TWO: ALASKA: THE GOLDEN PAST

1959, one of the first acts of the new legislature was to outlaw the hated fish traps.

When the Statehood Act was finally signed by President Dwight Eisenhower, one of the smiling onlookers was Vice President Richard Nixon. When Nixon moved into the White House, he played an even more pivotal role in Alaska's history. It was during his administration that the long-neglected question of Native land rights finally came to a head. During the mid-1960s, Natives from across the state had come together in a powerful political block to rectify a long list of trespass grievances in the courts and Congress. Their claims were substantially validated when the Secretary of Interior froze all land disposals in the state until the issue was resolved. In 1969, a super giant oil field was discovered at Prudhoe Bay, launching the state's modern era, but construction of a pipeline to get the oil to market

Goldstream Dredge #8 in Fairbanks, Alaska.

An Eskimo woman at Wainwright tends a copper seal oil lamp, circa 1920.

LEFT PAGE: *WWII relics remain in Dutch Harbor, in the Aleutian Islands.*
Ernst Schneider, photographer; courtesy of Alaska Division of Tourism.

CHAPTER TWO: ALASKA: THE GOLDEN PAST

This once hard-working steam shovel is now retired to Alaskaland, an amusement park in Fairbanks.

could not proceed with federal lands tied up in the Native claims dispute. Because of this convergence of factors, oil companies are often credited with tipping the balance of the land claims debate in favor of the Native settlement. In truth, the industry was forced to back a settlement because the Natives had so forcefully argued their claims before the judge who granted the injunction against pipeline construction.

Nixon signed the Alaska Native Claims Settlement Act of 1971 into law. Almost a decade later, President Jimmy Carter signed the Alaska National Interest Lands Conservation Act. These two statutes have resolved long-standing questions of land ownership and natural resource management in Alaska, even as they have stirred new controversies. Alaska has matured into statehood in a world vastly smaller and more complex than when it was acquired as an American territory. It is a world that still looks to Alaska as a source of minerals, timber, fisheries, oil and gas, but increasingly values the state's rich biological treasures and wilderness qualities. Alaskans have always faced their challenges with vigor and creativity. Despite the present-day complexities visited on Alaska by its past, it is the spirit of Alaskans, pulling together, that strongly suggest its bright future.

Getting from Here to There

by Mike Miller

Alaskan roads open up some of the world's most majestic country.
R.J. Hayes, photographer.

Chapter Three

"Alaska," someone noted a few years back, "is the State of Being in Motion."

It is true. Alaska, although truly the "Last Frontier" state of the U.S.A., has some of the mostmodern air fleets and sophisticated support networks in the nation for carrying people and cargo throughout the north country in big jets, intermediate aircraft, helicopters and smaller bush planes. The same can be said about the vast array of huge to little vessels that ply Alaska's ocean, inlet and river waterways and about the ports, harbors, and infrastructure that serve them. Also, the state's highways and railways, though limited in miles of road and track, nonetheless serve the vast majority of Alaska's residents and visitors quite successfully. If one wants to get somebody or something from here to there in Alaska there is a way to do it. Reliably. Safely. Quickly.

AIR TRAVEL

First, about Alaska's love affair with the airplane:

It all started in the 1920s, back in the days of Colonel Carl Ben Eielson who pioneered airborne mail service from Fairbanks into the bush and in 1928 made international history by flying across the top of the world from Alaska to Spitsbergen, Norway; and by the likes of Noel Wien, first pilot to land his plane on the north side of the Arctic Circle; and Joe Crosson, who brought out the bodies of Will Rogers and Wiley Post after the pair's tragic crash at Barrow in 1935. In Southeast Alaska, float plane pilots such as Bob Ellis of Ketchikan and Shell Simmons of Juneau connected island and mainland towns and villages in their float planes and amphibians.

Today, the legacy of these pioneers endures with modern jet service not only to Anchorage, Fairbanks, Juneau and other large cities but to smaller communities such as Wrangell and Petersburg in the southeast panhandle, Nome and Barrow in the far north, and Bethel and Dutch Harbor in the southwest.

The era of the "bush pilot" flying small, single-engine aircraft, however, is far from over. From one end of the state to another, serving the biggest communities and the tiniest, there remain numerous small-plane charter pilots and scheduled carriers ready and anxious to haul groceries to a remote prospector's cabin, or to

A moose takes time for a dip.
Alaska Division of Tourism.

Until the 1930s and beyond, when airlines like Pan American began their first tentative schedules between the Pacific Northwest and Alaska, steamship passenger and freight service provided the only real link between the United States and that nation's northernmost territory.

RIGHT PAGE: The services provided to the shipping industry by regional port authorities, such as the Port of Anchorage, are a key element to the expansion of international trade and the growth of the state's economy.
R.J. Hayes, photographer.

The Alaska Marine Highway System is vital for both the transportation and the shipping it provides.

transport a fly fisherman to the banks of a near-virgin lake, or to deliver a village patient to a big-city hospital. They will even take a passenger for a helicopter landing and a half hour's trek on the face of a frozen glacier.

WATERBORNE COMMERCE

The history of water transportation in Alaska begins with Native Alaskans and their ingenuous use of oomiaks, bidarkas, and long canoes to hunt seals, walrus, bowhead whales, sea otters and other bounty of the sea as well as to transport trade goods and people over vast stretches of water.

Beginning with Vitus Bering sailing from Siberia for the Russian czar in 1741, the first Europeans to visit Alaska arrived here, of course, by boat. A century and a half later, when gold was discovered in the Canadian Klondike, stampeders crowded aboard just about any West Coast hulk which could float in order to reach Alaska with its access to the Yukon goldfields. Until the 1930s and beyond, when airlines like Pan American began their first tentative schedules between the Pacific Northwest and Alaska, steamship passenger and freight service provided the only real link between the United States and that nation's northernmost territory.

Even today, ships, freighters, huge tankers, barges and ferries are the mainstay of the coastal Alaska transportation system, hauling foodstuffs, household goods, petroleum, and business-industrial supplies to the 49th state; and fish, timber, crude oil, petrochemicals, coal, and other Alaska goods outbound. Water transport may no longer be "the only game in town" for moving cargo and people around the state, but it remains a primary way to do so.

In recent decades, summer cruiseship and ferry travel has mushroomed to the point where more than three dozen cruiseliners and ferryliners carry hundreds of thousands of passengers each year from various west coast ports including Seattle and Bellingham in Washington state, Vancouver and Prince Rupert in British Columbia and between Alaskan communities. Among the cruiseliners, two type of vessels are popular. The mega liners (actually floating resorts) have the capacity to carry from 550 to 1,600 passengers and the smaller more intimate ships accommodate between 35 to 150 guests. Three basic itineraries have evolved: Traditional round trip or one way

In Kotzebue, getting to and from the grocery store is sometimes best done with a combination of old technology and new.

The Alaska Highway, though unquestionably the best known of Alaska's roadways, is only one of many, mostly in southcentral and interior Alaska, that link the state's communities to one another.

Helicopters provide needed access to Alaska's most remote and difficult-to-reach places.

CHAPTER THREE: GETTING FROM HERE TO THERE

The community of Indian, Alaska is located south of Anchorage on Turnagain Arm. Alaskans have developed a uniquely Alaskan network of shipping and transportation that reaches even the most remote of communities.

CHAPTER THREE: GETTING FROM HERE TO THERE

Monkey flowers.

"Inside Passage" voyages from Vancouver, Seattle or other west coast points to the southeast panhandle; "Glacier Route" trips that include the Inside Passage plus travel along the Gulf of Alaska to Prince William Sound, Seward, and even Anchorage; and intra-Alaska sailings, usually between ports in Southeast Alaska such as Ketchikan and Juneau.

ALASKAN HIGHWAYS

Alaska's highway connection with the contiguous 48 states began during World War II when, in order to establish a land link to the militarily-vital Territory of Alaska, the U.S. and Canada built the "Alcan Highway" (Alaskans, today, do not care for that name. They prefer "Alaska Highway"). Construction of the 1,400-mile military road was an incredible accomplishment. Officially, construction began on March 8, 1942 and reached completion October 25, 1942, an interval of only eight months and twelve days. It was hard, miserable work, with thousands of U.S. and Canadian construction troops and civilian workers enduring eight-hour shifts, seven days a week, in terrain that generated hordes of hungry mosquitoes and vicious black flies in the hot months of the summer and sub-zero temperatures in the winter.

Crews working from east and west converged and met at Contact Creek on September 25, 1942. Alaska would never again be the same. Road travel to and from the contiguous 48 states, at first reserved for the military but later opened to civilian use, became a reality.

Passengers take in Alaska's beauty from the solarium deck of an Alaska Marine Highway System ferry.

Modern cranes and transfer equipment are made available by port authorities to attract the business of major shippers.

CHAPTER THREE: GETTING FROM HERE TO THERE

Floatplanes, like this one in the Misty Fjords of the Inside Passage, are a major mode of transportation throughout the coastal areas of Alaska.

Today, the Alaska Highway is one of the north country's grand adventure roads. Between Mile 0 at Dawson Creek, B.C., Canada and the official end of the highway at Mile 1422 in Delta Junction it is almost entirely paved. It is the route of choice each year for tens of thousands of automobile drivers, RV campers, truckers, motorcoach visitors and even bicyclists.

The Alaska Highway, though unquestionably the best known of Alaska's roadways, is only one of many, mostly in southcentral and interior Alaska, that link the state's communities to one another. They range from high-speed paved and modern (the George Parks Highway, for instance, from its start thirty five miles out of Anchorage to Denali National Park and Fairbanks) to take-it-slow-and-easy gravel (for example, the McCarthy Road which leads from Chitina to the almost-ghost-town of McCarthy). Many of these roads are historic former sled dog and horse trails, such as the Richardson from Valdez to Fairbanks and the Haines Highway from Haines to Haines

LEFT PAGE: *Vehicles are loaded on an Alaska Marine Highway System ferry in Haines, Alaska.*
Linda Mickle, photographer; courtesy of Alaska Marine Highway System.

Huskies are specially bred as trail dogs adapted to the cold Alaskan winter conditions.

Wildflowers near Skagway.

Junction in the Yukon. Others are newly constructed for a specific purpose, like the Dalton Highway "haul road" to supply Prudhoe Bay on the North Slope and pipeline pump stations along the way.

One thing can be said for them all — they open up some of the world's most majestic country. Even truckers, negotiating their rigs on long hauls for the hundred and umpteenth time, revel in the mountain, forest, and water scenery they are privy to.

ALASKA'S RAILROADS

Railroading in Alaska is, well, different. Consider this report, by a nationally published travel writer, who took the state-owned Alaska Railroad from Anchorage to Fairbanks not long ago:

"They call it 'moosing' and what happens is this. Early in the afternoon at about the mid-point between Alaska's two largest cities, the northbound Alaska Railroad train out of Anchorage approaches the southbound train from Fairbanks on adjacent tracks. As the two trains pass one another, passengers who want to play 'moose' face out of their windows toward the other train with thumbs and fingers outstretched at right angles to their heads. The idea is to make their hands look like bull moose antlers. When the other train passes by, everyone wiggles their 'antlers' vigorously, laughing uproariously at the sight of others doing the same thing in the passing rail cars."

"Moosing" is just one of the features that sets Alaska rail travel apart from train transportation elsewhere. For a state not even accessible by train, Alaska offers a surprising number of options and surprises. Among them:

RIGHT: C47 for salmon transport from Egegik to Kodiak.

CHAPTER THREE: GETTING FROM HERE TO THERE

Even the vast rivers of ice such as Bering Glacier, shown here, are accessible. A helicopter pilot will take passengers out for an opportunity to walk on the frozen face of a glacier.

A young spectator takes in the sights at the Iditarod Trail Race.

Sixteen glaciers flow from the mountains into the waters of the spectacular Glacier Bay National Park in Southeast Alaska. Visitors can sightsee by cruise or "flightsee" by helicopter.
Alaska Division of Tourism.

CHAPTER THREE: GETTING FROM HERE TO THERE

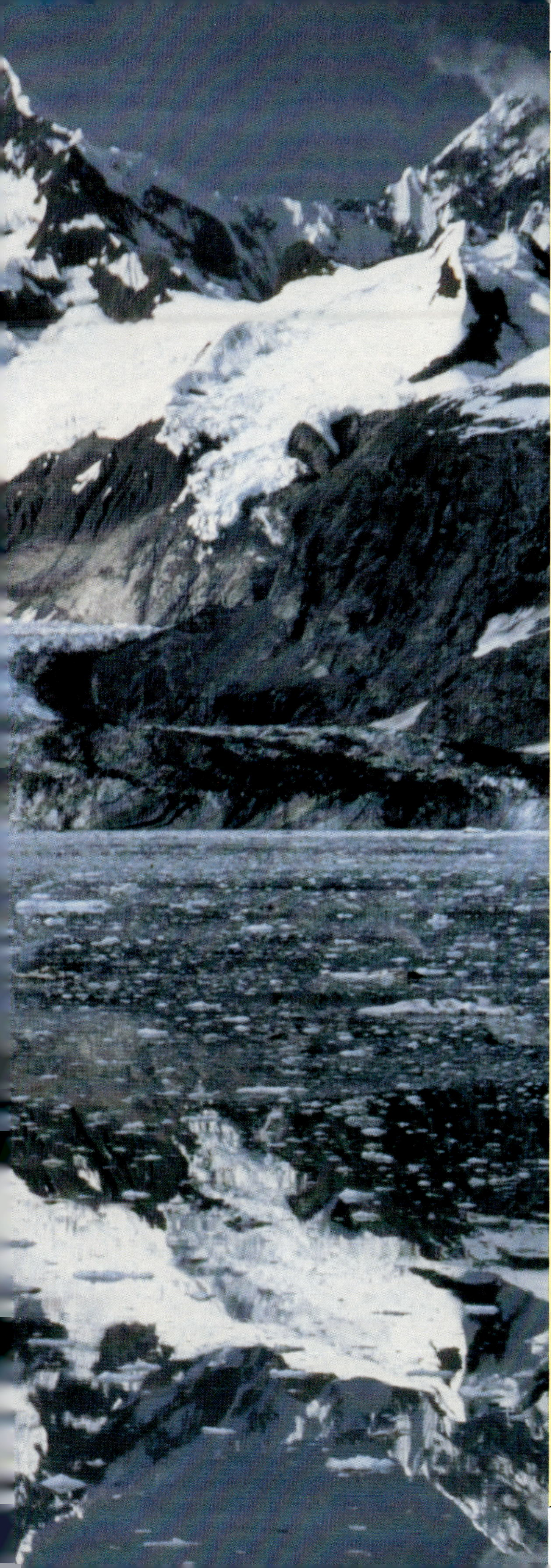

Ernst Schneider, photographer; courtesy of Alaska Division of Tourism.

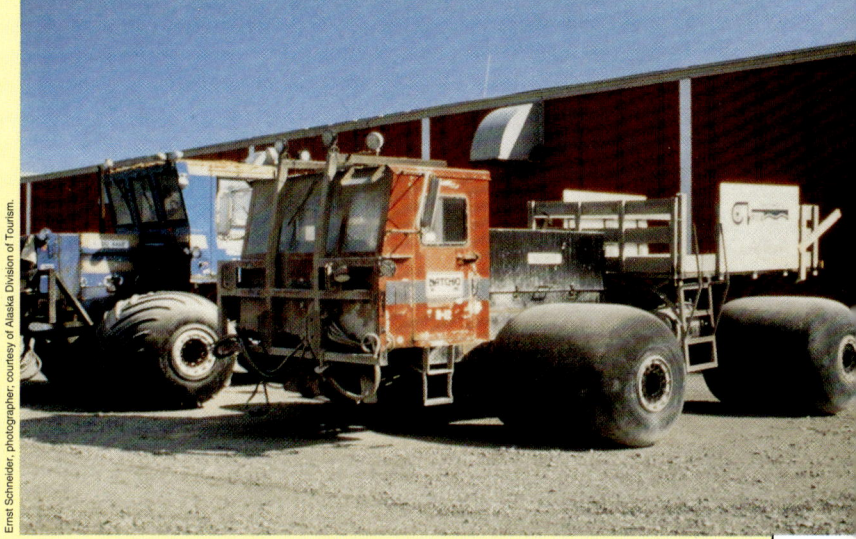

Special tundra trucks are often used in the North Slope area.

• The opportunity to drive the family vehicle aboard an Alaska Railroad flat car and ride "piggyback" along the coast of Cook Inlet and through tunnels to Whittier, where one can drive aboard an Alaska state ferry to Valdez.

• The choice of summer travel in privately-owned luxury dome cars attached to the rear of the ARR, with gourmet dining and special service en route to Denali National Park from Anchorage or Fairbanks.

• The option to book regular Alaska Railroad passenger service in comfortable standard coaches, with dining cars that feature Alaska seafood. Most Alaskan rail travelers choose this option.

• Even the opportunity to take off-the-beaten-path excursions in RDCs (for "rail diesel cars") that combine locomotive, coach, and caboose all in one unit. Among such adventures is the trip from Anchorage to breathtaking Hurricane Gulch. On this trip, if a passenger wants to get off with a fishing rod and some camping gear at a promising lake or stream, the passenger just needs to tell the conductor and he will literally stop the train. The passenger can flag the train and get back aboard the next day, or the next week.

Visitors can travel on the vintage 1890s cars of the White Pass & Yukon Route, one of the world's most scenic mountain railways.

CHAPTER THREE: GETTING FROM HERE TO THERE

• Further south, at the top of the Southeast Alaska panhandle, the venerable White Pass & Yukon Route, established in the gold rush days of 1898 and using coach cars with the look of that era, offers daily round trips in the summer from Skagway at sea level through rugged mountains to White Pass Summit, Inspiration Point, Dead Horse Gulch and Lake Bennett in British Columbia.

Passenger service, for Alaskans and visitors, is of course only one facet of the Alaskan rail picture. The role of the Alaska Railroad in hauling goods and resources, especially in the more heavily populated southcentral and interior regions, cannot be overlooked. The "rail belt," as Alaskans refer to it, extends nearly five hundred miles from saltwater at Whittier and Seward to Anchorage and on to Fairbanks. Freight service in these regions is frequent and dependable. Regular trains operate between Anchorage and Fairbanks; coal trains are scheduled from Healy to the port of Seward (where cargo is shipped to the Far East) and from Healy to Fairbanks; and trains regularly meet rail barges from Seattle and Prince Rupert, B.C. at Whittier. In addition, trains haul gravel from Palmer to Anchorage in the summer.

As was noted earlier, if one wants to get somebody or something from here to there in Alaska there is a way to do it - reliably, safely, and quickly. Especially in the area of transporting people, the process is sure to be a rich and memorable experience as well.

Jeff King, top center, poses with his support team on the first day of the 1994 Iditarod Trail Race. King is one of the highest ranked mushers in the state of Alaska.

Floatplanes on Auke Lake near Juneau.

CHAPTER THREE: GETTING FROM HERE TO THERE

Host to the World

by Jeffrey Richardson

These families are taking advantage of low tide for some clam digging, the result of which is a lot of fun and some good eating!
Alaska Division of Tourism.

Chapter Four

As long as people have been curious about Alaska, Alaskans have been willing to show them the sights that make the land such a rich, alluring destination. Chuck West, who deserves much of the credit for the birth of modern tourism in Alaska due to his pioneering efforts in developing tours by air, coach and all kinds of vessels, remembers the germ of an idea that came to him as he tundra-hopped by bush plane just after World War II:

"All the while during those bush pilot days—during the cargo flights, the passenger flights, the rescue flights—my enchantment with the land grew. And an idea grew along with it. If the land enchanted me, why not others? We could draw tourist travelers— just sightseers—from Fairbanks, take them round trip to Nome and Kotzebue, walk them through an Eskimo village, show them houses built on stilts, recount Nome's gold rush history, return to Fairbanks past the icy slopes of Mt. McKinley. In a single busy day, we could give travelers the flavor of this great land and a glimpse of the people who inhabit it."

The vast majority of the people lucky enough to have visited Alaska have come with dreams and left with memories packed into painfully short excursions. Although Alaska was built primarily by those who came expressly to open up the country and extract its riches, sometimes tourists became residents, lending their skills and talents to the community. This time-honored romance between Americans and their largest state continues to this day, as more and more people come to reap Alaska's wealth-in-place: its majestic scenery and unparalleled attractions.

EARLY ALASKA TOURISM

For those who put down roots in the Great Land, there is a special pride in showing off the beauty, the history and unique way of life that distinguishes Alaska from its southern relations. Combine this with the fabled hospitality of the north, where the arrival of a visitor or visitors has always brought at least a temporary respite from the isolation of remote communities and settlements, and one has the beginning of Alaska's visitor industry, a tradition dating almost to the time of the purchase of the territory from Russia. Certainly there

A sleepy Red Fox gives the photographer a yawn.
Robert Angell, photographer; courtesy of Alaska Division of Tourism.

For those who put down roots in the Great Land, there is a special pride in showing off the beauty, the history and unique way of life that distinguishes Alaska from its southern relations.

RIGHT PAGE: Many beautiful and scenic spots can be found near the University of Alaska Southeast Sitka campus.
University of Alaska.

A group of hikers pause on the historic Chilkoot Trail near Skagway in Southeast Alaska.

were travelers making their own adventurous way to Alaska before the advent of scheduled conveyances of formal accommodations, and precisely pinpointing tourism's modest beginnings is nearly impossible. However, it is known that in 1875, the Oregon Steamship Company took over a mail contract between San Francisco, Portland and southeast Alaska. In 1881, the Pacific Coast Steamship Company began to compete and that company's vessels, the *Ancon*, the *Idaho* and the *Eureka*, began to carry increasing numbers of passengers. By 1885, a book called *Journeys to Alaska*, which was comprised of newspaper columns and directed as much at the excursionist as at "business" travelers, was extolling the scenic splendor of the forested coast of the region with its evergreen-scented mists, abundant marine life and tidewater glaciers. Through such publicity, the ships themselves soon became draws. While they carried the rugged cargo of the territorial trade—food, building supplies, machinery, cattle, salt fish, gold—the vessels boasted fine

Dogsledding at Denali National Park and Preserve.

staterooms and other accommodations, at a cabin rate of $30 to Sitka, and steerage of $15.

It is interesting that many of the sights and activities which lure tourists to Alaska today were absorbing visitors one hundred years ago. Despite the rudimentary nature of the tours themselves, Indian villages, gold mining and scenery attracted those early tourists. Eliza Ruhamah Scidmore, author of *Journeys to Alaska*, described a visit to Taku Glacier that would curl the hair of a modern tour director. Passengers, who changed into more rugged attire, were rowed close to shore. Then crew members, who had been ferried over from the ship, carried them high and dry above the frigid surf to the beach. From there, the passengers climbed to a scenic spot and snacked on soda crackers in view of the river of ice. Crewmen were known to drop their burdens on occasion and given the vagaries of the tide, passengers had sometimes to wade in the shallows before regaining the ship.

The Egan Convention Center in Anchorage.

A popular excursion for visitors is a float trip, like this one on the Eagle River, near Anchorage.

In December, 1894, the Alaska Steamship Company was founded, ending the monopoly of the Pacific Coast line and inaugurating decades of loyal service to Alaska. Competition between the two was brisk and became even livelier as gold strikes began to draw thousands north. As the century drew to a close, Alaska Steamship Company put the 1500-ton, steel, twin screw *Dolphin* into service, a serious bid to cultivate the travel-for-pleasure trade. Pacific Coast responded by offering a thirty-day excursion to Nome by way of the White Pass and Yukon Railroad. Ever since, adding and deleting vessels and vehicles, developing rail and aircraft travel routes, constantly packaging and re-packaging tour options in response to the moods of the market, have been a hallmark of Alaska's visitor industry.

An Alaska Steamship Company flyer, a fancy piece of collateral worthy of today's glossy public relations, distributed at trade shows and other functions before the 1940s, may also sound familiar to the

A herd of bull caribou near the Colville River, in Arctic Alaska.
Bob Ritchie, photographer; courtesy of ABR.

Anchorage Visitor Information Center — the Log Cabin.

> Visitors and Alaskan residents could probably debate with vigor whether the state has retained its primeval character, but of true wilderness there is plenty.

Alaska visitor of today. Printed on the back of a colorful totemic cutout, the flyer read in part:

"Alaska is calling you! Visit the land of the Midnight Sun, dazzling Glaciers, inspiring fjords and weird Totems."

"See the Gold and Copper Mines, Fisheries and Salmon Canneries in operation."

"Sail Alaska's azure waters, flanked by evergreen shores and towering snow-capped mountains."

"Tour our Northern Wonderland while it is still primeval."

Visitors and Alaskan residents could probably debate with vigor whether the state has retained its primeval character, but of true wilderness there is plenty. The perception—largely correct—of Alaska being wild, pristine and full of adventure waiting to happen—continues to be a large part of its draw.

ALASKA TOURISM TODAY

Statistics regularly compiled by the Alaska Division of Tourism shed light on the tastes and attitudes of visitors to modern Alaska, now approaching one million annually. Nearly three quarters of these travel to the state strictly for pleasure; while eleven percent are visiting friends and relatives; ten percent come for business only; seven percent mix business and pleasure during their Alaska travels. On a scale of one-to-seven (with seven being excellent), seventy percent of Alaskan visitors rate their trip at six or seven! A high percentage also indicate the trip exceeded their high expectations and that they would readily recommend an Alaskan visit to their friends. The average visitor spends ten nights in Alaska.

Evidence of tourism's growing impact on Alaska's economy is graphically illustrated by the statistics. Spending by tourists has been steadily increasing. Recently, total summer season expenditures reached approximately $600 million in-state. On average, vacation/pleasure visitors spend $780 during their stay in Alaska, while those traveling for business and pleasure average $905 per trip. Visiting friends and relatives and those traveling to Alaska only for business spend an average of $419 and $399, respectively. Among all visitors,

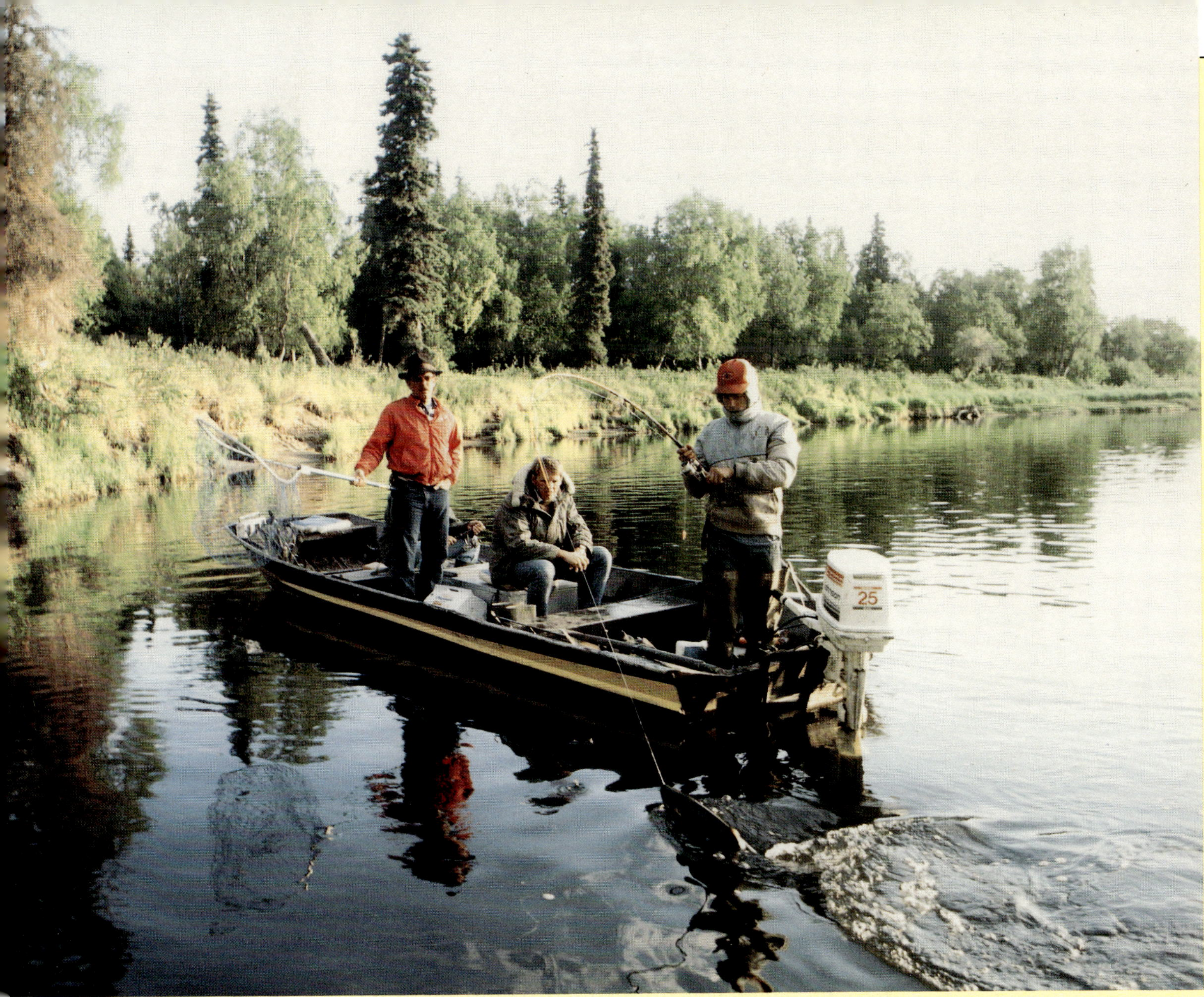

R.J. Hayes, photographer.

Alaska offers some of the finest fishing any angler could hope for.

the largest amount of money spent is for tours and recreation ($174.9 million annually), followed by transportation ($108.5 million), food and beverage ($78.5 million) and gifts and souvenirs ($77.5 million). The average vacation visitor spends $257 for tours (mostly day tours), $144 for transportation, $142 for lodging, $84 for food and beverage and $105 on souvenirs.

Glaciers are among the state's most prominent features; three of them are among the state's ten most visited attractions. Glaciers alone receive well over a million non-resident visitors drawn by these dynamic sheets of ice which continue to shape the land before our very eyes as they gouge valleys and push up ridges, sometimes advancing, sometimes retreating according to the dictates of nature. Many are accessible by road, including Mendenhall Glacier near Juneau, Portage and Matanuska Glaciers near Anchorage and Exit Glacier near Seward. Flight seeing, both by helicopter and fixed-

Alaska Division of Tourism.

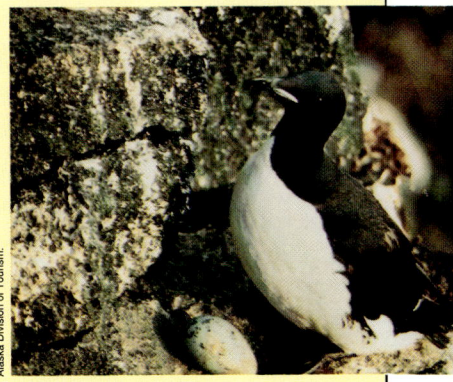

A mother looks after her precious egg on her rocky perch. The murre nests on rock ledges.

CHAPTER FOUR: HOST TO THE WORLD

The Sullivan Arena, in Anchorage, Alaska.

wing aircraft offers another cost-effective way to see the ice fields from a dramatic perspective, although watching the glaciers drop huge chunks of ice into the sea as an experienced skipper edges your vessel in close is hard to beat for excitement. Popular tidewater glaciers include the vast panorama of ice in Glacier Bay and those which sweep down to Prince William Sound.

There are also prominent glaciers draping the shoulders of North America's tallest mountain, Mt. McKinley. Mountains in general seem to hold a special attraction for Alaska's visitors and residents alike, and none more so than this giant, rising abruptly and without peer as the crown jewel of the Alaska Range. Because of its height and location, it actually spawns its own weather patterns and presents serious challenges to climbers. Before they go home, more than 300,000 visitors to the mountain each summer will know it by the name Alaskans prefer, the moniker bestowed by the Native people who first saw it—*Denali*, roughly and appropriately translated as the Great One.

While Native cultures have always been a curiosity to visitors, this curiosity is increasingly satisfied by attractions designed, owned and operated by Native communities and organizations. There is a growing emphasis on "living culture," exhibiting art, dance, history

LEFT PAGE: Portage Glacier flows into Portage Lake, creating this icy splendor. Portage Glacier is in Southcentral Alaska, near Anchorage.

These hikers are enjoying the greenery of Southeast Alaska, near Skagway.

Low bush cranberries.

and values in the context of daily life in many of Alaska's Native villages. The surging worldwide interest in eco-tourism has created an excellent opportunity to combine Native cultural experiences with air and river tours that also highlight scenic and natural wonders. High-quality attractions have been or are being developed by all of the state's major cultural groups. The elaborately-garbed dancers and carved totems of southeast Alaska draw visitors to America's largest rain forest. Several tours and exhibits highlight the survival ingenuity of Inupiat and Yupik Eskimo and Athabascan Indian peoples of the Arctic and sub-arctic. The Alutiiq Dancers of Kodiak have brought their ancient seagoing culture back from the

RIGHT PAGE: An ice climber faces the elements near Anchorage.

CHAPTER FOUR: HOST TO THE WORLD

This friendly face was part of the security team at the 1994 Iditarod Trail Race.

edge of oblivion at the hands of Russian fur hunters and gained considerable renown in the process.

Although the Russian chapter of Alaska's history has its dark side, it intrigues many visitors because of its rough parallels to the colonial heritage that sprang from the eastern seaboard. It also left behind quaint vestiges of a rich and aesthetically pleasing material culture. Major exhibits and activities and restored structures dating from the Russian era can be seen in Kodiak, Kenai and Sitka.

Many travelers just cannot seem to get enough Gold Rush mystique. Luckily, Alaska has a lot of it to share. From rustic ruins, working gold mines that welcome visitors and replicated saloons with can-can and melodrama to Gold Rush towns preserved in whole or in part, Alaska's prospecting trails are clearly marked. Sunshine, Hope, Independence, Chitina and Skagway are just a few of the venues for the visitor plagued with a case of gold fever. Railroads, too, are inseparable from Alaska's mining history. The state-owned Alaska Railroad was built to open up the country and

Ketchikan claims to have the largest collection of totem poles in the world located at the Totem Heritage Center, Saxman Park and Totem Bight State Park, where this totem can be seen.
Alaska Division of Tourism.

CHAPTER FOUR: HOST TO THE WORLD

threads its way from tidewater in Seward into the Golden Heart city of Fairbanks. The White Pass and Yukon Route Railway, which figured in those early package tours to Nome during its heyday, still provides a breathtaking narrow gauge route into the history of Alaska's golden beginnings.

Besides a railroad, the state owns and operates the Alaska Marine Highway, a ferry system that augments its modern air and highway routes, providing unique and cost-effective access to many communities along the southeast and southcentral coast. The state has also led the way in developing unique partnerships with the private sector to leverage Alaska's world-class assets into a first-class destination, able to compete with any other, bar none. If, for the enterprising traveler, there is no end of ways to get around or things to see, for Alaskans there seems to be no end to the ways they find to cater to visitors and show off their beloved state. Tourism is Alaska's third largest industry, out-ranked only by petroleum and commercial fishing. It has grown dramatically in recent years and contributes substantially to the state's economic well-being. Judging by some of the international players in tourism who have added their own resources to the state's growing tourist infrastructure, it is an industry that has come into its own, fully able to make its own way.

Horned Puffins.

CHAPTER FOUR: HOST TO THE WORLD

Communication Networks

by Scott Foster

A rural microwave station provides service to remote areas.
Alaska Division of Tourism.

Chapter Five

No phone booths exist on Baranof Island's rugged outer coast. At the shoreline, three kayakers in full rain gear lean against the wind. For the third day they are watching mountains of marching green waves roll off the North Pacific and crash on the beach.

The storm prevents them from continuing their paddle safely. The delay means they will miss their ferry connections and be late returning from their Alaska adventure.

Jenny pulls out her hand held VHF radio and switches it to channel 26. "WSR 5535. This is Jenny Johnson calling the marine operator, over." A moment later the answer comes.

"Jenny Johnson this is the marine operator. May I have the number you want to call?" Jenny calls her family in Virginia.

With the radio on a beach in the Alaska wilderness Jenny can call anywhere in the world, but like most communications it is more complicated than it appears. Jenny's voice goes from her radio to the automated VHF land station at Cape Spencer. It then moves via a radio transmitter to the Pt. Adolphus repeater, to the Hoonah repeater, to Lena Point in Juneau and to the marine operator.

Next her voice travels through a series of repeater stations to Whitehorse, Canada then along the Alaska Highway to Tok, Delta Junction and eventually to Anchorage. From there it goes on fiber optic cable to Seward and continues on an underwater cable to Oregon were it connects to a long distance carrier and is routed to Virginia.

"Hello, this is Jenny. I'm on a beach on Baranof Island. We're fine, but a storm has pinned us down and we're going to be late . . ."

OVERCOMING THE OBSTACLES

In Alaska, there is plenty of wilderness, plus many cities and towns, where effective communications has to overcome some barriers. Distance is one. Ketchikan to Barrow is 1,341 miles. Barrow to Adak is 1,493 miles. Adak to Ketchikan is 1,826 miles. This rough triangle connecting Alaska's corners cover about the same distance as going between Los Angeles and New York . . . twice.

Alaska's geography also gets in the way of communications. Contained within Alaska's 586,000 square miles is the Alaska Range anchored by Mt. McKinley, North America's highest peak. There are

A rainbow softens the sky beyond the spanning power lines.
R.J. Hayes, photographer.

A combination of public and private telecommunications systems have linked Alaskans to others via telephone, television, radio, newspapers and magazines.

RIGHT PAGE: 4th of July fireworks light-up the sky over the Alaska state capital of Juneau.
Mark Wayne, photographer; courtesy of Alaska Division of Tourism.

CHAPTER FIVE: COMMUNICATION NETWORKS

GCI.

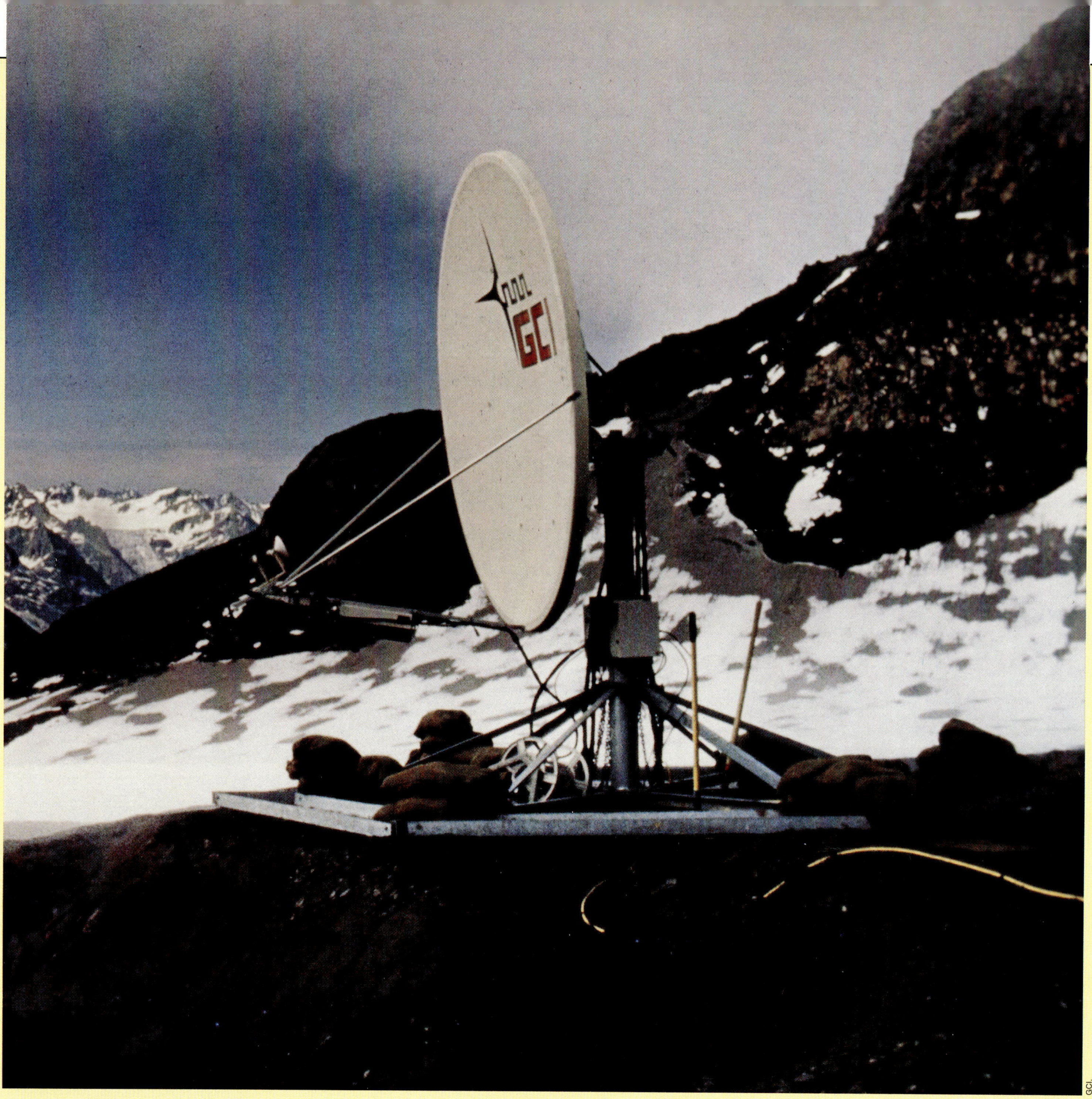

VSAT uplinks in remote locations such as this one are what many Alaskans depend upon for communication.

Alaska Division of Tourism.

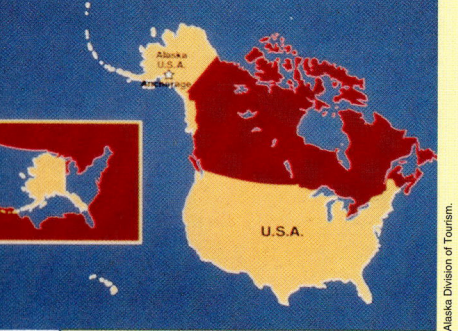

Alaska comprises approximately one fifth of the United States' land mass.

five thousand glaciers. Ice fields occupy nearly 30,000 square miles. Three thousand rivers cut through the state. More than three million lakes larger than twenty acres dot the landscape.

In addition to distance and geography, development of Alaska communications has been hindered by a small population which has effected the economy of scale. The state's 550,000 people total less than a medium sized city in many states. In Alaska there is less than one person per square mile.

Alaskans, however, have overcome these historic barriers, and today the state's communications infrastructure is robust and competitive. A combination of public and private telecommunications systems have linked Alaskans to others via telephone, television, radio, newspapers and magazines; to businesses around the world; to educational opportunities delivered via two way television; to legislators in the state capital through half a dozen distance cutting systems; and to news and entertainment from national networks and cable systems.

The first efforts to span Alaska's land with modern communications began in the 1860s. Western Union initiated a project to link major U.S. cities with the capitals of Europe by running an intercontinental cable through Alaska and continuing under the Bering Sea to Siberia and on to Europe. That project failed, but the need for communications with Alaska grew.

By the turn of the century, defense officials were working to

Since the beginning of the satellite revolution, the state government has used new technology to shrink distances and improve communications. In 1975, earth stations brought phone service to one hundred remote Alaska communities for the first time.

Wrangell, Alaska.

Communication can be a challenge when considering the remote locations so common in Alaska, such as this oil facility in Prudhoe Bay.

establish communications links between isolated military posts in Alaska and the United States. By 1905, 3,500 miles of land and submarine cables had been built. This military communications system changed over the years, and by 1935 it relied more on wireless stations than cables.

In 1971, the Department of Defense sold their communications system to a private company. The sale came just four years after communications around the world were forever changed. In 1967, the Russian's launched the first satellite. It is been described as the day distance died.

"Distance was no longer a penalty," Dr. Charles Northrip says. "All distance became 44,000 miles — 22,000 miles up and 22,000 miles down."

Northrip is a former executive director of the Alaska Public Broadcasting Commission and a communications consultant. "It doesn't matter if you live in Kotzebue or Ketchikan or Kalamazoo," he says. "Your proximity to information is exactly the same. Your ability to talk to, to interact with, is the same."

THE SATELLITE REVOLUTION

"Good evening. Let me make sure everyone is in the right class. This is Scope and Methods of Research in Business and Public Administration. Everyone's in the right class? No one's looking for Intro to Weight Lifting?"

There is nothing unusual in the university professor's opening words at the first class meeting. What is unusual is who is listening. Video and audio from the teacher on Juneau campus of the Univer-

RIGHT PAGE: The Aleutian Islands which sweep 1,500 miles toward Asia, have posed a difficult geographic obstacle in the effort to establish state-wide communications. Pictured here is a boat harbor at Dutch Harbor.

sity of Alaska is being sent by satellite to military personnel stationed across Alaska. The sites are as remote as Adak near the end of the Aleutian Chain. Students watch the Juneau based professor and can ask questions by audio hook up.

"People in the military are getting masters degrees without ever setting foot on campus," says university spokesman John Lindback. The advanced degree program is just one class being offered as part of a variety of Alaska distance education services to students from kindergarten to college that takes advantage of satellite technology.

Since the beginning of the satellite revolution, the state government has used new technology to shrink distances and improve communications. In 1975, earth stations brought phone service to one hundred remote Alaska communities for the first time.

In Alaska, there is plenty of wilderness, plus many cities and towns where effective communications has to overcome some barriers.

Hundreds of villages are as small and remote as Shaktoolik, Alaska. One of the barriers for effective communications is the lack of an economy of size. Such barriers have been overcome.

COMMUNICATION THROUGH THE MEDIA

A demonstration of satellite delivery television through a system of low-power television transmitters was funded. It grew into the Rural Alaska Television Network, a pioneering, state subsidized system that brings news and entertainment to any Alaska village of more than twenty-five people.

"RATNET made Alaska one big neighborhood," says public television station manager Bill Legere. Others involved in mass communications in Alaska have made similar observations.

"Alaska is kind of a community. To a surprising degree we know one another," says *Anchorage Daily News* editor Howard Weaver. His paper has won two prestigious Pulitzer Prizes. "We're used to dealing with one another. We have interests that transcend our geography."

Reporting on those interests in local communities falls to a cadre of professional reporters who use traditional media to communicate. Larry Persily is editor of the *Juneau Empire*. "Just about every small community of one thousand or more has their own paper," he says. "For the most part they are locally owned."

The broadcast media cover rural and urban Alaska. Public radio stations are found in large towns and many smaller communities. In addition, larger towns have enough advertising base to support commercial radio and television stations. Public television stations are located in Anchorage, Fairbanks, Juneau and Bethel.

"We communicate very well," says Dave Donaldson a reporter for the Alaska Public Radio Network. "We know more details about what's happening in people's lives around the state. In no other place I've lived do I know the name of the city manager in a town of four thousand."

A number of radio stations have found an Alaskan alternative to help their listeners in remote areas communicate with one another. The programs have different names on different radio stations. *Caribou Clatter, Yukon Wireless, Tundra Drums, Trapline Chatter,* . . . On KFSK in Petersburg it is called *Muskeg Messages.*

The Iditarod Trail Race is covered by television networks from all over the world.

CHAPTER FIVE: COMMUNICATION NETWORKS

Another indication of the growing interest in Alaska is the increasing popularity of the state as a location for feature films and documentaries, as well as photographers who take pictures in Alaska for national magazines, advertisements, and catalogues.

RIGHT: Anchorage, Alaska.

CHAPTER FIVE: COMMUNICATION NETWORKS

Greg Johnson, computer lab manager, shows a computer to Chancellor Joan Wadlow at the University of Alaska Fairbanks student computer lab.

Half a dozen times a day, the radio announcer reads the messages that have been phoned or mailed in to the station. "To Jim and Rusty. We have to get Robert's hand fixed. We'll be out when the storm breaks."

"To Terry. Dr. Johnson is unavailable for the Monday morning procedure. He's sick."

"To Barb Richardson. Did you know about the ceramics class starting Tuesday?"

KFSK volunteer Emily Merriam says the messages are sent and phoned in from local residents as well as friends from across the country. The station broadcasts the information to listeners.

Magazine publishers look for niches to attract readers and advertisers. A couple of dozen Alaska magazines cover subjects as varied as the arts, dog mushing, business, lifestyles, boats, the outdoors and more.

Matanuska Telephone Association.

CHAPTER FIVE: COMMUNICATION NETWORKS

CHAPTER FIVE: Communication Networks

Alaska Magazine was founded in 1935 and today rates as one of the top regional magazines in the country. Editor Tobin Morrison is optimistic about the future. "Interest in Alaska is growing. Our readership over the past year has grown by fifteen thousand." It is now about 245,000.

Another indication of the growing interest in Alaska is the increasing popularity of the state as a location for feature films and documentaries, as well as for photographers who take pictures in Alaska for national magazines, advertisements, and catalogues. In a recent four year period all or part of twelve feature films were shot in Alaska and accounted for a favorable $25 million dollar impact according to Mary Pignalberi, director of Alaska's Division of Tourism. International film makers are also coming to Alaska. "We've had crews from twelve different countries," she says. "They came from as different locations as Ecuador, Spain, Japan and Australia."

"They're here for the scenery and the glaciers," Pignalberi says. They also come for the unusual lighting conditions. "They call it the golden hour," Pignalberi says of the long lasting Alaskan summer twilight.

Alaskans have overcome the barriers of distance, geography, and relatively small population and today the state's communications infrastructure is robust and competitive.

INTRASTATE COMMUNICATION

While images of Alaska are increasingly being seen around the world, Alaska residents keep working to communicate with each other across the state.

Kotzebue has become a regional center like Barrow, 350 miles north, and Nome, 160 miles south. Like hundreds of other smaller communities in rural Alaska, Kotzebue residents are isolated. The nearest road system is in Fairbanks, 450 tundra covered miles to the east.

It is 1,100 air miles from Kotzebue to the state capital in Juneau. While it is expensive and time consuming to move people from towns like Kotzebue, it is easy to move information. A series of Legislative Information Offices have been established in nearly two-dozen hub communities like Kotzebue. The offices offer FAX equipment, provide computer access to committee and floor action

The Alaska state capitol, Juneau.

LEFT PAGE: *The Northern Lights dance over Fairbanks.*

White Birch.

on bills, allow computer searches of thirty relevant databases, send public opinion messages by electronic mail, and coordinate a Legislative Teleconference Network that allows home town participation in Juneau committee meetings.

During a recent 120 day legislative session more than 90,000 requests for information came from the various Legislative Information Offices. Alaskans sent more than 600,000 public opinion messages to express their views to legislators, and more than six hundred legislative teleconferences took place involving some 20,000 Alaskans.

Industry is also using telecommunications in unusual ways to meet unusual Alaskan conditions. Alaska Telecom Incorporated is an Anchorage based firm providing telecommunications systems to remote areas. For example, they have outfitted oil drilling ships in the Arctic ice pack with satellite communications, on board phones, back up radio systems, navigational aids to help supply helicopters find the ship, and have established two way communications systems with equipment barges.

At another remote oil drilling site, the company set up live, two-way video systems so officials in Tulsa and Anchorage could monitor on site developments. Company president Lloyd Morris says his crews have also installed alarm systems so the crews will be alerted if a polar bear comes into camp.

Not every Alaska communications problem means having to deal with polar bears. Sometimes communications experts "only" have to deal with the state's geography, distances and small population base. But today the surprise about communications in Alaska is there are not any surprises. Alaska uses telecommunications to tame the Great Land.

RIGHT PAGE: Anchorage night skyline.

Fairbanks, Alaska.

CHAPTER FIVE: COMMUNICATION NETWORKS

CHAPTER FIVE: COMMUNICATION NETWORKS

Entrepreneurial Spirit

by Sean Reid

Chapter Six

Alaska's modern history has been so inextricably woven with the fortunes of gold, copper, timber, fishing and oil that it may be hard to think of the state's commerce in other terms. Not surprising considering that the nation's awareness of Alaska was largely built from tales of fantastic mineral deposits, easy riches and natural bounty.

THE FIRST ENTREPRENEURS

The first "big business" in Alaska — the Russian-owned Russian America Company — was lured here by the coastal fur trade in the late 1700s. With an official government charter in hand, the company spent more than sixty years exploring and exploiting the territory. The Russians continued their fur seal harvest and initiated several new business ventures including exporting ice to San Francisco and prospecting for gold, copper, mica and coal, largely on the Kenai Peninsula. None of the ventures proved successful enough to counter the declining fur seal population which had been overhunted. The Russians started to consider selling their Alaskan interests to the Americans — a process which was consummated with the famous "Seward's Folly" purchase in 1868.

In 1880, a mild case of gold fever hit Alaska, when prospectors found gold in a couple streams in the northern part of Alaska's panhandle. Hundreds of gold seekers soon arrived and a town grew which came to be called Juneau in honor of one of those two original prospectors. But it was the 1896 discovery of huge gold fields in the Klondike that drew worldwide attention and thousands of people hoping to strike it rich. Most were unaware that the Klondike was in Canada's Yukon Territory, not Alaska. Nevertheless, Skagway was a suitable gateway to the interior. The rush built a pioneer infrastructure and Alaska had been "discovered."

A miner working on Prince of Wales Island.
Al Clough, photographer; courtesy of Alaska Division of Tourism.

> In spite of its image as a state that celebrates the spirit and freedom of the individual, Alaska has not been the business address associated with backyard inventors and young entrepreneurial daredevils.

RIGHT PAGE: *The Cook Inlet oil industry quickly grew to include what is now a fertilizer plant, a refinery, several on- and off-shore oil drilling and production platforms, natural gas and fuel pipelines to Anchorage, and a liquefied natural gas plant.*
Alaska Division of Tourism.

THE OIL AND TIMBER INDUSTRIES

Not until the 1970s did Alaska experience a similar boom. This time it was oil — fueled by the 1968 discovery of the world-class Prudhoe Bay field. But discoveries of Alaskan oil were made long ago. Eskimos, and later employees of the Hudson's Bay Company, observed oil seeping from the ground along the Arctic coast that would much later yield the Prudhoe Bay field. As early as 1853, Russian-American Company employees found oil and gas seeping from the ground along the west shore of Cook Inlet, across from what is now Homer. In 1896, seepages were noted in the Katalla area east of the Copper River and the Yakataga area, also along the coast of the Gulf of Alaska.

A few wells were drilled at promising sites around the state early this century, and some yielded small flows. The Chilkat Oil Company was the luckiest, drilling thirty-six shallow wells between 1902 and 1936 in the Katalla district. They built a small topping plant refinery and sold their petroleum products in nearby Cordova until a 1933 fire shut down the refinery.

In July 1957, Richfield Oil Corporation, later known as ARCO, established the first true commercial oil production when it discovered the Swanson River fields on the Kenai Peninsula. The Cook Inlet oil industry quickly grew to include what is now a Unocal fertilizer plant, a Tesoro refinery, several on- and off-shore oil drilling and production platforms, natural gas and fuel pipelines to Anchorage, and a liquefied natural gas plant.

Alaska's timber industry had grown on primarily a local level until 1954, when the first large pulp mill opened in Ketchikan.

Alaska Division of Tourism.

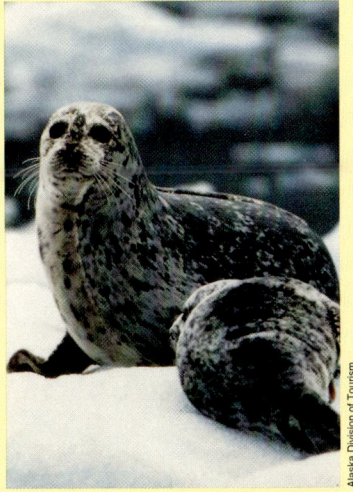

Harbor seals in Glacier Bay.

With less fanfare, Alaska's timber industry had been developing on primarily a local level until 1954 when the first large pulp mill opened in Ketchikan. Five years later, the Alaska Lumber and Pulp Company, financed largely by Japanese interests, opened in Sitka. Both mills relied on the vast stands of timber in the adjacent Tongass National Forest to produce lumber and pulp destined primarily for the export market.

THE NEW ALASKAN ENTREPRENEURS

Today, the key parts of the state's economy continue to be oil, fishing, tourism, mining, the military and logging. Support and peripheral industries — construction, telecommunications, retailers, government, airlines and others — also play an important role in the economy. Alaskan business has typically been defined by the big, resource extraction industries that ship raw materials somewhere else for processing and consumption.

However, some entrepreneurs, a couple of public corporations and a handful of young companies are researching and producing some surprisingly innovative products and services. One of the public corporations is the Alaska Science and Technology Foundation (ASTF) established by the state legislature in 1988 by setting

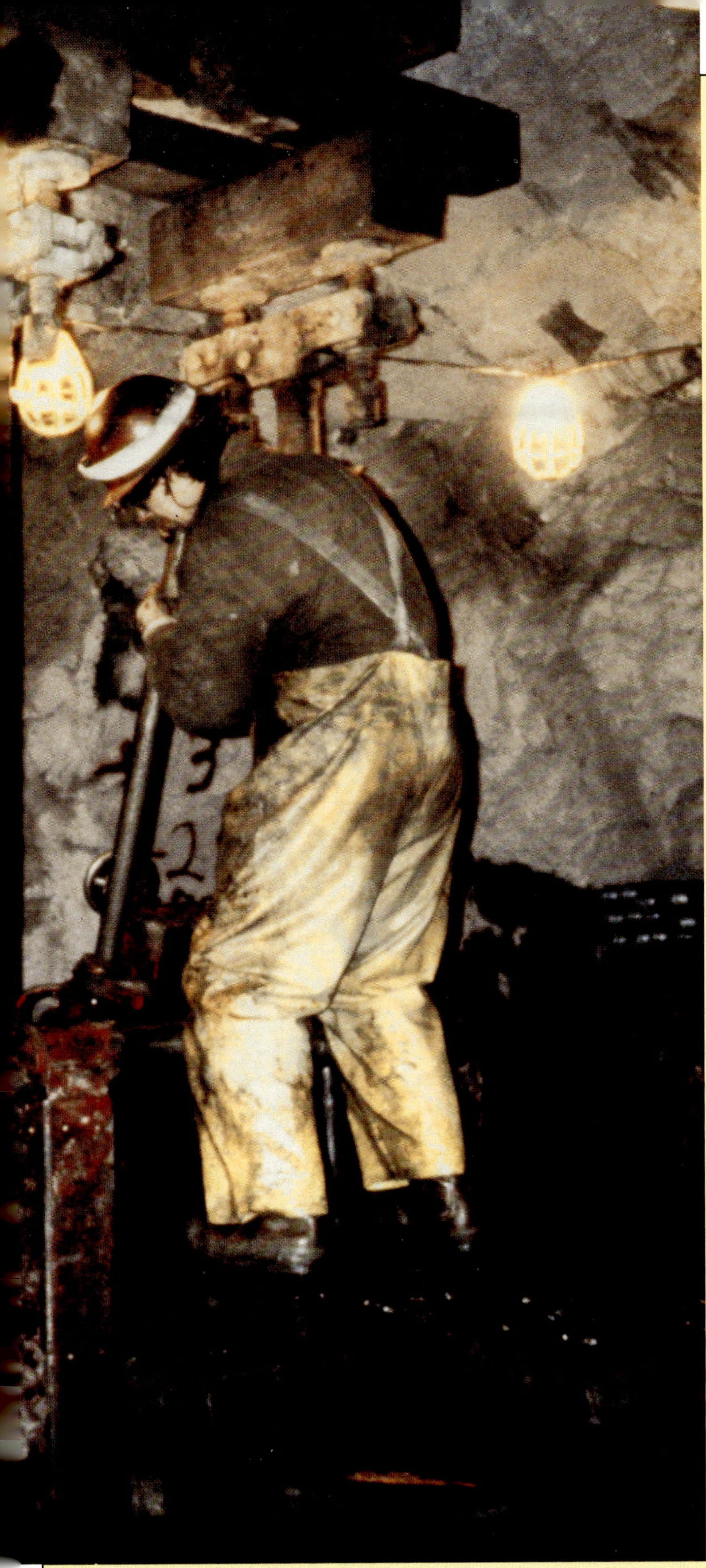

Al Clough, photographer; courtesy of Alaska Division of Tourism.

In 1880, prospectors found gold in a couple streams in the northern part of Alaska's panhandle. The town of Juneau was born. Here, miners are working the A-J Mine in Juneau.

aside a $100 million endowment. Operating within the Alaska Department of Revenue, the foundation's board of directors awards competitive grants to applicants working in applied and basic research. The goal is to enhance the state's long-term economic development and technological innovation, to build science and engineering capabilities, and to improve the public health of Alaskans.

Since its inception, ASTF has funded ninety major projects, awarded thirty-nine small grants and has provided technical assistance to ninety-five teachers statewide. Grants totaling some $14.4 million have been awarded. The largest was a 1992 grant of $1.1 million for the development of a high-temperature hazardous waste treatment system. The smallest was just under $5,000 for a study to establish the feasibility of a small business innovation center to assist entrepreneurs. All grants include provisions for matching support from grant recipients.

Although most of the ASTF-funded projects may have application in other parts of the world, all of them have a distinctly Alaskan ring to them — from low-cost district heating for rural Alaska communities, to Arctic oil spill bioremediation technology, to low-cost small hydroelectric power generation in remote areas — and they tend to address the problems familiar to many Alaskans.

The fact that several experimental projects focus, for example, on alternative forms of electrical power generation in rural Alaska should not be too surprising. Diesel power plants are currently the source of most electrical power in the villages, and it is expensive. One proposed alternative comes from a small company called Hydro Alaska in Anchorage. With assistance from ASTF, the firm is

Workers are processing lumber at Ketchikan Pulp and Timbermill. The opening of Ketchikan Pulp was a hallmark for the Alaska timber industry.

working on a small-scale barge-mounted hydroelectric generator suitable for use in tidal zones or rivers; areas near which many Alaskan villages are located.

Another of the ASTF projects is Arctic Pak Development spawned by LLR Technologies of Anchorage. LLR received a $130,000 grant to further develop and test an energy management device that charges a car's battery and controls engine block heaters and interior heaters used extensively in winter. The unit monitors air temperature and manages power to its multiple AC power outlets, turning devices on and off as necessary to save power.

"We sat down and started looking through some twenty years worth of research projects as well as current technology developments, looking for a gap that we could fill," explains Rex Plunkett, one of LLR's founders. "Our goals were to survive and to make a profit. Along that path we wanted to use and hire Alaskan talent, to help stop the exodus of the best Alaskan high school students."

Meanwhile, research done for the Arctic Pak has yielded a spin-off company and what may be an even more promising product for LLR. Wave Energy Corporation will soon begin marketing its Computer Power Saver.

AeroMap U.S., an aerialmapping and photography firm, takes aerial photographs of locations all over Alaska, such as Mt. Iliamna, a volcano located on the west side of Cook Inlet.

Looking much like a typical surge protector/power outlet box, the Computer Power Saver capitalizes on the same power-saving approach as the engine block heater device — it automatically turns equipment on and off. Computer peripherals such as the monitor, printer and scanner are plugged into the device which, like a familiar screen-saver program, detects when equipment is not in use. The unused equipment is powered-down until required. LLR estimates that the average office computer printer would be deactivated about seven hours per day and the average monitor would save about three hours of electricity every day, given a typical operator's lunch break, trips to the coffee pot, answering phone calls and chatting with fellow workers.

Across town at Anchorage's Merrill Field is another company working with computers. Since 1987, DAT/EM Systems International has been, as company literature proclaims, "... a guiding force behind the development of digital photogrammetic hardware and

The trans-Alaska pipeline crosses hundreds of miles of the Far North and Interior regions of Alaska.

software." For the uninitiated, that is the progressively high-tech world of aerial photography and mapping. And the company appears to be flying high among a handful of competing companies worldwide. In 1993, DAT/EM received the Governor's Exporter of the Year award — the first time the award has been given to a company not in resource development.

Now a division of aerial mapping and photography firm AeroMap U.S., also based at Merrill Field, DAT/EM was created in 1984 by three mapping firms to create a computer-aided mapping system based on the popular Auto CAD engineering and drafting software. A $180,000 grant from ASTF in 1991 sped development of the company's hardware and software packages which range from complete digital mapping systems and workstations to customized

The Northern Lights light the winter sky and cast a Tesoro Alaska sign into silhouette.

CHAPTER SIX: ENTREPRENEURIAL SPIRIT

These friendly faces work the Crackerjack Mine on Prince of Wales Island.

batch editing programs and foreign language mapping packages. The company also develops products marketed by other hardware manufacturers under their own label.

"We're gung-ho Alaskans," proclaims Jim Cucurull, DAT/EM's marketing specialist. "We're interested in showing the world that this can be a center for high-tech."

They are also showing how to run an apparently successful company. Sales in the U.S. and abroad have grown about eighty percent for the last couple years — mostly in the export market — to nearly $2.3 million.

Up in Fairbanks a small, uniquely-Alaskan-named company — Tundra Vole Software — is developing and selling another kind of

Shovellers are doing a water take-off.

CHAPTER SIX: ENTREPRENEURIAL SPIRIT

CHAPTER SIX: ENTREPRENEURIAL SPIRIT

mapping software called RangeMapper. Ask owner Kenelm Philip who the clientele for his Macintosh-based program are, and he will tell you it was designed specifically for the field or museum biologist wanting to easily produce species range maps for various organisms. Fact is, it appears anybody wanting to plot information on maps covering anyplace in the world may find the program useful. The latest version includes substantial world mapping files.

Software development seems to have captured much of the attention of Alaska Science and Technology Foundation folks. In 1991 they awarded a $124,000 grant to Finite Technologies of Anchorage to aid in the development of an accounting software package which can be used on a variety of computer systems including IBM-based PCs as well as Macintosh systems. Scott Henderson, president and founder of the firm, says most of the grant money was used to purchase computer equipment allowing ongoing development of their accounting software.

Two other software packages — one for doing building energy analysis and the other for water and drain system engineering — developed by Henderson and his three full-time and two part-time employees, are already on the market.

"We sell our software packages all over the world," states

LEFT PAGE: *Salt Chuck Mill on Prince of Wales Island.*

Alaskan Beer Brewery is a young company located in Juneau.

Henderson, an engineer and former Boeing employee. "The program is the best one in its field, but we have never sold a package in Alaska. I think there is a perception within Alaska that if a product is made in Alaska it's not any good. That's just not true. Some of the best programmers anywhere are right here in Alaska."

Fortunately this home-grown, anti-Alaskan bias is not shared by most people outside or internationally says Henderson. He points to his busy fax machine and orders from abroad as testimony to the quality of Alaskan products. While software development seems to be among the most active areas of new business development in the state — partially because the business traditionally has a high profit margin and is not geographically dependent — the list of innovative Alaskan products and services goes beyond software. There is work on a new two-piece archery longbow intended for Alaskan development and manufacture; an automatic system for controlling a state-of-the-art orthopedic process; an air-transportable research lab for use at remote sites; an improved permafrost soil detection method; geothermal power generation sources; and what are called fabricated food products from salmon muscle proteins.

Helping Alaskan inventors get their products patented, marketed and licensed has long been a problem, according to Alaska Inventors & Entrepreneurs Association, representing a group of

A laboratory worker tests mining samples at Montgomery Lab in Juneau.
Mark Wayne, photographer; courtesy of Alaska Division of Tourism.

The mills of Southeast Alaska rely primarily on the vast stands of timber in the adjacent Tongass National Forest to produce lumber and pulp destined primarily for the export market.

A young entrepreneur offers all-American fare to passersby in Anchorage.

business people, inventors and would-be inventors. Products designed or undergoing development by members of the self-help, grass-roots organization include a disposable cup holder; a rough-terrain wheel chair; a remote-control baby rocker; a machine that can photograph finger prints off small, difficult objects; and a tool to help people cut straight edges with a power saw.

Some of the most large scale "gee-whiz" planning is probably being done at the new Alaska Aerospace Development Corporation (AADC), a public company created to develop the final frontier space business opportunities in The Last Frontier. The AADC is working with private corporations, government agencies and universities to eventually build a comprehensive low-earth-orbit launch complex on Kodiak Island and an associated ground control facility in Fairbanks.

The Kodiak complex would launch rockets with medium weight communications, mapping and navigational satellite payloads (less than 5,000 pounds) into polar, low-earth-orbit.

Project supporters say that with its high latitude Alaska is an ideal location for launching satellites, and Kodiak in particular is an ideal spot. As one state economist observed, a rocket launched from Kodiak could safely climb out over the Pacific without going over any population center. "It's a perfect place to launch polar-orbit satellites." Supporters say the Kodiak launch complex and the associated ground control facility in Fairbanks is but one example of how twenty-first century thinking would open a new realm of scientific, educational and high-tech commercial opportunities in Alaska.

As developers and entrepreneurs focus on new products and services, it is clear that new technology and adaptive technology is

Eskimos, and later employees of the Hudson's Bay Company, observed oil seeping from the ground along the Arctic coast that would much later yield the Prudhoe Bay Field.

Placer mining equipment, often used in the Interior region of the state, uses water to separate material in order to isolate gold.

poised to join natural resource extraction on the forefront of Alaskan business in the future. While the new operations are not likely to mirror the huge scale of past construction and development projects, they do offer the advantages of diversifying state and local economies while attracting businesses that are less dependent upon natural resources.

Fortunately, the concept of doing business in Alaska is starting to change as the business environment continues to diversify. You do not even have to be a rocket scientist to see that backyard inventors and high-tech visionaries will help foster changes suited for the next century.

RIGHT PAGE: Floating logs wait for processing.
Alaska Division of Tourism.

Challenges in the Great Outdoors

by Mike Miller

Hiking on Mount McKinley at 11,500 feet is not an activity for the faint of heart or the inexperienced. However, Alaska has opportunities for adventure at every level of expertise.
Alaska Division of Tourism.

Chapter Seven

The lady from Kansas, a senior citizen and first time "river runner," steps hesitantly into the big rubber raft, looking to her husband for reassurance. He nods and smiles and shortly ten other passengers join the couple in the craft. Up and down the gravel shore of Mendenhall Lake near Juneau a few of the dozen other rafts are being launched for a trip across the lake and down the Mendenhall River. In the near distance, icebergs bob gently on the lake surface. They have "calved" recently from the very visible face of Mendenhall Glacier, a twelve-mile river of ice which descends into the lake from mountains nearby.

The trip starts peacefully, with a muscular young man on an elevated platform at the center of the raft rowing slowly toward the glacier. Soon the glacier's icy blue face looms close at hand, filling whole horizons in the viewing lenses of countless cameras. After turning the raft bow-to-stern, so everyone gets an unobstructed view and camera shot, the oarsman starts rowing for the entrance to the river. Moments later the raft picks up speed with its entry into the current.

One would never call this "whitewater" but there are rocks and whirlpools and rises and falls along the way, enough to send sprays of water into the raft — all to the loud and vocal delight of passengers who are protected by the ponchos and rubber boots their outfitter provided.

Now, getting into the spirit, the Kansas lady joins in the whooping and hollering as the oarsman displays his skill in maneuvering the craft. "Head for the choppy stuff!" she shouts as she sees a stretch of almost-rapids upcoming. "Wow!" she exclaims as the oarsman does her bidding.

About half way down the river the oarsman directs the raft to a sandy shore where smoked salmon, reindeer, and other Alaskan treats and beverages are laid out for a beach picnic. Shortly thereafter, the rafters return to their boats and the second half of their adventure begins. When it is all over, the Kansas lady will proudly claim her complimentary "I Shot the Mendenhall" pin, and proclaim for the balance of her vacation the joys of river running.

Festivities like the snow shoe race add to the fun and excitement during the Fur Rendezvous, a winter festival held every February in Anchorage.
Grant Klotz, photographer; courtesy of Anchorage Convention & Visitors Bureau and Alaska Division of Tourism.

In nearly every community and even in the Alaska bush country, a traveler will find outfitters who have packaged excursions in the outdoors which are tailored to a variety of visitor skill levels.

RIGHT PAGE: Winter balloons rise over Anchorage.
Alaska Division of Tourism.

CHAPTER SEVEN: CHALLENGES IN THE GREAT OUTDOORS

Skiing is the order of the day on these sunny slopes near Juneau.

This sled's built for one — and a small one at that! These children were having fun in the snow on the first day of the 1994 Iditarod Trail Race.

ADVENTURE FOR EVERYONE

The Mendenhall raft trip is, in many ways, typical of an evolving phenomena in Alaska travel: outdoor adventure, not only for the rugged, experienced outdoorsperson but for the uninitiated visitor as well. Add to this fishing lodges, fishing cruises, guided hunt services, ski resorts and other outdoor operations and it becomes evident that the great outdoors represents great opportunity in "the Great Land."

The development of such activity is widespread everywhere, and growing. The statewide Alaskan Wilderness Recreation and Tourism Association, in its directory of nearly two hundred business members, makes note of a revealing fact from the Adventure Travel Society. ATS, an international organization, estimates that this

CHAPTER SEVEN: CHALLENGES IN THE GREAT OUTDOORS

Anglers can reach remote fishing holes by way of float planes.

segment of the travel industry is increasing at a rate of twenty percent a year, and that it now accounts for ten percent of the $315 billion that Americans spend annually on travel.

Within the 49th State, the Alaska association estimates "there are over two thousand natural resource-dependent tourism businesses . . . Although a few of these businesses employ upwards of fifty people, many are small, supporting or contributing to the income of only a few families. They are, however, Alaska-based and vital to local employment, providing economic diversity and stability."

In nearly every community and even in the Alaska bush country, a traveler will find outfitters who have packaged excursions in the outdoors which are tailored to a variety of visitor skill levels. For example, a Juneau-based outdoor adventure firm lists among its eighteen tours two excursions down the Kobuk River in the Arctic.

RIGHT: Golf is not the first thing that comes to mind when one thinks of outdoor activities in Alaska. These golfers are teeing up in Anchorage.

CHAPTER SEVEN: CHALLENGES IN THE GREAT OUTDOORS

Most fishermen just dream of catching fine silver salmon like this angler. During the spawning season, it almost hard not to catch salmon.

One, for clients more physically fit, features a ten-day canoe trip that explores the headwaters of the Kobuk in Gates of the Arctic National Park. A less-strenuous seven-day tour utilizes motor boats through Kobuk Valley National Park, one of the most remote and the least visited of America's national parks. Day hikes during the tours can vary from rugged to relaxed, again depending on the inclination and the physical abilities of clients. During both tours, the likelihood of sighting bear, moose and caribou is strong. Travelers may well even witness the annual migration of literally half a million caribou as the Western Arctic Herd makes its annual trek across the tundra.

Another example is an outdoor adventure firm based in Girdwood near Anchorage which offers more than a dozen tour options. Those options range in ruggedness from a campout in which guests stay overnight in tents and help with camp chores to a considerably more assisted experience in which guests enjoy heated rooms and cabins with indoor facilities. In between, the company packages a range of tours that mix tent and cabin stays and offer rafting, canoe, yacht cruising, and hiking experiences in the backcountry.

The biggest contrast between soft and rugged adventure travel

RIGHT PAGE: These cross-country skiers are taking in the sights at Independence Mine in Palmer.

Challenges are waiting in Alaska for kayakers of every skill level.

110

CHAPTER SEVEN: CHALLENGES IN THE GREAT OUTDOORS

CHAPTER SEVEN: Challenges in the Great Outdoors

Kayakers dip their paddles into the pristine waters of Weird Bay.

CHAPTER SEVEN: CHALLENGES IN THE GREAT OUTDOORS

Alaska Division of Tourism.

CHAPTER SEVEN: CHALLENGES IN THE GREAT OUTDOORS

in Alaska probably shows up at Mt. McKinley in Denali National Park. From Talkeetna, about 130 miles south of the park, one can arrange a flightseeing excursion around North America's tallest peak, including a glacier landing at the principal base camp for climbing parties. Or, an adventurer can arrange to join a guided climbing expedition for an ascent on the 20,320-foot mountain. Casual climbers and weekend hikers need not apply.

AN ANGLER'S DESTINATION

What other opportunities are available for enjoying Alaska's great outdoors? The place abounds with them.

Alaska, for instance, has been the ultimate fishing destination for anglers for decades. In saltwater bays or freshwater streams and lakes, fishing enthusiasts come here from all over the world seeking lunker king, coho and other kinds of salmon; halibut that can weigh literally hundreds of pounds; world class trophy steelhead and rainbow trout; graceful grayling; chars; pike; and various other species.

Accommodations and services can range from near-primitive to luxurious. For instance, throughout the Tongass National Forest in Southeast Alaska and the Chugach National Forest in the southcentral region, the U.S. Forest Service maintains and reserves about two hundred plain but comfortable, weather-tight lake and streamside cabins that rent for the incredibly low price of only $30 per night per party. These are mostly fly-in sites; visitors bring their own food, sleeping bags, and gear.

At the spendier end of the spectrum one can reserve luxury accommodations where the guest finds rooms and cabins with all the comforts of home — and then some. Many resorts offer gourmet dining, the use of your own cabin cruiser and fish guide, and a setting that guests find to be awesome. Guided expeditions from these deluxe facilities often depart daily by float plane for the hottest, most productive fishing holes in the area.

Of course, all up and down the coast, and especially in Southeast Alaska, Prince William Sound, Resurrection Bay, and in Cook Inlet, saltwater charter operators take anglers in modest to magnifi-

LEFT PAGE: *This hopeful soul is gold panning by the Old Crow Creek Mine of Girdwood.*

Alaskans know the importance of dressing for the weather when activities take them outdoors.

A musher gets ready for his turn during the official start of the 1994 Iditarod Trail Race in Wasilla. The 1994 Anchorage start was ceremonial only because of an unusual lack of snow.

One does not need to go far to "get away from it all" in Alaska.

cent vessels on trips that last from a few hours to a couple of weeks or more.

Hunting lodges and guiding services are similarly widespread throughout Alaska, and serve the needs of big game hunters and photographers in search of brown bears, mountain goats, Dall mountain sheep, moose, caribou, and other animals.

WINTER WONDERLAND

The newest major attraction in outdoor Alaska travel is winter tourism. Only a short time ago, the last visitors of the year departed shortly before the first snow fell. Now, as the white stuff descends on Alaska, so do skiers, both downhill and cross-country, from all over the nation and the world. Joining the throngs of skiers are winter trekkers, snow machine buffs, and travelers wanting to try their hands at sled dog mushing, Alaska's official state sport. Alyeska Resort at Girdwood is the state's premier ski resort, but there are other excellent slopes also in the Anchorage area, the Matanuska Valley, Fairbanks, and Juneau. Nordic skiing is even more widespread, with locals and visitors sure to be found on trailways and frozen riverways wherever the snow falls.

RIGHT: Cross-country skiing is a sport that attracts enthusiasts of all ages and abilities.
R.J. Hayes, photographer.

Sled dog mushing can be as brief as a ten-minute spin around the park strip in downtown Anchorage in February during the annual Fur Rendezvous celebration or as long as a week's expedition in the remote Gates of the Arctic National Park. Other popular sites include the Kenai Peninsula, interior Alaska, and Denali National Park.

Perhaps the most spectacular winter outdoor recreation in Alaska is simply looking up to the evening sky — in search of the Aurora Borealis, more commonly known as the "Northern Lights." Whole tour groups arrive in Anchorage, Fairbanks, and other northern locales from as far away as Japan to see the breath-taking spectacle of the heavens alive with lighted curtains in shades of whites, blues, yellows, greens and reds. No picture nor painting, no matter how true to color or scope, has ever done it justice. It truly is, as they say in the brochures, one of the most memorable sights of a lifetime.

For the visitor, all of these myriad Alaska outdoor activities — from summertime rubber rafting and hiking on glaciers to fishing and mushing — fulfill the dreams of a lifetime. For the entrepreneur, they may represent the economic opportunity of a lifetime as Alaska becomes, more and more, one of the nation's last great outposts of wilderness and wild country.

Not all the boats in Alaska are for commercial fishing!

Bright Minds and Strong Ideas

by Sean Reid

A research survey team lands on a rocky beach on the Bering Sea.
Robert Angell, photographer; courtesy of Alaska Division of Tourism.

Chapter Eight

It will come as no surprise to any long time Alaskan that challenge can be the norm here. It is a land of nights that stretch into days. Where cold penetrates so deep that metal shatters like plastic. Where storms can peel roofs from buildings. It is a land so vast that no road, telephone line or electrical wires span the length or breadth of the state. In this beautiful but unforgiving place, it is the mix of determination and ingenuity that spell a person's success or failure. That was true when the first inhabitants arrived across the Bering land bridge and equally true now when more than a half million people call Alaska home.

To promote and reinforce those Alaskan hallmarks of determination and ingenuity, the people of the state are in the process of building an adaptive and innovative education and research system equal to the challenge of life in the north.

FAIRBANKS — A CENTER OF GLOBAL RESEARCH

Far from the glamour of California's famous Silicone Valley, thousands of miles distant in a town called Fairbanks, labors the second largest super-computer in the world. When the Cray Y-MP M98 was turned on a couple years ago, it was in fact the largest computer on the planet. Notably, it sports a huge disk storage capacity and an astonishing 8,192 megabytes of active memory — this in comparison to just four or eight megabytes for the average home or small business computer. It can perform 1.3 billion calculations per second, doing in one second what would take a person forty-one years to do on an adding machine.

The Cray is the heart of the Arctic Region Supercomputing Center (ARSC) located on the University of Alaska Fairbanks campus. Created in 1992 with a $25 million grant from the U.S. Department of Defense, the center facilitates a variety of projects, many of which are environmentally oriented. One of the conditions of the grant was that thirty percent of the research utilizing the massive computer be dedicated to Department of Defense projects, none of which are given top secret or classified status. The remaining seventy percent of the computer time is available freely to any researcher working on a qualified project.

At the facility there are twenty-five full-time staff providing

At Poker Flat Research Range, which is undergoing a major NASA-funded upgrade, scientists launch rockets to study the atmosphere and the Aurora Borealis.
Alaska Division of Tourism.

> To promote and reinforce those Alaskan hallmarks of determination and ingenuity, the people of the state are in the process of building an adaptive and innovative education and research system equal to the challenge of life in the north.

RIGHT PAGE: Bradley Lake Dam in Homer.
Alaska Energy Authority; Alaska Division of Tourism.

CHAPTER TWO: BRIGHT MINDS AND STRONG IDEAS

A signpost gives students at the University of Alaska Fairbanks a sense of perspective — and direction.

computer-use assistance to some three hundred scientists and engineers from around the world. Attracted to the research facility because of the Cray computer's superior ability to process immense amounts of data contained in complex studies, scientists at ARSC are studying Arctic ice-ocean-atmosphere modeling, global climate modeling, polar ice sheet research, volcanic plume modeling, solar-terrestrial physics, Arctic engineering and Arctic biology, among other projects. Another high-capacity Cray computer was added at the center in 1994, providing even more opportunities for complex studies.

STUDYING HIGH LATITUDES AND HIGH ALTITUDES

Not far from the Supercomputing Center is another home to researchers studying the planet and its environment. The Geophysical Institute, established by an Act of Congress in 1946, has earned an international reputation for its high-latitude research. Here scientists study a whole spectrum of geophysical processes ranging from the center of the earth to the center of the sun and beyond.

Eskimo children attending school in Northern Alaska.

CHAPTER TWO: BRIGHT MINDS AND STRONG IDEAS

An University of Alaska Fairbanks anthropologist on a dig.
Samuel Winch, photographer; University of Alaska Fairbanks; Alaska Division of Tourism.

Research facilities include Poker Flat Research Range, where they launch rockets to study the atmosphere and the Aurora Borealis. In January, 1994 the 250th major sounding rocket was launched from the small complex carrying instruments high into the stratosphere to measure atmospheric chemical reactions associated with global climate change. Joining other research efforts at the institute, global warming is the subject of a ten-year joint international research project at Poker Flat, which is undergoing a major NASA-funded upgrade.

Other Geophysical Institute facilities include the Poker Flat Optical Observatory; the GeoSpace Environmental Data Display Center; the Alaska Volcano Observatory; the Alaska Earthquake Information Center; and several other units dedicated to better understanding earth and its northern regions. The institute also operates many field stations across Alaska, Canada, Greenland, Antarctica and elsewhere.

In the 1980s, the state — flush with new-found oil money — embarked on a program of building a statewide television network devoted entirely to the delivery of educational programs.

CHAPTER EIGHT: BRIGHT MINDS AND STRONG IDEAS

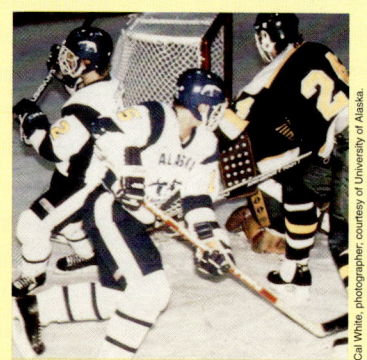

Hockey is a big sport on the University of Alaska Fairbanks campus. The UAF Nanooks (Eskimo for "Polar Bear") compete in the Central Collegiate Hockey Association, Division I.

Cal White, photographer; courtesy of University of Alaska.

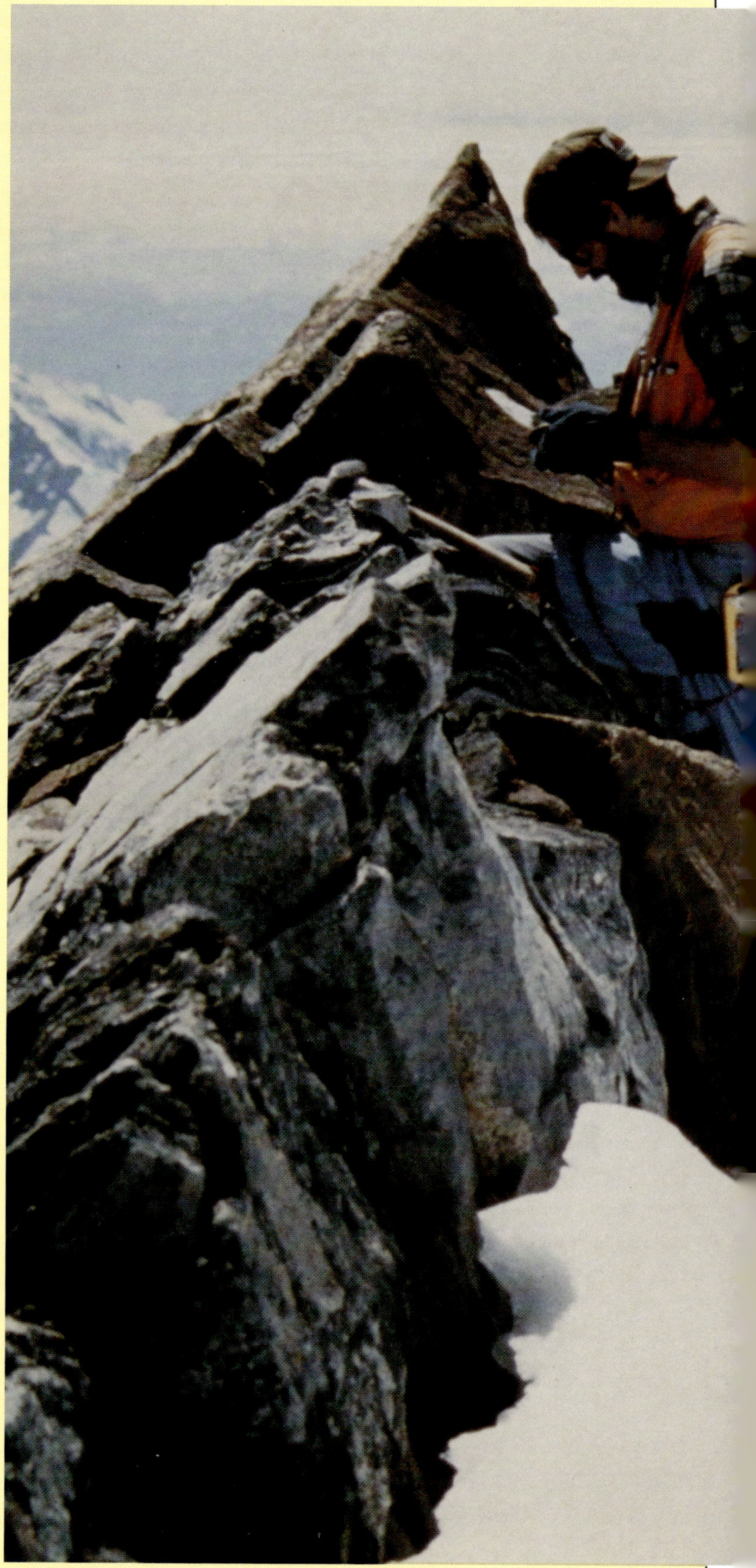

Geologists brave the peaks of Mount Fairweather.

A STATEWIDE SYSTEM OF RESEARCH AND HIGHER EDUCATION

The Geophysical Institute and the ARSC are but two components of the larger University of Alaska system, the only public institution of higher learning in the state. In addition to the Fairbanks campus, there are two other multi-mission universities — at Anchorage and Juneau — plus extended satellite colleges and sites across Alaska, including more than one-hundred extension and research sites.

The university opened its doors in 1915 in Fairbanks as the Alaska Agricultural College and School of Mines; in 1935 it was renamed the University of Alaska. At the Fairbanks campus there are now five professional schools and three colleges offering bachelors degrees in more than sixty-five major areas, recognized master's degrees in professional disciplines, and doctorates in the sciences and mathematics. The university's main library collection contains more than 750,000 hardcover volumes, in addition to extensive collections at the Anchorage and other branch sites. Meanwhile, the university's Otto Geist Museum, also in Fairbanks, is the only teaching museum in the state and is one of the state's most popular tourist attractions, with more than 100,000 visitors annually.

The University of Alaska Anchorage offers baccalaureate and associate degrees, as well as certificate programs, through its colleges of arts and sciences, career and vocational education, and nursing and health sciences. There are also the schools of business, education, engineering and public affairs. Master's degrees are also offered.

The University of Alaska Southeast is a comprehensive regional university focused on providing post-secondary education, offering certificate and associate programs. It has campuses in Juneau, Ketchikan and Sitka, as well as several outreach locations.

CHAPTER EIGHT: BRIGHT MINDS AND STRONG IDEAS

Scientists conduct a research survey of sea lions in the Aleutian Islands.

SOLVING HEALTH PROBLEMS OF ALASKANS AND OTHER NORTHERN PEOPLES

It is no secret that health problems of depression, alcoholism and suicide are endemic to Alaska and other northern regions around the world. While millions of dollars have been spent to address these problems in Alaska and other circumpolar regions, major successes have not generally been forthcoming. So, in a major step toward addressing and finding solutions to these health problems, Alaska's governor signed a bill in 1988 authorizing the creation of a new university branch — the Institute for Circumpolar Health Studies (ICHS). The institute would be based at the Anchorage campus, and consist of a research and instruction branch, as well as an administration and information branch. The ICHS is proving to be one of several world headquarters for circumpolar health studies, providing information, coordination, research, training and professional development for the international medical and health sciences community.

The fledgling institute was an early participant in the efforts to melt the social and political barriers separating Alaska and the far eastern regions of the nearby former Soviet Union. In 1990, the institute helped facilitate the first-ever medical evacuation from the USSR to the U.S. when a critically burned Soviet boy was transferred to Anchorage and on to the burn unit at the Shriners Hospital in Galveston, Texas for treatment. Building stronger ties to the people of the former Soviet Union, ICHS in the ensuing years has initiated several international and regional agreements including the exchange of specialists between the Russian Academy of Sciences, the Russian Magadan region Ministry of Health, the Alaska Department of Health and Social Services, and the institute's own specialists.

A laboratory technician tests mining samples at Montgomery Lab in Juneau.

LONG DISTANCE EDUCATION

In a land one-fifth the size of the Lower 48 states, more than twice the size of Texas, where there are hundreds of communities with less than a hundred residents and no roads in or out, it is little wonder that providing access to higher education is more complicated here than elsewhere. The contemporary solution has been what the experts call "distance delivery." This long distance education can utilize a variety of technologies and formats — and some have proven more successful than others.

In the 1980s, the state — flush with new-found oil money — embarked on a program of building a statewide television network devoted entirely to the delivery of educational programs. In every village of twenty-five or more people, satellite dishes down-linked educational television programs from an orbiting satellite. This educational network was a complement to a companion entertainment network also reaching Bush communities. But unlike the entertainment network which continues to this day, the educational network floundered for lack of popular support and ongoing legislative funding.

Chocolate Lily.

CHAPTER TWO: BRIGHT MINDS AND STRONG IDEAS

The academic community has not given up on the idea of distance delivery, however. These telecourses offer an educational option to students who cannot attend regularly-scheduled on-campus classes. By watching televised programs or viewing courses on videotape, students can learn and earn credit hundreds of miles off campus. Several distance delivery education programs are in use across the state, including ones that reach isolated military bases.

At the University of Alaska Anchorage, a typical telecourse lesson requires students to consult a study guide, read a textbook chapter and view a related television program. Students communicate with the instructor by telephone, mail, and optional discussion groups. While most student work can be done off campus, assignments and exams are mailed or faxed in.

Another long distance option offered from the Anchorage campus is called TeleClass. These are live broadcasts from UAA classrooms which off-campus students participate in via cable television. Students are required to watch the live course and phone in to participate when called on by the instructor, or phone in with questions and discussion items.

Research on agricultural possibilities for northern regions takes place at the University of Alaska Fairbanks' experimental farm.

LEFT PAGE: *Alaska's rich geology has been a boon to the state's resource based economy.*

CHAPTER EIGHT: BRIGHT MINDS AND STRONG IDEAS

Each year since the 1950s, the University of Alaska engineering students have tested their cold weather design and construction abilities. This hyperbolic paraboliod was built by UAF students.

In 1991, the state launched an ambitious effort called Alaska 2000 Education Initiative, a plan of action to restructure the public schools to make them the best in the world.

BASIC EDUCATION — BEYOND THE THREE R'S

Alaska has fifty-four school districts, plus the state-operated Mt. Edgecumbe residential school in Sitka and the Alyeska Central School, a state-operated correspondence school serving students across Alaska. There are some 119,000 students enrolled in the public system attending 467 schools. Five districts (Anchorage, Fairbanks, Juneau, Kenai and Matanuska-Susitna) enroll approximately seventy percent of all students statewide. Two thirds of the students are Caucasian-American; twenty-two percent are Alaska Native or American Indian; almost five percent are African-American; four percent are Asian-American; and just over two percent are Hispanic-American. Statewide the average pupil-to-teacher ratio is about 16:1, although the ratio tends to be much higher in the urban communities.

Graduate student Tracey Martinson is a PH.D. candidate in oceanography at the University of Alaska Fairbanks. She is examining cultures of algae that will be used for biochemical studies.

LEFT PAGE: *Neal Brown, professor at the University of Alaska Fairbanks, is working with Alaska teachers and students to improve the quality of science education in Alaska schools. Alaska Space Academies, currently in its second year, taps youngsters' natural curiosity and the appeal of space exploration to teach mathematics, science, and physics. In addition to mapping and exploring other worlds, campers build and launch their own rockets.*

In 1991, the state launched an ambitious effort called Alaska 2000 Education Initiative, a plan of action to restructure the public schools to make them the best in the world. As the report concedes, "Some people think our public schools are doing a good job; others think they are mediocre. Nearly everyone, however, believes our schools can do better."

In keeping with the goal of improving the state's public schools, numerous recommendations have been generated by the Alaska 2000 program and are proceeding on four fronts: the Legislature, the State Board of Education, the Department of Education, and various ad hoc committees appointed to develop action plans. Some recommendations have been accomplished. Others are in progress. Several are stalled or have not begun.

Among those recommendations that have been accomplished include adopting a goal statement for public education; assessing the need for additional residential high schools; establishing waivers for state education regulations for innovative approaches to improve learning; and clearing a backlog of funding requests for schools.

Innovation does not have to wait for grand plans, however. High school students in the small rural community of Galena on the banks of the Yukon River are taking home more than homework these days. Each of the thirty-three students will be issued a portable, laptop computer free of charge.

"Children in the Bush have a difficult enough time trying to find work when they go to town," said school board member Roland Chadbourne said in a recent newspaper article about the new program. "This way, they might have a notch up."

Out in the Yupiit School District in southwestern Alaska, Superintendent Leland Dishman has a different approach for his 367 students. "I came from a district that had the highest test numbers in the state to this district which had the lowest," remarks Dishman. "Fortunately we're off the bottom now, but with a long way to go."

The University of Alaska Fairbanks Museum.

CHAPTER TWO: BRIGHT MINDS AND STRONG IDEAS

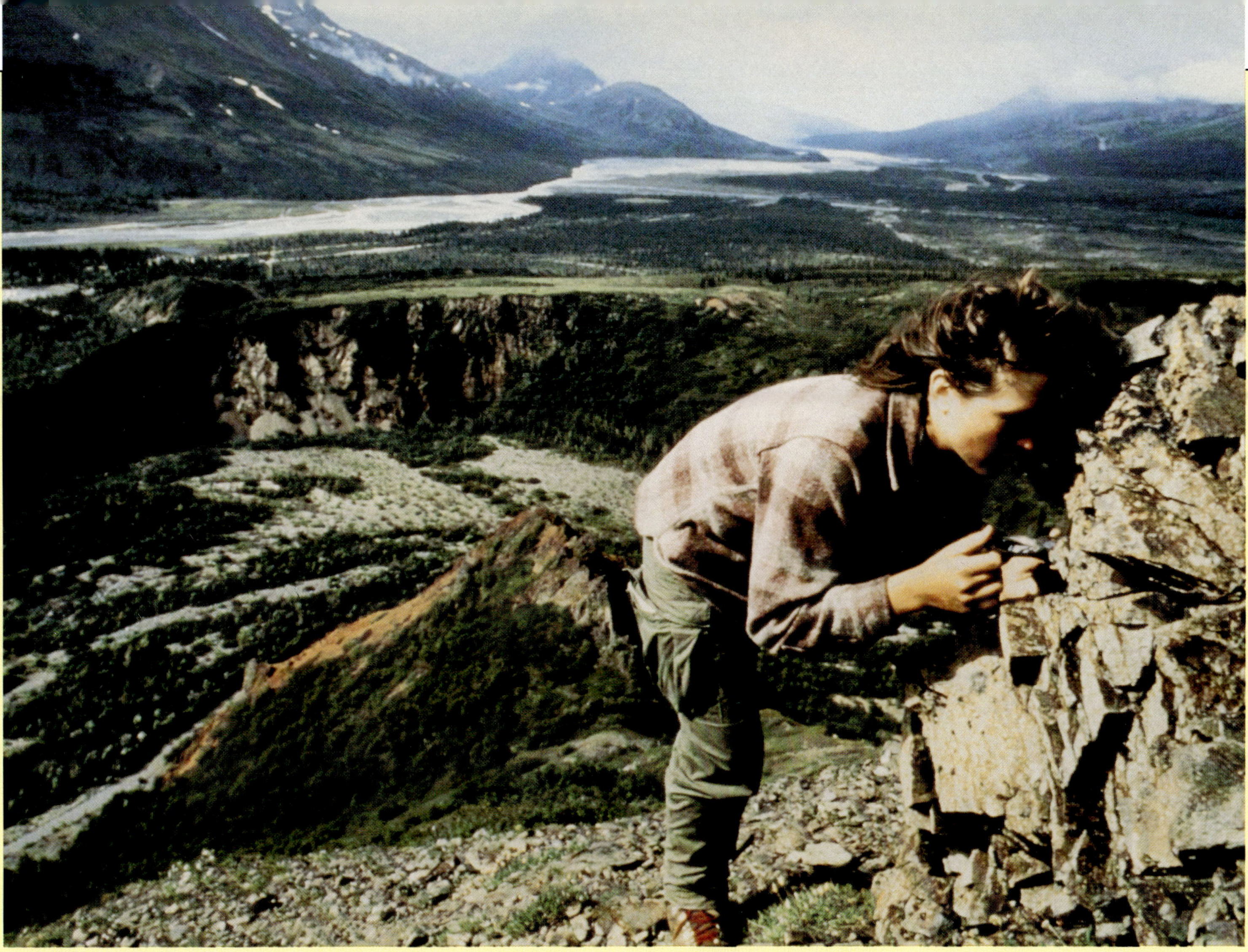

Samuel Winch, photographer; University of Alaska Fairbanks; Alaska Division of Tourism.

The Geophysical Institute at the University of Alaska Fairbanks has earned and international reputation for its high-latitude research.

During the past three years students of the Yupiit School District have improved their standardized test scores by more than one hundred percent. At the same time, student attendance has dramatically improved. "The first thing you've got to do is get the kids in school," continues Dishman. "But there's no panacea for achieving quality education. No substitute for hard work, getting parents and students involved and motivated."

Dishman might have added that the same simple spirit of determination and ingenuity has been a guiding light to generations of Alaskans surviving and thriving in this demanding and wondrous land. For the Last Frontier is truly a land that rewards bright minds and strong ideas.

University of Alaska.

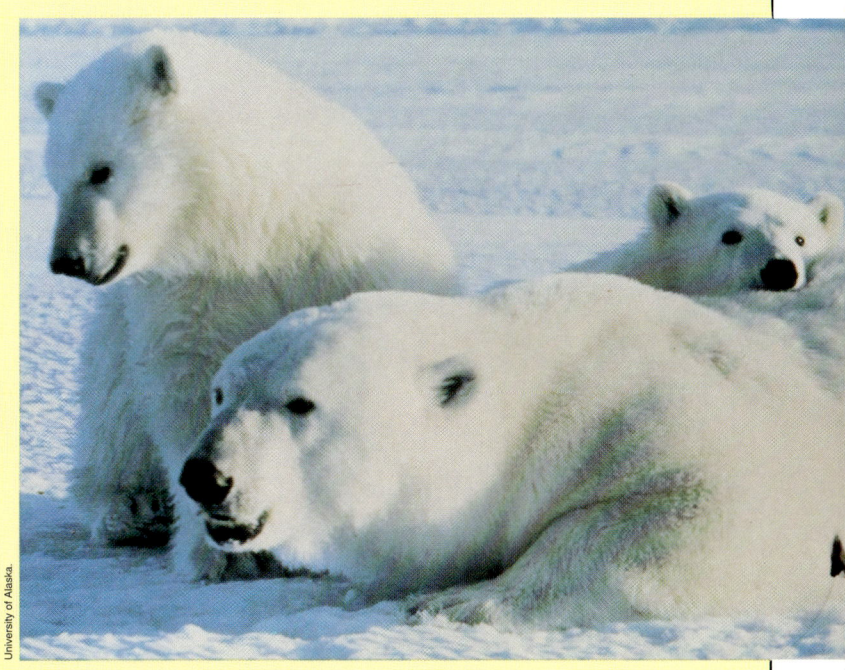

A polar bear and her cubs relax on the high Arctic ice pack.

Harvesting the Ocean

by Mike Miller

The F/V Aleutian Ballad fishing for opilio crab during the winter on the Bering Sea in Western Alaska.
Tony Lara, photographer; courtesy of Alaska Seafood Marketing Institute.

Chapter Nine

Back in the late 1890s, when gold in the Klondike set off a mad, frenzied stampede to Alaska and the Canadian Yukon, Peter Buschmann had a better idea.

Fishing, not gold seeking, lured the Norwegian-born Buschmann north to Alaskan waters in 1897. He liked what he saw at the north end of Wrangell Narrows and settled there with the aim of establishing a fishing and seafood processing enterprise.

The site could not have been better for his purpose, with a natural harbor, close proximity to rich fishing grounds, abundant timber for construction lumber, and a constant, unlimited supply of ice from nearby LeConte Glacier. Icy Straits Packing Company built a sawmill to cut lumber for the first salmon cannery in the area and completed it in 1900. Docks, warehouses, salteries, homes and a school followed as more pioneers arrived to fish and log.

The community in 1910 became the City of Petersburg, named for the fisherman who saw in the harvest of the ocean a future much more stable and enduring than the search for stampeder's gold. The city continues to this day as a premier producer of seafoods for the world, processing not only salmon but halibut, shrimp and crab as well. It is one of dozens of Alaskan communities whose mainstay is the taking and processing of bounty from the sea.

Alaska's Dutch Harbor is another. This community at the eastern end of the Aleutian Islands chain is, in fact, the number one harbor in the entire United States in terms of pounds of fish landed each year. Other Alaskan ports usually ranked in the nation's top twenty include Kodiak, Naknek, Cordova, Petersburg, Ketchikan, Egegik, and Seward.

As a state, Alaska ranks as undisputed first in the nation, with typical annual landings well in excess of five billion pounds of fish. This compares with the second-place southeastern gulf states region at around a billion and a half pounds and other regions (Pacific Coast and Hawaii, New England, Mid-Atlantic, Chesapeake, and South Atlantic) harvesting fish only in the hundreds of millions of pounds.

In terms of people, Chuck Meacham (deputy commissioner, Alaska Department of Fish and Game) reported not long ago in

Spawning salmon return to their fresh water stream near Seward.
Alaska Division of Tourism.

Another plus for salmon's future and — for that matter other species — is that the market for the state's seafood has become not only nationwide but worldwide. Markets today inlcude Asia, Europe, and Australia.

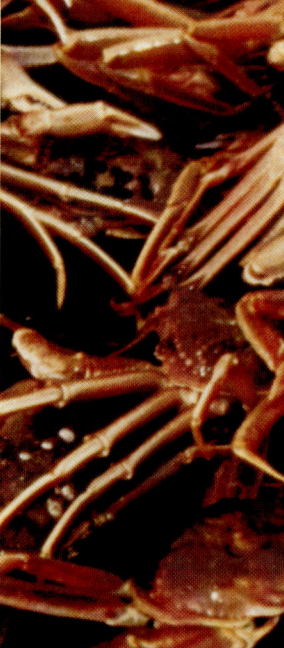

RIGHT PAGE: *Ben Kapp sorts opilio crab aboard the F/V Comelia Marie on the Bering Sea in Western Alaska.*
Tony Lara, photographer; courtesy of Alaska Seafood Marketing Institute.

CHAPTER NINE: HARVESTING THE OCEAN

Some Alaskans prefer to use a traditional method for drying salmon.

Alaska's Wildlife magazine that the commercial fishing industry is Alaska's largest private employer, providing jobs for 75,000 people during the peak of the season. During one recent year, he noted, "fishermen were paid about $1.3 billion for their catch which, after processing, provided over $2.5 billion in fisheries products at first wholesale value."

He also noted, almost as an aside, that Alaska's largest city, Anchorage, has so many resident commercial fishermen that it ranks as "Alaska's largest fishing village."

The deputy commissioner noted as well that even the humble herring fishery has, over the years, provided a total of 8.4 billion pounds of fish, and that in a single hectic three-hour sac-roe herring fishery in Unakwik Inlet, Prince William Sound, "processors paid fishermen more for herring than the United States paid Russia for

LEFT PAGE: *Commercial fishermen bring up their nets filled with salmon. As recently as 1993, the industry reached an all-time high of 846 million pounds of salmon.*

This rig is off-loading fresh halibut in Cordova. Halibut is one of Alaska's oldest and most profitable species.

the purchase of Alaska!" (That figure was $7.2 million.)

There are, no question about it, real opportunities to be realized in the field of Alaska fisheries. There are, truth to tell, entrepreneurial risks as well. The Alaska salmon story is instructive.

SALMON

During the days before Alaska Statehood (in 1959) salmon management was characterized by fish traps (tremendously unpopular with Alaskans), resource over-exploitation, long distance federal management, and political conflict. With Statehood, Alaskans assumed control of their nearshore fisheries, including salmon, and established biological management, created limited entry and other programs in the fishery, and saw a near-miraculous recovery of the once-depleted resource.

Killer whale.

"WHAT'S IN A NAME?"
A GLOSSARY OF WORDS YOU NEED TO KNOW IN ORDER TO TELL A TRAWL FROM A TROLL

In the world of Alaska fishtalk, things may not always be what they seem. A run, for instance, is not a race; it is a group of fish migrating to spawning areas in order to reproduce. A fry has nothing to do with cooking; it is a recently hatched fish. Stock is not the number of shares you own in a corporation; it is a group of fish you can distinguish by their distinct location and time of spawning. And a pot is not something you cook in; it is a box-like or conical trap covered with mesh for catching fish or shellfish.

Similarly, bycatch is not telling an escaping fish "goodbye;" it is the incidental catch of a non-targeted species, such as crab in a halibut fishery. Escapement, on the other hand, is that portion of a run of fish which passes through various fisheries and escapes to spawn.

You cannot tell a trawl from a troll? A trawl is a large conical net dragged along the sea bottom; used as a verb it means to fish with a trawl. To troll, on the other hand, is to fish with hook and line drawn through the water.

Groundfish do not spend any time on the ground; instead, in Alaskan waters they are Pacific cod, Alaskan pollack, sablefish (black cod), rockfish, and other similar bottom dwellers. Recruitment is not the act of enlisting for anything; it is an upcoming or next generation of fish.

Finally, roe has nothing to do with propelling a vessel (as in "Row, row, row your boat"). It is the eggs of a fish.

Commercial fishing boats.

Another plus for salmon's future and — for that matter other species — is that the market for the state's seafood has become not only nation-wide but worldwide. Markets today inlcude Asia, Europe, and Australia.

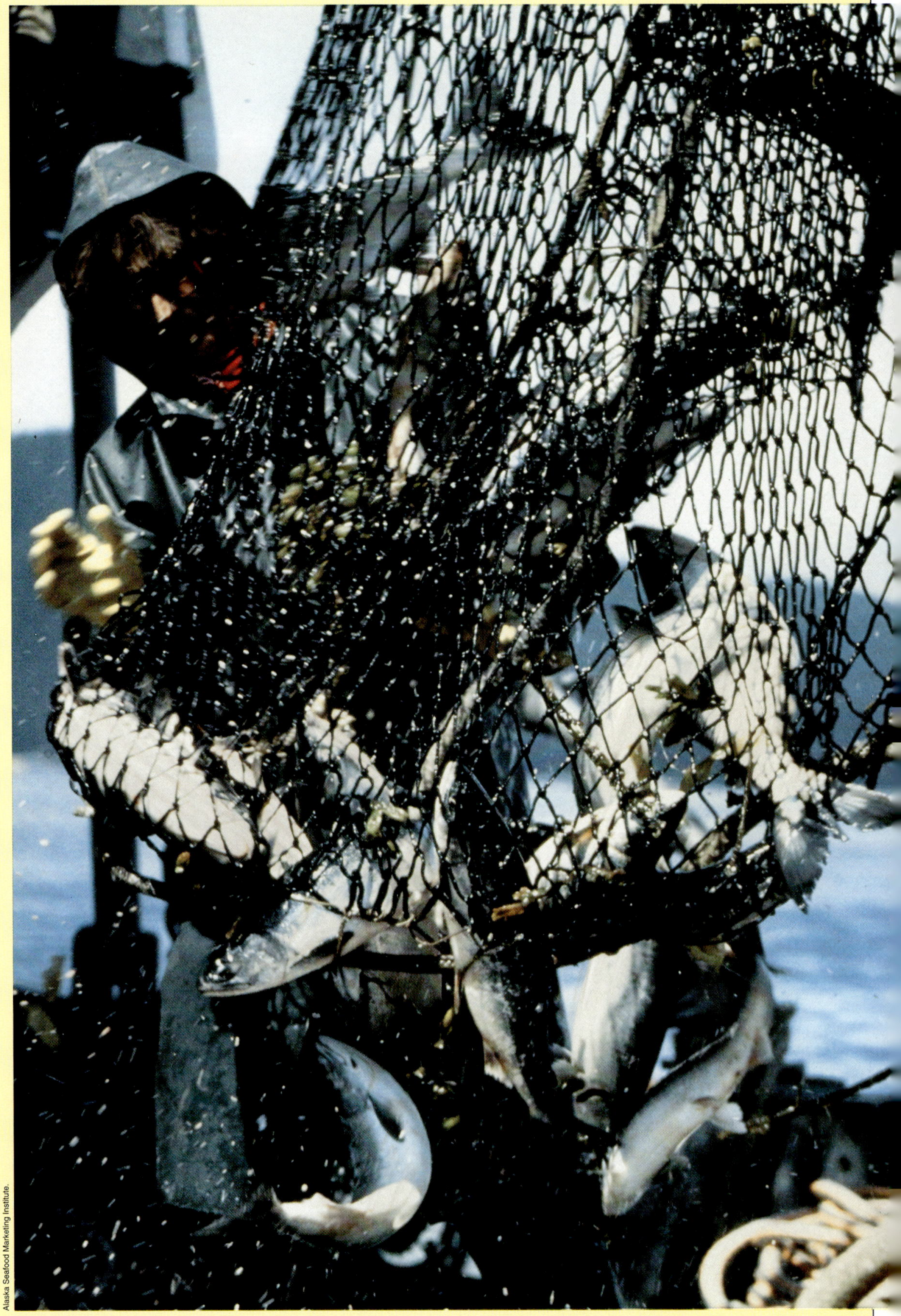

Alaska Seafood Marketing Institute.

Fresh caught salmon being picked from the net.

The iced over crab boat continues its work under adverse conditions.

Although subject to considerable "peak" and "valley" cycles over the years, the salmon catch as recently as 1993 reached an all-time high of 846 million pounds of fish. That is the good news; the not-so-good news was that the sales value of the salmon that year dropped substantially, due to a sharp increase in the world production of salmon and the fact that a significant portion of Alaska's harvest was comprised of lower-value pink salmon. Alaskans harvest five distinct species of salmon: king, also called chinook; silver, or coho; red, or sockeye; chum, or dog; and pink, or humpy.

So what might be the solution to this dilemma? A cutback in production to drive prices higher?

Hardly. In an annual report to its membership and to the state, the Alaska Seafood Marketing Institute (called ASMI and pronounced "As-me;" it is the official organization charged with generically promoting the sale and use of Alaska seafood) asserted that "the long-term solution for Alaska's economy is not cutting back production — it is increasing consumption."

Actually, ASMI has been doing just that in recent years — and

These workers are processing fresh fish. Alaska's market for seafood has become not only nationwide, but worldwide.

doing it well. Retiring ASMI executive director Kim Elton, in the same annual report, noted that "we have expanded into new markets overseas, convinced the U.S. Department of Agriculture to purchase canned salmon for federal lunch programs, countered attacks from consumer magazines regarding seafood safety, and accomplished the mundane and exciting elements of commodity marketing."

One of the elements that make the future look bright for Alaska salmon is the introduction in recent years of new specialty salmon products like custom smoked lox in presentation gift boxes and even the creation of salmon "ham" which compares more than favorably with meat from traditional pork farms.

Another plus for salmon's future and — for that matter other species — is that the market for the state's seafood has become not only nationwide but worldwide. Markets today include Asia, Europe, and Australia.

Presently, Japan is the industry's best importing customer, purchasing in excess of eighty-five percent of the state's exported

A proud catch of halibut displayed at Homer Spit in Southcentral Alaska.

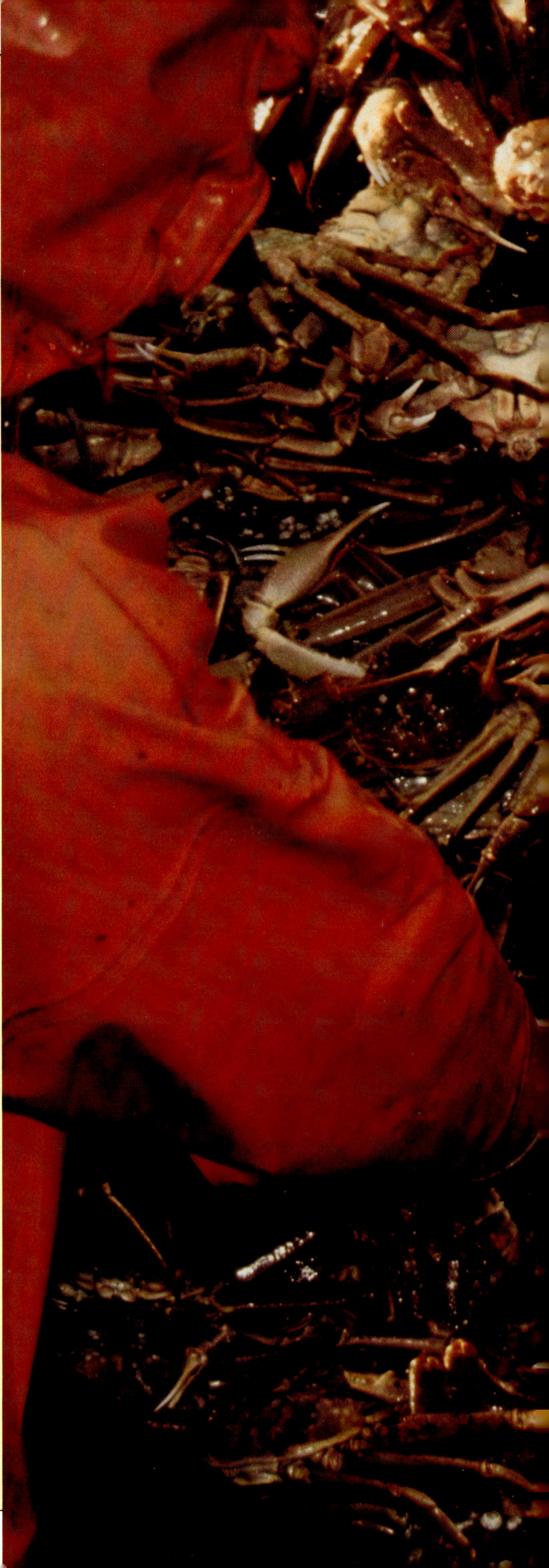

RIGHT PAGE: *On the Bering Sea in Western Alaska, crewmembers aboard the F/V Cornelia Marie sort opilio crab.*
Tony Lara, photographer; courtesy of Alaska Seafood Marketing Institute.

CHAPTER NINE: HARVESTING THE OCEAN

fresh and frozen salmon, herring, and crab. In the past, most groundfish from Alaska waters was processed as surimi and exported to Japan (Surimi is sort of a "minced fish" made into a paste which can be flavored to taste surprisingly like crab, lobster, shrimp, scallops, even bologna.) Recently, however, markets for groundfish blocks and fillets have developed in the U.S. and Europe as well. The United Kingdom, Canada, and Australia provide the biggest overseas markets for canned salmon.

Here, species by species, is a rundown of Alaska's other major fisheries:

HALIBUT

It has got to be one of the least pretty creatures in the sea (how many animals do you know that have two eyes on one side of its head?); but it is also one of Alaska's oldest and most profitable species. The commercial harvest goes back to the early 1900s when Puget Sound halibut schooners first ventured into North Pacific waters.

These days a whopping ten thousand or more skippers and crew participate in the chase for this species. This is a bait fishery, with halibut fishermen using longline gear with baited hooks to attract individual fish which may range from ten pounds to five hundred pounds (a record). Many are in the one hundred to three hundred pound range.

Alaska-caught landings in the 1990s typically run from forty-eight to fifty-million pounds or more each year. Quotas for this fishery, incidentally, are set by the International Pacific Halibut Commission. The fishery is managed by the National Marine Fisheries Service.

A commercial fishing crew readies their nets.

HERRING

They may be little, and the "season" for herring is measured within a single day instead of weeks or months, but the economic value of Alaskan herring is considerable. Historically, the fishery dates back to the 1890s and the now long-gone days of salteries. The fishery was reborn and became a major factor with the development in the 1970s of a Japanese market for herring sac roe (eggs) as a highly valued holiday delicacy. Alaskan herring is also sold for bait and food.

These days there are some 2,900 limited-entry herring permits issued to fishermen most of whom use seine and gillnet gear and usually catch the allowable quota in a matter of hours. Even so, the ex-vessel value (meaning the total amount of money paid to vessels at the dock) can run to $20 million or more annually.

SHELLFISH

The Alaska shellfish fishery takes in three kinds of crab (king, Tanner, and Dungeness) plus shrimp, scallops, clams and other species. Nearly three thousand permit holders seek these creatures. They use baited wire mesh pots on the ocean bottom to bring in crabs; shrimp and scallops are usually caught in trawls.

The king crab fishery started out as primarily a Japanese and Soviet fishery in the 1930s and 1940s. It became a major domestic fishery in the 1950s, rising from about five million pounds in 1953 to 188 million in 1980. The king crab harvest plummeted only five years later to 15 million pounds. Now, however, the fishery is showing signs of sustained recovery and annual harvest reports run in the neighborhood of 27 million pounds. Total shellfish harvests typically approximate three hundred million-plus pounds per year.

Petersburg Harbor.

A seiner "making set."

GROUNDFISH

Perhaps nowhere has change in Alaska's seafood industry been more apparent than in the groundfish fishery. Previously the catch of Alaska pollack, Pacific cod, sablefish (black cod), rockfish, and similar species was heavily dominated by foreign operators utilizing offshore factory ships. In recent years, with the expansion of the United States' jurisdiction offshore, the fishery has become a pronounced American undertaking. Domestic groundfish harvests, in fact, have virtually exploded from 69 million pounds of fish landed in the early 1980s to four billion pounds with the advent of American fishermen and processors taking over the fishery.

Groundfish, though lower in value on a per-pound basis than other Alaskan fisheries, accounts for a huge percentage of the fish caught in Alaska's ocean waters and is used in the making of fish and chips and surimi as well as being served in white tablecloth restaurants across the nation.

The fishery will become even more economically valuable to Alaska in the future as more shore-based plants (as opposed to floating factory ships) process the groundfish caught off Alaska's shores.

SUMMING UP

They are fast-changing, these varied components of the Alaska fisheries industry. Huge improvements have taken place — in fishing gear, in ways to process the catch, in quality of the catch, and in ways to market the finished product — since the days a near-century

Fishing gear is neatly packed and ready for the next trip.

RIGHT PAGE: *King crab fishing with the F/V Cornelia Marie on Bristol Bay in Western Alaska.*
Tony Lara, photographer; courtesy of Alaska Seafood Marketing Institute.

Groundfish, though lower in value on a per-pound basis than other Alaskan fisheries, accounts for a huge percentage of the fish caught in Alaska's ocean waters and is used in the making of fish and chips and surimi as well as being served in white tablecloth restaurants across the nation.

Alaska-caught landings of halibut in the 1990s typically run from forty-eight to fifty-million pounds or more each year.

ago when Peter Buschmann came sailing to Alaska in search of opportunity and a likely base for his operation.

Further change is certain, and new challenges lie ahead. As a recent study by the Alaska Division of Economic Development, simply called *Alaska Seafood Industry*, points out, "Alaska seems likely to retain a prominent role in U.S. and world fisheries, but the complexion of the industry will be very different in the year 2000 from what it is today."

The bow of the crabber F/V Aleutian Ballad breaks a wave during the winter on the Bering Sea in Western Alaska.

Alaskan fishermen and the Alaska seafood industry accept that forecast. They have embraced change and new opportunities in the past. They are more than willing to do so in the future.

For example, lest anyone think all the new ideas possible in Alaska's fisheries have been used up, consider an innovative shellfish company in Juneau. This enterprising company has invested in oyster spat and is busily and profitably engaged in raising the little critters in nets and long lines at Otter Sound on the west coast of Prince of Wales Island. The company then markets and sells mature fresh oysters in the Juneau area, Anchorage, Skagway, Seattle, and San Francisco. Response from the market, and the dinner table, has been extremely favorable. The firm is one of a small handful of Alaska enterprises testing the economic waters in this new field.

The prognosis is excellent. It is, a local booster noted, an absolute gem of a product, even if the company has not yet come up with any pearls in its shells.

ALYESKA:
Its Great People
by Scott Foster

An Eskimo watches the Arctic sun in an umiak (skin boat).
Alaska Division of Tourism.

Chapter Ten

A home in the Alaska wilderness. The nearest town is thirty miles away and accessible only by boat or plane. When the weather kicks up like it did for five straight weeks last winter, the Franklins are stuck.

Jeff and Anne Franklin are retired Alaskans. But not to an RV. Not to an Arizona planned community. The Franklins retired to four acres of certified, isolated, Alaska wilderness.

Living in the Alaska wilderness is a reality for some and a dream for others. Alaska has always attracted dreamers. For some, the dream has been to taste a life where strength, survival skills and grit count for more than corporate ladder climbing, 70 mph lane changes in heavy traffic, or deftness in cocktail party chatter.

Alaska is not just a place for dreamers though. The land is too tough for that. It demands too much. Fifty below zero happens during Fairbanks' winters. Alaska is a state of extremes that are apparent in many ways: life with city convenience and rural homes without plumbing; Arctic treeless tundra and Inside Passage rain forests; city traffic congestion and wilderness quiet; Valdez mountains and Bethel flats; Kodiak fisherman and Anchorage businessmen; conservative Fairbanks shop owner and liberal Juneau state employee.

Ron Clark spent part of the '70s and '80s in Fairbanks. "They've got a real curious mix of the most progressive thinking in the country, things that haven't been tried before," Clark says. "That exists with ideas right out of the 14th century."

These differences seem more an asset than a liability. "You can argue hammer and tongs with someone at a city council meeting. You think they hate you," Clark says. "Then the next morning they'll pick you up on the road when it's fifty below." It is a story repeated across Alaska with geographic variations.

THE ALASKAN SPIRIT

Gustavus is home to a few hundred people. It is the closest community to Glacier Bay National Park. There is one main road and dozens of dead end side roads. No road is paved. No road connects to another town. Ride with a local in his rusty "beater" and one will see another comfortable throwback to America's more gentle days. The wave. In Alaska it is not a big production performed by crowds

Handlers keep the excited huskies calm before their turn to start in the Iditarod Trail Race.
Wyndham Images.

> Alaska Natives are descendants of the people who traveled across the Bering Land Bridge some twenty thousand years ago and, scientists generally believe, populated the rest of North and South America.

RIGHT PAGE: An Eskimo woman makes preparations for drying fish.
Alaska Division of Tourism.

in a football stadium. In Gustavus and hundreds of other small Alaska towns, the wave is simply a friendly greeting; an acknowledgment of a neighbor, a friend, another human as he or she passes. Meet again ten minutes later going in opposite directions and wave again. "Hello."

Another part of Alaska community life that also harkens back to a more peaceful time is trust. One thirty-year resident returning from a Seattle trip told Juneau friends his surprise at a feature on his new rental car. "As soon as you put it into drive," he said, "all the doors automatically lock!" In twenty years, he has never locked his car or his downtown home.

Panning for gold is hard work! It's time to take a break at the Old Crow Creek Mine in Girdwood.

Chilkat dancers preserve their culture through traditional ceremonies.

It would be a mistake to think all of Alaska is friendly waves and people trusting unlocked doors. No invisible barrier has spared Alaska from the rude realities of American life. Residents of large and small communities struggle with too often tragic problems. But one difference is that there is still surprise that some of America's ills are actually occurring in Alaska, and when they do, they still make the news.

Of course, there are problems, but in Alaska, there is still hope. That hope comes from the opportunities in the Great Land and the kind of people the land attracts. Take a chance. Give it a try. Come for a summer job. Stay forever.

There is a spirit among those who stay in Alaska. In part it is a reflection of why they came. Randy Burton moved from West Virginia to Alaska in 1981. "People in Alaska have the chance to make their own destiny rather than accepting one," he says. "It is the 'Last Frontier.' What brings people to Alaska today is the same thing that brought people on wagon trains across the country."

Alaska's modern lure also carries some old fashioned realities. "Alaskans have to be good at a lot of things," says one long-time resident. "You put on a suit, tie, and shiny shoes for work, but then you turn around and have to fix a greasy diesel at home."

In the more remote areas, the land, weather and isolation demand that flexibility. Those who have it survive just fine. Those who do not probably head back where they came from. It is a self-selecting system that has produced the character of Alaska's people. Call it a wilderness spirit. Alaska is big enough to allow plenty of space to implement that spirit. If Alaska were placed over the continental U.S., Ketchikan loggers and fishermen would go to work

A musher develops strong bonds with the dogs that he or she works with.

CHAPTER TEN: ALYESKA: ITS GREAT PEOPLE

CHAPTER TEN: ALYESKA: ITS GREAT PEOPLE

An Eskimo girl hides in the family's fishing nets.

near Jacksonville. Juneau state workers would punch a clock in Atlanta. Anchorage clerks would earn a living near Kansas City. Shemya Air Force personnel would fly out of Bemidji, Minnesota.

At a time when the sheer numbers of people threaten to clog many American cities, Alaskans have room to spread out. If every Alaskan received an equal share of land, each would have about a square mile to call their own.

Although it contradicts the stereotype, most Alaskans actually live in the cities, not in the wilderness. Half of the state's 550,000 people will be found in the greater Anchorage area. Fairbanks, with 75,000 residents, is Alaska's second largest city, followed by Juneau, the capital city, with 28,000 residents.

Alaska's cities have all the modern amenities. What makes them different is what is beyond the city limits. There is an old Alaskan joke about frustrated people having to live in the city, but at least being able to see the wilderness from the office window.

To earn a paycheck, many Alaskans have to locate their bodies in the city but keep their minds in the wilderness. They share the desire of many Alaskans to get out rather than stay in. While the end

The Russian Orthodox Church still has a great deal of influence in many regions of Alaska.

LEFT PAGE: *One compensation for the long winter nights that Alaskans can look forward to is the performance of the Aurora Borealis.*

Totem carver Nathan Jackson puts the finishing touches on another work of art.
Alaska Division of Tourism.

Many people in the remote regions of Alaska still use reliable dog sleds in the winter months.

results are the same, dozens of different reasons lure these north-land dwellers outside. For many it is hunting or fishing. Others hike, or ski, or snow machine, or mush dogs, or fly small planes, or . . .

"Usually, it takes me at least one night in a tent to get away," says one outdoor adventurer. "It takes that long to get away from the electricity that powers our conveniences, away from the entertainment distractions, away from the houses and cars that separate us from the weather. It takes that long before I can feel myself shedding the trappings of civilization and entering into a more natural state."

People enter that "state" all across Alaska in all types of weather. Check out Bethel, a regional hub of 4,500 in western Alaska, during the "Kuskokwin 300." This is no mega horse-powered assemblage of

CHAPTER TEN: ALYESKA: ITS GREAT PEOPLE

Permitted through international agreement, the whale hunt continues for Eskimos whose subsistence lifestyle requires it. Every part of the whale is used.

metal hurling around ovals, but rather teams of howling dogs pulling wooden sleds and mushers across the frozen tundra.

Or take off for a big game hunt from any town. Join the salmon or halibut derby frenzy in any coastal community. Race up Seward's 4,603 foot Mt. Marathon with other masochists on the Fourth of July. Decorate the boat and take part in Sitka's Christmas boat parade. Vacation in Anchorage in February and get caught up in the Fur Rendezvous — a good reason for a winter party. Wind surf in Juneau's Mendenhall Lake with a glacier backdrop. Cross country ski or run, depending on the season, between home and work on Anchorage's extensive trail system. Sea kayak to tidewater glaciers or along the outer coast.

Craig Peterson of Seattle spent a summer kayaking and camping on a solo seven hundred mile paddle from Port Hardy, British Columbia to Glacier Bay along Southeast Alaska's outer coast. "It's a very basic lifestyle. For me, it's very satisfying. There's a feeling of

An Eskimo family brings home groceries in Kotzebue.

161

CHAPTER TEN: ALYESKA: ITS GREAT PEOPLE

being more alive. You can bring it back to your twentieth century life in terms of what do you really need."

Roy Scott returned to Alaska after a two year absence to make a second attempt on Mt. McKinley. "We had to carry four loads of gear just to move everything from one camp to the next. We forded rivers, fought mosquitoes, complained about being nothing more than dumb pack animals. But we kept going."

The four climbers crossed crevasse fields, climbed avalanche-prone slopes, gingerly navigated a long approach ridge with a 5,000 foot drop on one side and 7,500 foot drop on the other. They also suffered altitude sickness at their high camp. Scott was the 313th person to stand on North America's 20,320 foot summit.

"We spent thirty days getting there, thirty minutes on the top, and a day and a half getting down. It was the highlight of my life, both literally and figuratively. When I die, I'd like my ashes to be spread on Mt. McKinley."

The locals get into the spirit of the festivities during Petersburg's Little Norway Festival.

CHAPTER TEN: ALYESKA: ITS GREAT PEOPLE

Sometimes the spirit of those who live in Alaska manifests itself in the oddest — and funniest of ways.

Sometimes Alaskans' work brings as much adventure as their play. Commercial fishers lead a fiercely independent life and make their living challenging the power of Alaska's sometimes treacherous waters. A helicopter pilot lands tourists on a glacier several times a day. A long-haul trucker carries heavy equipment from Fairbanks, across the Arctic Circle, to Prudhoe Bay. Alaska Natives hunt whales as a traditional food, a practice allowed by international agreement.

The "Arctic Sounder," a Kotzebue-based newspaper, reported on a hunt from Kaktovik on Alaska's North Slope. "The first whale was landed on September 9th by James Killbear, Sr. and was thirty feet, ten inches. On September 13, Herman Aishanna landed a thirty-one-foot, three-inch whale. It's been very windy and the seas have been running high, so they are waiting for the weather to die down to try for their final strikes."

Alaska Natives are descendants of the people who traveled across the Bering Land Bridge some twenty thousand years ago and, scientists generally believe, populated the rest of North and South America. Natives are involved in all aspects of Alaska life and comprise fifteen percent of the state population.

Many Natives live in smaller, remote villages and still practice subsistence food gathering. Jeff Nickerson is a Tlingit from the coastal village of Klawock. "Right now we're doing the fish eggs. That's herring spawn on kelp. In May we'll start looking at seaweed and right after that we start looking at sea cucumbers."

The bi-annual Celebration held in Juneau attracts Natives from all over to take part in the festivities.

CHAPTER TEN: ALYESKA: ITS GREAT PEOPLE

Sitting on her stoop in the sunshine, an Eskimo woman gives a friendly smile to a passerby.

Alaska Natives are descendants of the people who traveled across the Bering Land Bridge some twenty thousand years ago and, scientists generally believe, populated the rest of North and South America.

Nickerson's annual subsistence cycle also includes gathering wild asparagus, berries, and sockeye salmon through July. Then the deer-hunting season opens, which is followed by fishing for coho salmon. "In October we try to put up a couple of seals," he says. "We start looking for halibut up to January and of course we eat a lot of clams. February is pretty slow and we start again in March right where we are (gathering fish eggs.) I don't know if I left anything out."

Compared to Alaska Natives, every other Alaskan is a newcomer. Many of these "newcomers" came because of Alaska's resources. Fur, gold, fish, timber and oil each brought new groups and each group brought new diversity to Alaska's character.

The population diversification continues. A strong military presence introduces a changing cross section of American society to bases near Anchorage, Fairbanks, Kodiak and Juneau. As the world's economy changes, Japanese business people have become more common in Anchorage board rooms, Dillingham fishing plants, and Wrangell saw mills. Other Asian and European businesses add to Alaska's expanding international flavor.

One Alaskan has direct experience with an Alaska business attraction that does not have to do with resource development. "The trend in business down south is to escape the city. If a company can do the job in Montana rather Los Angeles then they're moving. Successful business people in Alaska have known that about this state for years. It's a well kept secret."

One Alaska secret that is not being kept is tourism development. They come for the mountain scenery, the wildlife, the fishing and the wilderness.

"Maybe it's just a little too cold out today!"

An Athabascan woman prepares salmon for drying at a camp along the Yukon River.

It is that wilderness. The unending emptiness. The forever of the country that helps define people who live in Alaska. It also says something about the people who chose to live here.

Jeff and Anne Franklin's isolated home is bathed in the soft gold of evening. Jeff has finished another repair project. He relaxes on the porch. Anne sits nearby on a chair, quietly talking to a visitor about the realities of retiring in the wilderness. "We've wondered about getting a place closer to medical attention," she admits.

Anne Franklin pauses. Her eyes mist. Her voice is hardly more than a whisper. "I doubt we'll ever move. I don't want to leave."

The Rich Future

by Jeffrey Richardson

Mount McKinley reflects in a small pond surrounded by cotton grass.
Alaska Division of Tourism

Chapter Eleven

As the 21st century dawns over Alaska, much has changed, and much remains the same as it was a century ago. Much, too, has come full circle. Though strangers are less likely to ask where they can see igloos, Alaska is still widely viewed as a treasure trove of natural resources that can fuel, supply and house a needy and somewhat depleted world. Among its many natural assets, Alaska's pristine wilderness and relative emptiness may arguably have increased in value due to the tremedous growth of the tourism industry. This has further complicated Alaska's efforts to realize its economic destiny on its own terms, even as it provides the seeds of a burgeoning industry just coming into its own. The expectations of tourists sometimes clash with industrial activities. But it is equally true that tourism presents an excellent opportunity for Alaska to continue its economic diversification against those times when the fortunes of such mainstays as the timber and oil industries fluctuate in response to access challenges and market conditions.

With the pragmatism and inventiveness that are the hallmarks of many northern peoples, Alaskans are building their future on well-defined strengths, but not letting those strengths alone dictate the path of their ingenuity. Old ideas are being examined in the light of new information. Tourism is not a new industry in Alaska since it actually pre-dates oil and gas development by many years. However, it is growing at an unprecedented rate, and creating new opportunities in the process. Oil exploration dates to the turn of the century, but Alaskans are leading the way in innovating cold-region engineering solutions to make oil development safer and more cost-effective. In addition to the mainstays of the Alaskan economy, there are new industries being born in Alaska with a tremendous potential to help carry its residents into the next century with prosperity and distinction. These include a number of initiatives in telecommunications, applied space technology and science, to name a few. In some communities, industries long dormant are gaining new life due to technological innovations.

Accompanying this vital economic maturity is a coming of age in Alaska political and social institutions, with the result that Alaskans often find themselves, in essence, re-inventing society. An illustration would be useful. While oil exploration has a long history

Sea Lions.
R.J. Hayes, photographer.

Oil exploration dates to the turn of the century, but Alaskans are leading the way in innovating cold-region engineering solutions to make oil development safer and more cost-effective.

RIGHT PAGE: *The Northern Lights dance behind the Synthetic Aperture Radar dish atop the Geophysical Institute at the University of Alaska Fairbanks.*
Jim Connor, photographer; courtesy of University of Alaska.

Crewmembers Murray Gamrath (R), Todd Weisenbeck (C) and Roger Jencen (L) sort Tanner crab aboard the F/V Comelia Marie on the Bering Sea in Western Alaska.
Tony Lara, photographer; courtesy of Alaska Seafood Marketing Institute.

in Alaska, dating back to the turn of the century, the state profoundly remade its image in the eyes of the world with the discovery of the huge oil field at Prudhoe Bay. Overnight Alaska became an oil giant that continues to produce about twenty percent of all the oil consumed by the United States. The strike gave rise to an engineering marvel—the trans-Alaska pipeline, and made the young state suddenly wealthy. With the same forethought that characterized the shaping of its modern and progressive constitution, Alaskans rose to the challenge of prudently managing its windfall. While urgent social and infrastructural needs received the consideration they deserved, a Permanent Fund was created which established a substantial savings account for the future. A portion of investment earnings from the fund are paid out each year as a dividend to residents. The idea behind the concept is as simple as it is striking, and tailored to a land of individualists: every citizen is entitled to decide how a fraction of the collective royalty wealth is spent, or saved, without the consent of a legislative body. This is not simply a symbolic gesture. The Permanent Fund dividends have circulated throughout the state's economy, helping it mature, giving it resilience. New business startups have been leveraged and college educations have been financed. For many people, the dividends have helped ease transitions brought on by contractions in one economic sector or another.

INDUSTRY IN ALASKA

The oil industry is among those that have undergone periodic changes, sometimes expanding, sometimes slowing. The Prudhoe Bay field has years of active life remaining, but oil companies have pursued new basins in promising areas. Additional discoveries are likely. They have engineered better ways to recover more oil from dwindling fields. There is hope, too, that a large field of gas associated with the oil at Prudhoe will be developed in the next century. Extensive planning has already been completed and aggressive marketing is underway. The growth in population and the economics of Asia point to a huge potential market for Alaska's natural gas. It is plentiful, clean and relatively close to those who need it. Oil and gas will continue to be important mainstays in Alaska's "adolescent" economy, but other sectors have also come into their own as efforts to diversify the state's economy have begun to bear fruit.

Tanks at a Prudhoe Bay oil facility.

While enough is known of Alaska's mineral potential to predict a prosperous future, until recently, that potential had not been explored in depth. That is beginning to change. Here, a miner checks samples at the Crackerjack Mine on Prince of Wales Island.

After fur trapping, commercial fishing is Alaska's oldest economic pursuit. Today it has grown far beyond the traditional harvest of salmon, halibut, herring and cod to target a host of species known for their high-quality taste, texture and nutritional quality. Pollock, sole, flounder and rock fish occur in huge numbers in the biologically rich waters of the Gulf of Alaska and Bering Sea. Heightened awareness of resource limitations have resulted in new strategies to conserve and perpetuate these remarkable fisheries, including expanded research and cooperative management projects with other nations. Alaskans have also become value-added leaders, developing new technological processes and finding new market niches for products made from Alaskan fish, adding a new measure of stability to an industry that historically is very cyclical.

With the advent of more clearly defined land management regimes in recent years, and the transfer of large tracts of land into private ownership, mining has been receiving renewed interest in

While oil exploration has a long history in Alaska, the state's image was profoundly changed with the discovery of the huge oil field at Prudhoe Bay.

Alaskans are leading the way in developing safer and more cost-effective oil development in cold regions.

Alaskans are also in the forefront of many innovations in land use planning, engineering and architectural techniques and telecommunications, government and social progress.

Alaska. While enough is known of Alaska's mineral potential to predict a prosperous future, until recently, that potential had not been explored in depth. That is beginning to change. With the opening of the world-class Red Dog zinc mine in northwest Alaska, efforts to re-open several mines in southeast Alaska and the application of increasingly sophisticated technologies to known gold deposits near Fairbanks, Alaska promises to be a major contributor to world metal markets in years to come.

Surprisingly, large scale logging did not get underway in the vast forests of southeast and southcentral Alaska until the 1950s, although small sawmill operations have always been a feature of both the economic and natural landscape of the state. Management of

these forests has been profoundly influenced by the national debate over management of national forests and the interplay of social, environmental and economic values. This has brought difficult changes to logging communities in Alaska, as elsewhere. While the outcome of this debate is uncertain, there are ample indications that logging will continue to be an economic mainstay of the state. A shift to more diverse value-added processing techniques could open up new niche markets for Alaska's fine spruce and hardwood timber.

Poker Flat Research Range is the only rocket launch facility in the U.S. polar regions and the only university-operated range in the world. It is dedicated primarily to launching rockets to investigate the aurora and other middle-to-upper atmosphere phenomena for research at the University of Alaska Fairbanks Geophysical Institute.

173

CHAPTER ELEVEN: THE RICH FUTURE

Alaska continues to produce about 20% of all the oil consumed by the United States.

Timber is just one of many Alaskan industries in which technological innovation will play a key role in securing a brighter future for the state, and there have been many initiatives by Alaskans to use their oil wealth to expand opportunities in the wise utilization of renewable resources. Just one example is the Alaska Science and Technology Foundation, a state-endowed entity whose mission is to fund research into technologies that will create economic opportunities and improve the lives of Alaskans. With a top-flight staff to review proposals and monitor progress of independent innovators, ASTF has sponsored research on projects as diverse as medical engineering, solid waste disposal and food processing, lumber manufacturing, calibration and computer software applications,

LEFT PAGE: Tourism has grown to be Alaska's third largest industry. Shown here is the Crown Princess cruising Alaska's Inside Passage.
Princess Tours.

creating a highly successful track record in the process. The foundation is an excellent vehicle for transforming brainstorms and inventions into marketable products that can form the basis of a business and create new employment opportunities. Independent of state government, the foundation is a model of disciplined flexibility and a key player in devising the state's high-tech future.

A DIVERSE SOCIETY

That future is already being born in the imaginations of Alaskans who are determined that the state take its rightful place not only as an economic leader, but a leader in building a healthy, sustainable

As Alaska's economy continues to grow and diversify, so too does its trading relationships outside of the state.

CHAPTER ELEVEN: THE RICH FUTURE

The discovery of the huge oil field at Prudhoe Bay gave rise to an engineering marvel — the trans-Alaska pipeline.

society, in which all have equal opportunity. As they conceive and build their future, Alaskans are also in the forefront of many innovations in land use planning, engineering and architectural techniques and telecommunications, government and social progress. Alaskans are coming to terms with the role that preceding generations played in traumatizing indigenous cultures and they are working toward an even more diverse and tolerant society. For their part, Native peoples throughout Alaska, drawing on a rich cultural legacy, are investing their villages and other institutions with new vigor and resilience based on traditional values, as well as assuming greater roles of leadership. This promising trend is also evident among the many Asian, Latin and European peoples for whom Alaska has been like a magnet as they have sought new opportunities. Since its early days, Alaska has boasted a vital African-American community whose members have left their mark on the life and culture of both the territory and the state, and will continue to do so. From this great diversity is coming the talent to devise Alaska's future.

Though not widely known, Alaska has always been a strikingly cosmopolitan place. The late Alaskan journalist, Kay Kennedy, reflecting on life in frontier Fairbanks in the early 1900s, often made this point and took a measure of pride in listing some of the luminaries of the day—people with international reputations— who called Alaska their home in that distant time. The state will continue to draw bright and accomplished people from all over the world into its warm and promising community, and will also give birth to its own sons and daughters who will lead the state to a future that works for everyone.

Bald eagles.

PART TWO

Puffins inhabit the rocky cliffs of Alaska's coastal waters.
Alaska Division of Tourism.

Governmental and Community Organizations

Windham Harbor near Juneau.
Alaska Division of Tourism.

Alaska Credit Union League

The Alaska Credit Union League (ACUL) is an industry trade association whose membership is comprised of Alaska's 17 state or federally chartered credit unions. The ACUL was first organized as an association in 1970 and was officially designated a League when it affiliated with the Credit Union National Association in 1974.

The ACUL's goals are to assist with the establishment, improvement, and growth of credit unions in the state of Alaska; to promote credit union interests; and to facilitate cooperation among credit unions and other state, national, and international credit union associations. The ACUL pursues these goals by providing assistance to groups interested in chartering new credit unions; by coordinating and sharing operational, technical and educational expertise with existing credit unions; by providing a forum for credit unions to come to consensus on local, state, and national

Donna J. Rylander, President.

legislative and regulatory issues; and by fostering the public's understanding of credit unions and the many benefits they provide their members and the communities within which they operate.

The ACUL employs a professional staff and utilized a working committee structure with credit union staff and volunteer officials from throughout Alaska appointed as committee members. This cooperative, broad-based committee structure provides a wide range of experience that all credit unions can draw upon, learn from, and utilize.

The ACUL's cooperative operating approach is similar to the cooperative structure of credit unions and their "People Helping People" philosophy. Unlike other financial institutions, a credit union is a member-owned, not-for-profit cooperative financial institution formed to permit those in the field of membership specified in its charter to pool their savings, lend them to one another, and own the organization where they save, borrow, and obtain related financial services. Members democratically operate the credit union under state or federal law and regulation. Alaskans have long recognized the value of this approach to obtaining financial services versus the "for profit" structure of other financial institutions.

The development and success of credit unions in Alaska began after the second World War when people began to settle the "Last Frontier." These people needed small amounts of money to get settled and established in their households. Since banks were reluctant to lend to these newcomers, the only alternative the people had was to borrow from one another. The credit union structure was an excellent vehicle for doing that. Alaskans pooled their resources through their credit union to help one another and improve their financial well being. It was a classic example of the credit union philosophy and the frontier spirit so prevalent in Alaska. Credit unions were perfect for the situation in Alaska and still are.

With over 330,000 credit union members, Alaska holds the distinction of having more credit union members per capita than any other state in the nation. Credit unions in Alaska provide a wide range of financial services to their members who come from all walks of life and from throughout the state. They hold more than 135,000 consumer loans, $1.5 billion in member deposits, and operate 60 branch locations in 15 Alaska communities.

Helping members improve their financial well being is not the only job of credit unions. Part of the credit union tradition of helping people includes social responsibility. Credit unions take pride in their communities and the people who live and work there as they share their history and their success. Not everyone is a member, but everyone is a neighbor. As an extension of the commitment to helping one another, credit unions, their staffs and officials donate significant amounts of time and money to numerous civic, charitable, and educational programs in communities throughout the state. It is with the spirit of cooperation that credit unions make a difference in the lives of members and others in the communities they serve.

In recognition of the increasingly interrelated world environment, the ACUL in the early 1990s became involved with credit union development on a global scale. In coordination with the World Council of Credit Unions, the University of Alaska's American Russia Center and the Russian Committee for Credit Union Development, the ACUL developed and entered into a long-term project to provide credit union training and internship opportunities to individuals from the Russian Far East. Because of Alaska's geographic proximity and cultural similarities to Russia, and the Russian peoples' desire to develop alternatives to their government-run banks, Alaska's credit unions seized the unique opportunity to help the Russian people develop a better financial future for themselves through democratically-operated credit unions.

The power of cooperation is evidenced by the success of credit unions in serving their members and the communities where they live. It is also evidenced by the success the ACUL has had in helping credit unions and promoting credit union ideals over the years. The strength of the ACUL and the credit unions it represents is their commitment to cooperative principles and to the philosophy of "People Helping People."

Join a credit union . . . it's where Alaskans belong.

Alaska Public Radio Network

Everyday, some 80,000 Alaskans hear the voice of public broadcasting on the Alaska Public Radio Network. It is a voice that speaks many languages, that celebrates many cultures. A voice that entertains. That educates. A voice that draws together the most culturally and geographically diverse state in the union.

Alaska Public Radio Network (APRN) broadcasts to nearly thirty member stations across the state and reaches more than 330 communities. Remote translators allow even tiny settlements of less than ten people hear public radio.

In addition to its six daily programs, APRN has grown to provide professional training and other services, including:

• **National Native News**, the country's only daily news service focused on Native issues;

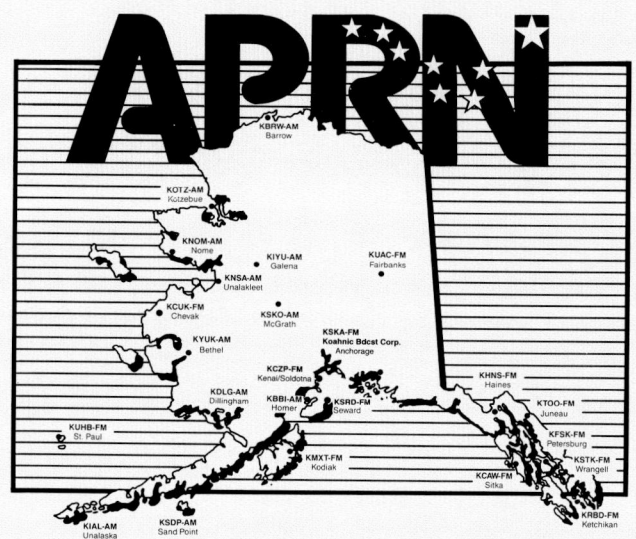

• The "**Indigenous Broadcast Center**," providing media training for Natives across the U.S.;
• "**Advanced Strategic Management Program**," funded by the Corporation for Public Broadcasting, training professionals in public broadcasting management, nationwide;
• "**Native America Calling**," debuting in 1995, the nation's first daily call-in program to discuss issues relevant to present day Native life.

APRN is supported, in part, by corporate sponsors. APRN's corporate underwriting program offers an opportunity to join in a unique partnership by which the corporation receives unmatched state- or nation-wide exposure as well as affiliation with APRN's popular, widely-acclaimed news service.

Board members of APRN's indigenous broadcast center honor National Endowment for the Arts chair, Jane Alexander, with an award of framed Alaskan dance fans, in appreciation for NEA's support. Shown from left to right are: IBC administrative assistant, Linda Mack; IBC board member and general manager of KCUK-FM, Peter Tuluk; IBC director, Jaclyn Sallee; National Endowment for the Arts chair, Jane Alexander; IBC board member and radio manager KYUK-Bethel, Peter Twetchell and IBC board member and general manager KSTK-Wrangell, Tis Peterman.

Alaska Division of Tourism

SELLING ALASKA TO THE WORLD

Created in 1962 as the Alaska Travel Division, the **Alaska Division of Tourism** is charged with stimulating economic growth, diversification, and increased job opportunities in Alaska's visitor industry. In 1989, the legislature created the Alaska Tourism Marketing Council, a committee make up of 21 private and public sector members, responsible for administrating the state's domestic marketing program. The Division of Tourism has a separate budget to promote Alaska as a visitor destination to emerging markets, to answer inquiries from prospective visitors, and to provide technical assistance for the development of infrastructure and visitor attractions.

Alaska visitors enjoy seeing glaciers up close. Mendenhall Glacier, 13 miles from downtown Juneau, is one of Alaska's top attractions.

Alaska's vast expanse of pristine wilderness and abundance of wildlife draws visitors from all over the world. Mt. McKinley in Denali National Park and Preserve is a favorite attraction for visitors to Alaska.

The division promotes Alaska to consumers and the travel trade through contract offices in developing foreign markets. Through its affiliation with Tourism North, a consortium of Alaska, Yukon and British Columbia, the division also promotes the development of highway travel to and within Alaska. Staff members provide technical assistance to individuals, communities and local organizations for the development and marketing of visitor attractions and facilities. Staff members also attend key trade and travel shows in the U.S. and abroad. The division administers the AlaskaHost hospitality training program, and maintains and staffs the Alaska Public Land Information Center in Tok. Other marketing tools provided by the Division of Tourism include published reports outlining the results of an extensive visitor research program, the maintenance of a public slide bank, and distribution of a biannual newsletter.

The Anchorage office of the Division of Tourism administers the Alaska Film Office which attracts commercial, feature, and photographic production to the state. The Juneau office maintains an inquiry section to respond to approximately 120,000 inquiries annually from individuals and organizations seeking information about Alaska.

World Trade Center

On June 1, 1987, Alaska's international trade leaders welcomed the newest international site for a World Trade Center in Anchorage! These leaders knew then what we are observing today. Alaska's strategic position within the Pacific Rim would play a greater and greater role in enhancing Alaska's trade picture. The World Trade Center Alaska offered a unique tool to access these opportunities to individual companies through a variety of educational and trade facilitation services.

World Trade Center Alaska is a member of the World Trade Centers Association, headquartered in New York, which is an organization that stands outside of politics and across national boundaries in service to those who develop and facilitate international trade. As one of the world's premier international business organizations, it currently serves over 400,000 individual businesses through 274 World Trade Centers throughout the world.

Companies now "Join the World" to access trade education programs and information, as well as to become an active member of Alaska's international trade community. World Trade Center Alaska members are located throughout the state from Barrow to Kodiak and St. Paul to Sitka. They represent diversified industries including small manufacturers, international air cargo companies and Alaska Native Corporations. These companies begin their journey to master international business by using the services of the World Trade Center as an integral part of their international business savvy and expand their worldwide contacts through services that make trade happen.

The World Trade Center works hard to create a stronger relationship for these firms with international trade partners, but equally important is to create a strong trade team, within Alaska, of international experts, economic development organizations and international trade facilitators. The World Trade Center Alaska is proud to work with a trade team in Alaska that works consistently and proactively with Alaska's small, medium and large firms and organizations to positively affect the bottom line of these firms and enhance their position in international trade.

The outlook is bright for these and most Alaskan firms who make the commitment to open the door to international opportunities and expand their business knowledge and experience. As international trade looks less foreign, the skills they have developed will give them the competitive advantage to have increased success. It is evident that as these same firms have success, they will encourage the next generation of firms to follow their path of good fortune.

Anchorage, Alaska.

Alaska Division of Economic Development

An oil facility and pipeline are glowing in the dim winter sunshine at Prudhoe Bay, Alaska.

A PARTNERSHIP FOR PROGRESS

Simply stated, the business of the Division of Economic Development is the business of the state of Alaska, and everyone in it. As part of the Department of Commerce & Economic Development, the DED has the responsibility of monitoring and assessing business activities and the economic climate within Alaska. The Division must also act as a working partner with all those doing business, or thinking of doing business, in the 49th state. And business has never been easier to do here. Alaska's state government, unlike many others, is dedicated to working closely with business and industry to energize and advocate, rather than simply to regulate. In these rapidly changing times, it's an approach that works. The state can also offer a young, highly skilled and trained workforce; and boasts an enviable reputation for being able to balance environmental awareness and respect with the continuing needs of the population.

For most of Alaska's history, the extraction and marketing of its natural resources (including seafood), together with recreation- and tourism-related industries, have always formed the backbone of the state's economy. While these are still areas of vital importance, the 1990's have already been making significant changes in that traditional picture. For example, Pacific Rim trade, in all of the above industries, is a major area of growth and development, especially in the extremely competitive world marketplace of today. The same is true of international transportation and shipping. The modern communications industry has made great strides in Alaska, and a high-tech presence is also beginning to emerge.

From gold-rush days to the time of the oil & gas boom, Alaska has always been known as the land of opportunity — and the DED's mission, as part of an ongoing partnership for progress, is to make sure that such opportunities continue to be available to every person and company making an investment in Alaska's future — a future of tough challenges and bright new goals. Working together, with an emphasis on innovation and flexibility, individuals, business, and government can meet those challenges and achieve those goals — throughout the rest of this decade, and on into the 21st century. On behalf of The Last Frontier, the DED welcomes all those who are ready and willing to give it a try.

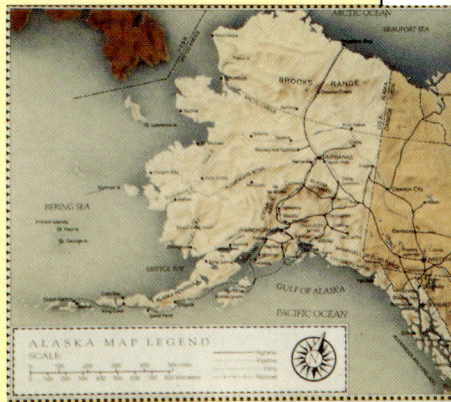

Alaska Humanities Forum

Alaska is a land of great human richness and diversity. In almost every community in the state — whether a remote fishing village or a hurried urban center — Alaskans come face to face with contrasting cultures, values, purposes, and needs. The goal of the Alaska Humanities Forum is to create dialogue among Alaskans through the methods and perspectives of the humanities, and to allow residents to learn from one another through projects that explore what it means to be human.

Since its creation in 1972, the Alaska Humanities Forum has awarded more than $7 million to non-profit organizations and individuals to engage in humanities projects of significance to Alaskans. These projects vary tremendously in topic and scope. Some of the projects the Forum funded in 1993 and 1994 include a multi-faceted program on prejudice, a video documentary on the life of a Tlingit tradition-bearer, a public forum on northern architecture, a planning session for a Yup'ik cultural center, and a conference on balancing jobs and the environment in Alaska.

Examples of various publications supported by Alaska Humanities Forum.

The Forum also serves Alaskans by sponsoring its own projects. The Forum offers a Speakers Bureau through which scholars, Native culture bearers, poets, and others travel throughout the state sharing their unique perspectives. In 1994, the Forum launched a major new project, "Communities of Memory," enabling Alaskans to meet and share their thoughts and stories about their communities. The Forum also publishes a regular journal, "Frame of Reference," which includes articles on projects funded by the Forum, essays and scholarly reflections.

The Alaska Humanities Forum is dedicated to cultivating the enjoyment of the humanities among Alaskans. The humanities include such disciplines as history, anthropology, linguistics, archeology, philosophy and comparative religions. But the humanities do not just belong to scholars or academic institutions. They are rooted as well in the everyday experiences and concerns of individuals. The humanities are concerned with enduring human questions about the meaning of life and with making intellectual, moral and spiritual sense of the world.

Projects funded by the Forum enable Alaskans to apply traditional wisdom to present concerns, search for a sense of personal identity and place, explore divergent points of view and engage in community-based discussions of public policy.

Through its works in partnership with museums, libraries, historical societies and other interested organizations, the Alaska Humanities Forum is by far the most important private source of financial support for humanities projects in Alaska.

The Alaska Humanities Forum is a private, non-profit corporation affiliated with the National Endowment for the Humanities (NEH). To support its work, the Forum depends on financial support from the NEH, grants from private corporations and foundations, and contributions from individuals.

The Forum is guided by a thirteen-member State Committee, which is made up of Alaskans from diverse walks of life and all regions of the state. The State Committee is divided between humanities scholars and members of the general public. Three members are appointed by the governor. Members of the committee serve a three-year term, renewable once.

Alaska Forest Association

Since 1957, the Alaska timber industry has spoken with a common voice; first as the Alaska Loggers Association, and more recently as the Alaska Forest Association. The name change reflects the expansion of membership to include private timber owners, mills, processors and suppliers throughout the state.

The Alaska Forest Association advocates a stable, strong forest products industry based on the sound development of natural timber resources. AFA finances research programs to ensure that forest management practices are compatible with wildlife values, recreation, watershed management, and economics. AFA provides public information to schools, the public, the media, and to its membership to increase awareness of forestry issues, and to accurately portray Alaska's forest facts. The Alaska Forest Association cooperates with federal and state legislative and regulatory bodies to assure a healthy, growing forest-based industry. The AFA is proud of the productivity of Alaskan forests, and its members' responsible stewardship.

AFA members produce the resources needed to manufacture thousands of wood-based products to meet a global demand. The following products, and thousands more, are examples of forest products:

- acetate • acetic acid • acetone
- activated carbon • adhesives
- alcohol • ammunition • anti-foaming agents • artificial snow
- artificial vanilla flavoring
- asphalt • asbestos replacement
- auto instrument panels
- baking cups • boat caulking
- bread wrapping • cellophane
- cement dispersant
- ceramics • charcoal
- cleaning compounds
- corks • cosmetics • creosote
- draperies • enamel
- epoxy resins • eyeglass frames
- fishing tackle • flashlight cases
- foundry cores • football helmets • foam rubber • fuel
- garment bags • gummed tape
- hairspray • insecticide
- laxatives • linoleum • lubricants • luggage • medicines
- missile and radar domes
- mobile homes • nail polish
- oxygen • paint • paint remover
- photographic film and slides
- pingpong balls • piano keys
- pine oil disinfectant
- poultry feed • printing ink
- purified water • rayon
- rubber tires • sausage casing
- shoe insoles and heels
- spacecraft reentry shields
- steering wheels • tanned leather • turpentine • vacuum bags • vinegar • wood stain
- world globes

*Regeneration promotes healthy, productive timbered lands to benefit people **and** the environment.*

Land Managers work closely with regulatory agencies to provide for wildlife, recreation, water and wood.

Governmental and Community Organizations

Katmai National Park.
Alaska Division of Tourism

GCI

When GCI brought long distance telephone competition to Alaska with state-of-the-art technology, it was just the beginning. During the past 15 years, the company has literally changed the way Alaskans think about communications, and how they communicate among themselves and with the rest of the world. While offering the highest quality technical and customer service, GCI has positioned itself as the low-cost leader in Alaska. The impact of this historic development has been tangible: Alaskans saved $200 million in the first decade of GCI's presence. As importantly, the company is anticipating a new era of growth by expanding into the telecommunication frontiers of the 21st century.

Founded by Alaskans and strongly committed to the Alaska market in all of its burgeoning vitality, GCI has the kind of qualities that make it a natural leader among the state's top corporations: stability, innovation, perseverance, a competitive spirit. Especially important for Alaskans, these qualities have been greatly enhanced through GCI's affiliation with the vast global network of MCI. This vital strategic alliance gives Alaskans direct access to a universe of telecommunications capabilities with resulting efficiencies and convenience. The two companies cooperate closely in the provision of services, research and new products by sharing certain marketing, engineering and operating resources. Alaskans receive the benefits of MCI's sophisticated intelligent network services. The relationship allows GCI to develop and deploy locally driven communications solutions based on global applications.

"Our strategic alliance with MCI puts us on a global playing field and gives us access to several billion dollars worth of networking software. In essence, we are Alaska's doorway to that rich resource," says Ronald A. Duncan, GCI's president and co-founder.

As the trend towards more competition in long distance service grows, GCI has continued to balance current strategies

Customer satisfaction is the highest priority among GCI's 400 employees. In fact, GCI employees own 15 percent of the company's common stock. This means its employees have a personal interest in the reputation and ability of the company to provide the best telecommunication service available.

and offerings against the long-term horizon with deftness, always keeping the needs of customers uppermost. Indeed customer needs have directly influenced the extensive menu of products and services GCI currently offers. Founded in 1979, the company is engaged in the transmission of interstate and intrastate switched message toll service and private line and private network communication service between the major communities in Alaska, the other 49 states and foreign countries. In response to the changing needs of its customers, GCI provides originating calling card and 800 toll services, as well as termination of north-bound toll service for MCI, Sprint and other interexchange carriers who don't have facilities in Alaska.

Service is provided from facilities in Adak, Anchorage, the Mat-Su Valley, Seward, Glennallen, Homer, Kenai, Soldotna, Eagle River, Fairbanks, Juneau, Ketchikan, Prudhoe Bay, Valdez, Kodiak, Sitka, Unalaska and Cordova, all in Alaska, and at Issaquah, Washington. An operator service center is maintained in Wasilla, Alaska, near Anchorage.

In 1991, GCI made fiber optic transmission available to its customers. Linked to a fiber optic cable extending from Oregon to Japan, a 700-mile Alaska spur is linked to GCI's statewide network at Seward. This advanced technology greatly enhances voice and data transmission quality. Also, as a result of careful market research, and with attention to detail, GCI has devised a variety of savings plans for residential and business customers covering both intrastate, interstate and international calls.

While high-quality long distance telephone service at reasonable rates has given GCI its enviable position in the Alaska market, it is the restless and ongoing pursuit of technological innovation and more efficient, cost-effective communication applications for Alaskan households and businesses that is driving the company towards the future.

"When we say we're committed to Alaska, we mean just that, in the most direct, pragmatic terms," says Duncan. "Part of our mission, perhaps our most important service, is to make Alaskan companies competitive in the global market. Every time we succeed, the entire Alaska economy benefits."

The company's strategy to fulfill this mission involves a unique, focused partnership with each of its business customers to develop the most cost-effective communication strategies possible, with emerging technologies tailored expressly to the needs of each client. Portable satellite technology, telecomputing and wireless communications services are just three areas in which GCI's highly trained personnel are breaking new ground.

VSATs–Recognizing the profound effect of geography

In 1992, GCI instituted RELAYalaska — the first telecommunication relay service for deaf, hard-of-hearing and speech impaired callers in Alaska.

and other natural factors on Alaskan businesses, GCI has moved aggressively in providing satellite earth stations with small antennae called Very Small Aperture Terminals (VSATs). These versatile units provide high-quality communications similar to standard earth stations, but because of their small size, they can provide a significant logistical advantage and cost savings for applications of short durations such as news coverage, construction projects and resource exploration. They provide tremendous flexibility by enabling users in remote areas to communicate in a cost-effective manner with larger, permanent networks and facilities. GCI is providing reliable VSAT services to a growing number of retail

A significant contributor to community activities, GCI is the official communication sponsor for Alaska's premier sporting event, the 1,049-mile Iditarod Trail Sled Dog Race. The race showcases GCI's abilities to establish state-of-the-art communication links in remote locations.

operations that use VSAT technology to link multiple locations directly to a central computing facility to track product inventories, verify credit, approve check cashing and similar functions. Other technology is being combined with VSATs to produce a wide variety of services including facsimile, video, broadcast program distribution and data distribution for wire services and stocks.

GCI utilizes fiber optics technology — the latest in advanced telecommunications.

Computer Networking– Being competitive today, and tomorrow, requires the ability to transfer information— sometimes on a private line, sometimes on a switched circuit — instantaneously, accurately and consistently. Billing, payables, tax preparation, inventory control and ordering, supply and logistics planning, operational trouble shooting and other management functions are just a few of the tasks now being done entirely or with the substantial assistance of computers. GCI specializes in providing and supporting integrated communication systems to customers throughout Alaska. The company sells, services and operates dedicated communication and computer networking equipment.

Wireless Communications Services–Wireless telecommunications is another area of tremendous growth potential for GCI, signaling another era of profound change in the way communications services are delivered. Today, a telephone number is connected to a single physical location. In the new wireless system, a telephone number will designate one person, and will allow that person to receive or make calls from any location. By the end of the century, users may not have to go to an office to conduct business, but may do it from any place they choose. For Alaskans, this could mean more direct participation in economic, cultural and educational activities elsewhere in the world, and allow Alaskans to share the state's creativity, talent and expertise with other regions.

Not all of GCI's expertise is reflected in its packaged services. Behind the scenes, the quest for improvements and greater customer satisfaction has the highest priority. "Increasingly, people want to come to one place for a full range of services. They want to be sure

GCI-4: When NASA explored the crater floor of Mt. Spurr, an active Alaska volcano, with an experimental robot, GCI provided communication links between the robot and the outside world.

all the pieces fit together. We can give that assurance. Affordable peace of mind is another name for what we do so well," says Duncan.

In large measure, that peace of mind derives from the individual and collective efforts of GCI's team of professionals. The company places a high value on all of its employees and strives to recognize their achievements, their hard work and loyalty. A high priority is given to nurturing a workplace conducive to high performance as well as personal and professional growth. A strong employee orientation extends from the progressive policies of daily management to making employees co-owners in the company through stock-purchase and profit sharing plans. This practice helps bring out the competitive spirit in GCI's professionals and helps foster productivity and creativity in their work.

"We welcome competition because it makes the economy grow, to the benefit of everyone," says Duncan. "Competition tends to keep prices down, which is certainly a boon to business, but it also spurs new technological developments. It drives the search for more efficient ways to provide an existing service, or to provide a service where none existed before, and if we can provide those services less expensively, while maintaining or enhancing quality, then our customers become more competitive in their respective arenas. Competition creates a ripple effect throughout the economy with enormous implications."

Although GCI's customers benefit considerably from the company's outlook on the marketplace, GCI managers believe strongly that their responsibility as a corporate citizen extends beyond the day-to-day transactions involving its high-tech services. GCI has also made its resources available to the community in a spirit of charity and goodwill, as reflected in its mission statement and "declaration of principles." In addition to embracing qualities such as innovation, efficiency, trustworthiness and promptness, in its operations, the declaration pledges the company to "responsible, ethical and honest participation in the community" in order to "carry out legal and ethical obligations, and to

GCI introduced digital transmission technology to Alaska in 1979, and now offers access to the Lower 49 states as well as 220 countries.

GCI has 14 major earth stations throughout Alaska and Washington. Fiber optic and terrestrial microwave links carry the majority of interstate and inter-urban traffic. Satellite links carry most of GCI's intrastate traffic.

support the dignity of each employee."

It is this spirit which has led GCI to investing in community events, charities and activities throughout Alaska. One of GCI's most notable and visible community contributions has been its wholehearted support of the Iditarod Trail Sled Dog Race. This exciting international event has not only provided a means for field testing a variety of communications solutions under rigorous conditions, it has come to symbolize the company's fervent belief in the benefits of competition to the company, its customers and the Alaska economy as a whole.

"We feel the pride and accomplishments of our employees, and their enthusiastic implementation of our customer service philosophy, has more than vindicated our investment in competition," says Duncan. "With this kind of teamwork, we are strongly positioned for future growth."

Weaver Brothers

Weaver Brothers' petroleum tanker fleet consists of 30 units, including this linehaul truck with fuel tanker.

Family trucking is alive and well at Weaver Brothers. The firm is owned by the Doyle family. James H. (Jim) and Trina live in Kenai and Jimmy operates the Anchorage terminal. Other family members also contribute talents to the profitable management of the company.

Weaver Brothers is a major player in supplying Alaska's oil fields from Swanson River on the Kenai Peninsula to the North Slope. As a common carrier, this support comes through winch trucks, chemical and petroleum tankers, drilling mud bulkers and various types of flatbeds and lowboys. The line-haul portion of their business adds to the variety of trucking services they provide along with the contract work they do for the water-carriers which dock at the Port of Anchorage.

Jim Doyle actually got his start in the home-to-home fuel delivery business in 1957, in Moose Pass. In the spring of 1958, he moved to Kenai to run the fuel delivery business for Ed Estes. In his spare time he hauled freight around the Kenai area with a two-ton flatbed he bought. Finally in 1962, he started his own fuel business, Doyle's Fuel Service. From there he branched out mostly into gas station deliveries over the Kenai Peninsula. In 1978, just following the completion of the Trans-Alaskan Pipeline, the owners of Weaver Bros. shut the company down. At the time, the trucking industry in Alaska was regulated, so the only viable opportunity for Doyle to expand was to buy an existing trucking permit from an existing company. In October of 1978, the deal was completed for the purchase and Doyle quickly opened up additional terminals in Anchorage and Fairbanks to go

The local drivers, linehaul drivers and dispatchers have proven to be both a loyal crew and the backbone of the company. Some of the drivers have been with Weaver Brothers for 20 years.

Weaver Brothers delivered hot oil used in making road asphalt to a highway construction job on the Seward Highway on the Kenai Peninsula. WBI has 25 asphalt semis/pups.

along with his home terminal in Kenai. Jim remembers throughout the 60s and 70s when he would see the Weaver Bros. trucks busily hauling past his home on the Kenai Spur, never thinking that someday he might own that company.

While many of his then competitors in the industry have since departed due to attrition and competition, the Doyles have exhibited the ability to balance the search for new business while keeping the level of service they provide as high as they can.

The quality of employees that they have is one reason they feel they have been successful. "If we didn't have the drivers, office, shop and management people that we have, we couldn't provide the type of top service that we feel we give our customers. A lot of these people have been around here a long time and are like family to us," says the younger Doyle. "Some of the employees have been here as long as 26 years."

They feel the same way about their customers. "Our customers know that Alaska is our home and we're here to stay," says Jim Sr. Establishing good service at a fair price is one way Weaver Bros. kept some long-time customers. One such customer is Jim Burns of Petro Marine Services. Burns explains, "My most recent agreement with Weaver involved hauling heavy fuel oil from Nikiski to Seward for cruise ships that call at Seward. There were unique problems with our terminal, truck configurations, handling of the fuel oil and timing of each delivery. As I expected, Weaver delivered on time and safely, steadily, and competently. I wanted excellent performance and I got it."

To all of its customers, regardless of the cargo-handling needs, Weaver offers the special and increasingly rare combination of traits that mark old-time Alaskan companies: innovative, forward-looking, competent, caring and neighborly.

The owners of the company from right to left: Jim and wife Trina Doyle, and Jimmy with wife Sharon Doyle. Jim Sr. lives in Kenai and Jim Jr. oversees the Anchorage terminal.

"Those qualities may be old-fashioned," says Burns, "But as far as we're concerned, they comprise a sure-fire formula for the future. I can rely on Weaver to do it exactly as we agreed to. Their word is good. That kind of trust and dependability is priceless."

Northern Television

Northern Television is a pioneer Alaskan firm, but that does not keep it from being a progressive, forward-thinking leader in Alaska's economy. In fact, a visit with founder and chairman Augie Hiebert makes it clear that providing opportunities for youth to gain wide and diverse experience in broadcasting has long been part of the company's formula for success.

Another is its savvy blend of diversified ventures, a key factor in its success in a crowded, competitive market. It is the only firm with AM and FM stations as well as television. Northern Television also operates a very profitable Muzak franchise. Although Hiebert and his team make it look easy, and Northern Television has been thriving since the 1950s, success is the fruit of long and difficult labor, attended by the kind of calamities that a frontier territory can dish out, including floods and earthquakes, to say nothing of competitors.

Hiebert came to Alaska in 1939 to help build the first radio station in Fairbanks. In 1947, it was on to Anchorage, where he helped design and build radio station KENI-AM. Although radio greatly enhanced communication and entertainment in Alaska, Hiebert saw a bright future for television. The conventional wisdom, however, was that television could never compete with radio and film. Putting his money, and that of several other backers, where his faith pointed, Hiebert founded the state's first TV station (KTVA-TV, initially an NBC affiliate that switched to CBS in July, 1955) in Anchorage in 1953. A transcript of that first broadcast by announcer Frank Brink reveals the primitive state of both the medium and the market in which Hiebert had launched his enterprise:

KNIK-FM 105.3 The Breeze, Anchorage. From left to right: Duane Millsap, Chief Engineer and Jennifer Summers, Radio Announcer in new KNIK-FM studio adjoining KBYR 700-AM.

KTVA-TV, Channel 11, Anchorage. From left to right: Duane Millsap, Chief Engineer; Augie Hiebert, Chairman/CEO; Julianna Guy, President/General Manager; Bruce Sloan, Vice President - TV Programming/Operations at dedication of new CBS Ku Band Satellite uplink to CBS Newspath.

"To many of you, television will be a completely new experience but as time goes by, I'm sure it will become a regular and necessary part of your daily life. It won't be long until you will be talking a new language filled with expressions like 'snow,' 'ghosts,' 'fringe area,' 'diffusion,' and others having to do with quality and performance of your TV set and your reception. We sincerely hope that your reception will be trouble free at least most of the time . . ."

This was only the first of several history-making ventures initiated by Northern Television. Hiebert also flipped the switch on the first television station in Fairbanks in 1955, KTVF-TV, the same year he acquired affiliation with CBS, a happy partnership that has endured to this day. He introduced television translators to Alaska and brought FM radio to Anchorage when KNIK-FM went on the air in 1960 (originally as KTVA-FM).

Despite dramatic damage to broadcasting facilities as a result of the Good Friday earthquake in Anchorage in 1964 and the great Fairbanks flood of 1967, Hiebert and his staff persevered. The massive quake damaged the building that housed the radio and TV stations, along with the antenna. Water from broken pipes flooded the transmitters.

But a week later they were beaming their signals into the shattered community as Alaskans began to pull their lives together.

"We had to wear hard hats on the air," Hiebert recalls. "The building had no heat and no water. We got little stoves for the offices and space heaters for the big studio, and put chimneys out the side of the building, but strange air currents blew the soot and smell into the building."

The Fairbanks flood was even more devastating. But every time adversity visited Northern Television, the firm seemed to bounce back even stronger; usually another historic broadcasting innovation was not far behind. In 1971, it was the KTVA-CBS satellite coverage of the trans-Alaska pipeline hearings, beamed live from Alaska to the Lower 48 — the first successful commercial satellite transmission going south from Alaska.

"I think what we've done stands on its own feet," says Hiebert, who is already laying the groundwork for another advance in television programming with the advent of high-definition technology. "The thing that sets us apart is the diversification. It's not easy to do but we're probably more profitable than stations in other markets that get grandiose ideas. Instead of constantly trying to repackage ourselves, we simply focus on improving performance and sticking to what customers want and what we do best."

Hiebert's vision of the future encompasses far more than technological concerns. Northern Television remains a progressive firm, dedicated to its employees and searching out new, young talent.

"This provides opportunities for young people to get a broad-based taste of what's going on. I'm pretty proud of that. This is the entry level for people in the industry. They can learn it and learn it very well. What's very important to us is to hire in-state," says Hiebert.

Perhaps no better tribute has been paid to Hiebert's visionary efforts than that voiced by America's dean of broadcasters, Walter Cronkite. Reflecting on a tour of Alaska, Cronkite wrote:

"When I think of those people at the far reaches of the North Slope, and out west of Kotzebue, and down on the little cove near Homer, I know what Augie Hiebert has meant to them. He, as much as any single person, has brought them in touch with one another and with the great outside world. He was one of the pioneers who brought them radio, and now television."

KTVF-TV, Channel 11, Fairbanks. For efficient operations, Master Control, Satellite Control and Production Control are located in one central location. Frank Bascom, Master Control Operator.

KTVF-TV, Channel 11, Fairbanks. Two sets in one! "Good Morning Fairbanks" set on the left, and News set on the right in new studios.

Sealand Service

On May 9, 1964, just weeks after Alaska's devastating Good Friday Earthquake, the Sea-Land New Orleans docked at the Port of Anchorage carrying relief supplies. This marked the beginning of year-round waterborne container service to Alaska. For the first time, with regularly scheduled arrivals, Alaska's merchants could restock their shelves on a frequent basis. The new service was not only reliable, it was cost effective.

Since those dramatic beginnings, Sea-Land has brought more than a million containers to the state, keeping pace with the Alaskan market by increasing the frequency of

Sea-Land's Alaska fleet consists of three world class vessels constructed especially to meet the rigors of Alaskan service.

Sea-Land has brought more than a million containers to Alaska, keeping pace with the Alaskan market by increasing the frequency of arrivals and number of ports served over the years.

arrivals and number of ports served over the years. Today, Sea-Land's Alaska fleet consists of three world class vessels constructed especially to meet the rigors of Alaskan service. Commissioned in 1987, the Sea-Land Anchorage, Tacoma and Kodiak each have a capacity of 706 containers. They call the ports of Anchorage, Kodiak and Tacoma twice weekly and the Aleutian port of Dutch Harbor once a week. Sea-Land also operates feeder barge service to Akutan, Sand Point, St. Paul, Cordova and points in Bristol Bay. Sea-Land Freight Service, a Sea-Land subsidiary, provides trucking and terminal service from Anchorage to the cities of Fairbanks and Kenai.

In 1993, Sea-Land began calling Dutch Harbor weekly with vessels from its PSW string which connects America's West Coast with Asia. This new link provides express service directly to Japan from the seafood-rich Alaskan waters.

Alaskan ports are fed by Sea-Land's worldwide shipping network which serves 120 ports in 80 countries. Sea-Land's intermodal service from the continental United States is especially important to the Alaskan customer. When Sea-Land became a unit of CSX Corporation in 1986, the combination of ocean and rail transportation leaders created the world's most sophisticated intermodal network. Containers can be loaded at any city or town in the continental United States, quickly railed on one of the more than 240 weekly dedicated container trains or trucked to Tacoma and then lifted aboard an Alaska Service vessel. The same container is then delivered to the customer in Alaska, eliminating any rehandling of freight from the original point of loading to the final destination. Similar service is also available to or from Canada, Europe and Asia.

Safety of employees, vessels and customer's cargo is Sea-Land's number one priority. Storms in the Gulf of Alaska can create high winds and waves in excess of 65 feet high. While some companies may focus on arrival time, Sea-Land believes that the safe arrival of its vessels, crews and their freight, all in good condition, is its primary goal. Under this policy, the stability of the D-7 vessels and Sea-Land's patented hinged frame stacking system, Sea-Land experiences very little cargo loss at sea.

Sea-Land pioneered the containerized shipping industry in 1956 and continues to lead in innovation and technology. Sea-Land has introduced a series of state-of-the-art refrigerated containers ("reefers") whose platinum sensors provide precision response to temperature changes. Recent versions even include a remote monitoring capability. These containers can maintain a constant environment ranging from -15F degrees to +75F degrees, have

In 1993, Sea-Land began calling Dutch Harbor weekly with vessels from its PSW string which connects America's West Coast with Asia.

Sea-Land Freight Service, a Sea-Land subsidiary, provides trucking and terminal service from Anchorage to the cities of Fairbanks and Kenai.

fresh air exchange capabilities and regulate internal humidity. "Dual-temp" reefers feature separate compartments within the same container that can maintain different temperature settings.

A dedicated Alaska sales team for general commodities and a special seafood sales group comprise the most professional and knowledgeable sales organization in the Alaska trade. The team prides itself on long-term customer relationships and expertise in specific commodity shipments. Special Customer Service groups based in Anchorage, Kodiak, Dutch Harbor and Tacoma are linked to the company's mainframe. Full-time personnel work with customer data and Sea-Land schedules giving one-on-one attention to shippers' questions and booking requests. No problem is too large or too small to solve.

Alaskan customers choose Sea-Land equipment that meets their needs. The standard and high cube 40-foot container pool is supplemented high cube 45-foot containers, 20-foot containers, the sophisticated line of "intelligent" reefers, insulated containers, car-tainers, and flatbeds.

Sea-Land is proud of its thirty-year partnership with Alaskans. Their ships have provided reliable transportation through good time and bad, boom and bust, in sunshine and snowstorm. Sea-Land will continue to seek new ways to serve the changing needs of its customers.

Avis

Trying harder takes on a whole other dimension in Alaska, especially in vehicle renting and leasing. But that extra effort, for which Avis Rent-a-Car is so famous, has on many occasions made a big difference to customers residing in or visiting Alaska.

"Driving conditions here can be widely variable. We pride ourselves on being able to provide the right vehicle to our customers for the conditions and for their needs, whether it's biological field studies, or sales calls or fishing on the Kenai Peninsula," says Andrew Halcro, the company's director of sales and marketing for the state. He notes that with a fleet of over 1,400 vehicles, ranging from sedans and 4x4's to Suburbans and pickup trucks, Avis provides flexibility. This also stems from years of hands-on Alaskan experience. Established in 1955, the locally owned Avis agency was renting cars before Alaska became a state!

Halcro recalls the frantic days of the Exxon Valdez oil spill when the inventory handled by the Valdez office soared from 20 to 120 vehicles. The spill was the largest in U.S. history and required a massive clean-up effort. An unbelievable amount of equipment and supplies had to be shipped into the area. Even as the cleanup got underway, Avis personnel swung into action, doing their part with characteristic professionalism. The company handles individual and project customers with equal dispatch. During the recent filming of a major motion picture, Avis had two days to stage 40 vehicles of all descriptions for a remote location. The occasion was location shooting for "On Deadly Ground," Steven Segal's blockbuster directorial debut. On a tight schedule and on a budget, the vehicles were an indispensable part of the logistical framework for the picture. Once again, Avis delivered.

"Projects like that are challenging. We get a chance to demonstrate what we're made of, and a chance to be really proud of our employees," says Halcro. "But I'd have to say that we treat our everyday customers with the same level of service, the same attention to detail, if not more so. They're really the backbone of our business."

As the only statewide agency in Alaska, Avis is able to provide seamless integrated service across an area one-fifth the size of the Lower 48 states. A customer can rent a vehicle in Juneau and return it in Fairbanks, or rent in Fairbanks and return it in Skagway, or

AVIS' fleet is perfect for winter conditions. Besides 4-wheel drives, the majority of their fleet are sure-footed front-wheel drives.

AVIS features GM vehicles like the all new 1995 4-wheel drive GMC Jimmy. AVIS has a wide range of 4X4 vehicles from Minivans to Sedans.

rent in Anchorage and return it there after having completed a driving tour of Central Alaska. Literally dozens of combinations are possible, says Halcro.

"We do this year round," he adds. "People commute between Anchorage and Fairbanks for winter festivals, rural folks come into town to shop, people are always heading out of town to ski or see friends, and that's just the residents. We also have a large business clientele, some of which is based on a very healthy year round convention market."

Avis also serves an increasingly large number of non-resident visitors drawn to Alaska's vivid scenery and rich culture. These visitors are discovering there is a lot to see from the 14,000 miles of road system in Alaska, from vacation hideaways and fabulous fishing holes, to Native villages, national parks and forest and numerous activities for every season of the year.

Regardless of their travel needs, customers have come to expect a high standard of performance from Avis. Service is friendly, punctual and well-

Corporate and convention services distinguish AVIS in a class by itself.

informed. Cars are clean and ready on schedule. Despite its large territory, the company stands ready to assist any customer with mechanical difficulty, promptly and free of charge. Halcro notes with satisfaction that such services are rarely required since the fleet is new and maintained to high standards. The list of other amenities offered by Avis is long and includes:

• the same corporate rates that customers have come to expect from Avis agencies outside Alaska;

• an airport shuttle for visitors arriving at the newly-enlarged Anchorage International Airport;

• a high-quality vehicle sales program; and

• 13 locations statewide, centrally managed by a modern computer network that affords fast reliable service.

Although the computers are essential, Halcro says people are still the heart of Avis. Twenty of the 100-plus employees have been with the firm for more than 10 years, a strong testament to Avis' stability and growth.

"That says a lot about our employees and the service we provide. The people we have working at Avis are enthusiastic, helpful, and courteous: this in turn creates a pleasant and comfortable transaction for our customers," says Halcro.

Matanuska Telephone Association

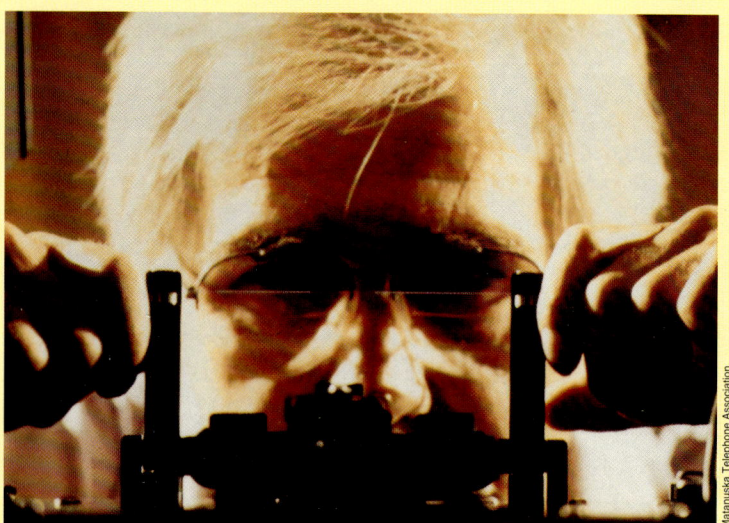

The old days of solder and connectors are gone — today's telephone cable splicers use laser fusion devices to join continuous glass fibers into the roadways of the "information highway."

When one thinks of Alaska . . . especially rural Alaska, they think of snow covered peaks, giant cabbages, and teeming salmon in the streams. They dream of bears and eagles, great mountains and dog sled teams. If they have never been to Alaska, they envision an often dark, foreboding land covered with ice and snow, winter nights under the Northern Lights, and tales of the sourdoughs. In reality, Alaska is all of these things — and today it is so much more.

Today's Alaska truly is the last frontier . . . a collage of historic gold mining towns, fishing villages, great rain forests, snow covered peaks and spectacular rivers of ice. There are just over a half million people who inhabit Alaska, and they are spread out over the nation's largest state in a cosmopolitan mixture of quaint bush towns and modern cities. The very nature of Alaska's vastness and diversity demands an efficient information highway. Before that phrase was ever coined, many Alaskans had already begun their journey down the fiber optic freeways and through the digital interchanges of Alaska's most modern local telephone service provider. That journey between cities and onto the ionospheric relays connecting families and businesses around the state and the world is provided by the nation's fourth largest telephone cooperative, Matanuska Telephone Association, Inc. (MTA).

No ordinary rural American telephone cooperative, this architect of telecommunications pathways for the 1990s and beyond, is a nationally recognized leader in the telecommunications industry.

Because of MTA's location in the heart of Alaska's historic Matanuska Valley, the organization was created and nurtured by the members of the local farmer grange. That small seedling, which they planted nearly forty years ago, has bloomed and prospered under the midnight sun. Today, MTA has become the key to voice and data communications along the railbelt corridor, from Anchorage to Denali National Park, just south of Fairbanks.

North America's highest peak, Mt. McKinley lies in the heart of Matanuska Telephone's service area. MTA serves Denali with digital technology and fiber optic transmission lines.

With its newly constructed state-of-the-art headquarters facility located in Palmer, Alaska, a scenic hour drive from Anchorage, Matanuska Telephone is ideally situated to provide 21st century telecommunications to the largest growth area of the state.

For years, publications from around the world have wondered at the ninety-eight pound cabbages and three hundred pound winter squash that grow huge during Alaska's never ending summer days. The crop being planted by this progressive co-op is state-of-the-art telecommunications and the harvest has been good. The

The Chugach Mountains remind Alaskans of a time when telephone cables were stretched from fence-post to fence-post. Today, fiber optics serve MTA's 36,000 access lines.

environment and rapidly growing residential areas of this picturesque and prosperous area of Alaska. They provide the warmth and comfort of instant communications to the mobile, as well as to the sourdoughs, who inhabit the farthest reaches of this great land.

Yes, all of this and more is Alaska. Ever since those midwestern pioneers came to the Matanuska Valley in the 1930s, the "Greatland" has provided for their needs. For forty of those years, MTA has continued planting the telecommunications seedlings that have grown into one of the nation's fastest growing telephone cooperatives. Whether it is communication with the "lower 48" or telecommuting to another Alaska city or the rest of the world, Matanuska Telephone is the telecommunications leader that provides the vehicle for your journey into the 21st century.

miles and miles of fiber optic cables that have been planted in the rich Alaskan soil link MTA's central office digital equipment to its 36,000 plus access lines. It provides a rich bounty of custom service features and digital data links.

Even more than telecommunications have grown from this "network's" planting. Education is springing up all around MTA's service area. The state's first fully interactive educational TV system, linking rural high schools, is out of the ground, taking its fledgling steps toward a future rich with real time medical links, teleconferences, and switched broadband services.

The fence posts of today are stainless steel, each covered with microwave relays and cellular antennas. They surround the fertile business

MTA's Eagle River Central Office was the first in the nation to provide Equal Access for long distance service. Now virtually all MTA subscribers enjoy the digital technology of the 21st century.

Municipal Light and Power

Providing electricity to Anchorage since 1932 with vision and quality service, Municipal Light and Power (ML&P) is a leading partner in developing the city's economic strength.

"It's a fact that our performance record, customer orientation and technological innovation have made us one of the strongest utilities in the state and a key participant in the railbelt power grid of central Alaska," says Tom Stahr, ML&P's general manager. "We believe that we provide the most reliable power in Alaska and we're in a position to supply large quantities of electricity to industrial as well as new commercial and residential customers."

Although ML&P's service area of twenty square miles is relatively small compared to neighboring utilities, the city is literally the commercial, industrial and transportation nerve center of the state, as well as home to more than half its population.

Jan Blanchard, senior systems analyst, displays the computer-controlled radio equipment used for automatic meter reading.

"This is the state's primary growth center and has been for a long time. We're proud that we've kept pace and helped make that growth possible," declares Stahr. "Even better, our projections indicate that this vibrant market will continue to grow."

The Alaska Railroad maintains its primary yarding facilities and is aggressively developing several commercial projects on land it owns in the service area. The projects will support substantial increases already occurring in year-round tourism and convention industries. Large-scale improvements to the Port of Anchorage will accommodate larger traffic volumes and downtown businesses and facilities are working to meet new demands.

"Even though we're smaller in geographical size, we've got nearly 30,000 customers and counting, and the same climatic and seasonal challenges to cope with as larger utilities. In essence, the job of our very committed staff is to insure that the vagaries of weather and a long winter don't interfere with the well-being of our customers; and they perform that function very well," states Stahr.

Increased demand, environmental factors and a fundamental commitment to efficiency have all contributed to ML&P's never-ending quest for technological innovation. This has provided excellent results for customers and has sharpened ML&P's competitive edge in Alaska's power market. "We've tried to stay in the forefront of technology without sacrificing service. That balance is key and I think we've maintained that very effectively," says Stahr.

ML&P was the first Alaska utility to use natural gas turbines for base load applications in 1962, and later achieved success in bringing turbine emissions within new limits. The utility was also the first to develop automatic meter reading on a large application basis. But according to Stahr, innovation hasn't been limited to the basic operations. In 1993, President Bill Clinton announced the selection of ML&P, along with partner Babock & Wilcox, to become the frontrunners in electrical storage

One of ML&P's generators is cleaned using a method called air blasting. The method uses carbon dioxide pellets and leaves no mess to clean up.

ML&P's 1994 Electrical Safety Poster Contest winner, Mike Sabo, and his fifth grade classmates, display his "award-winning" entry, which was enlarged into bus signs.

technology by constructing and installing a midsize Superconducting Magnetic Energy Storage project. This selection was made under the Federal Technology Reinvestment program's joint funding to develop dual use technologies with both military and commercial applications. The storage device is sized for a 30 MW power rating and 1800 Megajoule storage capacity. ML&P projects the device could save up to $2 million per year through generation fuel cost reductions to customers and power outages of shorter duration. Reduced combustion turbine emissions will provide an additional benefit.

"This is the first such device of its size and nature to be installed on an electric utility system anywhere in the world, and we feel our selection is a strong testament to our commitment to stay on the cutting edge of developments that will measurably improve cost-effective service delivery," explains Stahr. "We've also been looking at the feasibility of operating electric cars in northern climates. We're working with Chrysler to develop data for some of their research and development work."

As important as technological performance, is ML&P's relationship with its customers—commercial, industrial and residential. In this area, ML&P's excellence is reflected in the broad intentions of its mission statement and in the myriad, sometimes minuscule, sometimes major, actions of professional staff who answer questions, reconcile statements, respond to emergencies, explain procedures, perform data entry and troubleshoot a thousand contingencies.

The mission statement gives direction to strategies that recognize the needs of the customer not only for reliable power, but cost-effective electricity as well: *To commit to being Alaska's energy leader by being innovative and trustworthy in responding to our customers' needs for safe, economical and reliable electrical service.*

In a characteristically progressive move, ML&P offered the public an opportunity to acquire a greater sense of ownership by offering a tax free "mini-bond" sale, complete with a mini prospectus. The bonds, which had five, seven and ten-year maturities, will be worth $1,000 each at the date the bond matures. The five-year bonds sold for approximately $750 each, the seven-year bonds for about $660 and the ten-year mini-bonds for about $540.

The bond sale was extremely unique as the bonds were offered to the public without the customary use of a broker. Underwritten by Bank of America, the bonds were offered at a minimum of $1,000 of face value and a maximum of $5,000 of face value per invetor, thereby boosting opportunities for the general public to participate. The sale was a huge success, netting the utility nearly $1 million and providing a vehicle for long-term goodwill between ML&P and its customers.

"Activities such as these are basically tokens of our dedication, albeit important tokens. They're gestures intended to strengthen our bond with customers," Stahr remarks "In the final analysis, we owe our success to a marvelous cadre of

An American bald eagle sits majestically on a post which has a weathered electric meter mounted to it.

professionals who know what they're doing, and enjoy doing it. Customer satisfaction gives them satisfaction."

Stahr says customers, those who make Anchorage their home, can be proud that such dedication makes employees the key to ML&P's future, a future as bright as Anchorage, Alaska's own ascending star.

MACtel Cellular System

With customer service that is fast becoming a tradition, MACtel Cellular System is proving that Alaska may no longer be the Last Frontier after all. MACtel is the purveyor of choice for many Alaskans seeking the best in portable telephone technology, networking and rate structures.

"We feel we've played a key role in putting the state in the forefront of the very latest in applied telecommunications technology," says Scott Davis, General Manager of the Alaska-owned firm. "In order to maximize the benefits of this technology, it is critical that customers know we not only back up the equipment we provide, but also the technical assistance, and counsel to access and utilize the network effectively."

Davis says the very qualities that have fostered Alaska's frontier image make it a natural market for cellular systems. The country is big, with great distances between population centers. Infrastructure is relatively limited in some areas, with many people living and working in remote locations off the main communications and utility grid. These people range from trappers and placer miners to oil rig crews, loggers, government officials and aviators. Geography and climate are diverse and demanding from region to region. The state is young, with a vigorous economy and active population that values independence, self-reliance and the rigorous challenge.

Because of MACtel's broad coverage, cellular phones can be taken off the beaten path.

"Alaska was ready for us, and we were ready for Alaska," says Davis. "Like so many of our customers, we have overcome the challenges of operating in difficult circumstances, and we're thriving in a competitive environment."

MACtel's sales figures tell a remarkable tale, with business growing by as much as fifty percent in recent years. The firm increased its customer base in Anchorage and developed new clientele from Cantwell on the north and Kenai Peninsula, to the south of Anchorage as new transmission equipment came on line.

"We started out with two cell sites in the Anchorage area," says Davis. "The last couple of years, we've increased that to ten cell sites. In addition to our main switching system in Anchorage, we've installed a switching system on Soldotna and tied the two together. That way, in case of a power outage, earthquake or other factor, the switch in Soldotna could stand alone and provide service to Anchorage, or the other way around. And, our system connects with the system in the Matanuska-Susitna Valley area, which means that our customers can travel anywhere from our cellular coverage zone and to the valley up to the Cantwell area, making calls at no additional charge on a per call basis."

Although company officials foresaw southcentral Alaska as a high growth market, results to date have virtually eclipsed expectations. Some Alaskans remember the not-too-distant days of the 1970s when some television programming arrived in the state as much as two weeks after it was seen in the Lower 48 states. In a smaller and more competitive, fast-paced world, and with the aggressive leadership of firms like MACtel, Alaskans enjoy the benefits of new technological developments to the same degree and quality as everyone else as soon as it is available.

"We've worked hard to make our system as simple and user friendly as possible," says Davis. "We know our customers are busy and their time is valuable. Efficiency is what we're all about and that's how we've designed our offerings."

One of the greatest assets of the MACtel Cellular System is the ability it gives cellular customers in Alaska to connect with the rest of the world using the same portable technology they use for their in-state business. "We're part of a nationwide 'roaming' system whereby our customers can travel outside Alaska without having to change numbers all the time. You can use the phone wherever there is cellular service which is just about universal in communities throughout North America."

Although technology is obviously a driving force in MACtel's line of work, the firm has distinguished itself as a people-oriented business that cares as much about its employees as it does its valued customers. This is based in large measure on the notion that the company can only be as profitable as its 25 employees are productive. This has promoted development of a progressive management system that affords each employee the chance to perform effectively as he or she cultivates individual strengths and learn new skills.

"We have management staff, but all our employees are managed a little bit differently than in other companies," says Davis. "We operate as a team and provide cross-training so that we can help each other with whatever is needed in each department. The theme is what I refer to as a 'can-do group,' so that everyone enjoys their job. There are four main managers covering sales and marketing, customer service, engineering and fiscal management/administration."

Davis says experience has shown the company's system works, "It does make a difference, both behind the scenes and up front in customer relations."

While many businesses falter in the middle of change, MACtel has been thriving on it, and looking forward to more advances in technology and system capabilities in all forms of communications," says Davis. "We see it as our mission to bring those improvements to our customers just as fast as possible so they can remain competitive. We're going to

Although personal use is increasing rapidly, MACtel phones remain an important business tool.

keep doing just that, in the friendliest, most cost-effective way possible. After all, Alaska is our home, and our neighbors expect nothing less from us."

MACtel customers are finding that the service is affordable, useful, and fun.

Carlile Enterprises Incorporated

Co-owner Jeff Allen discusses procedures with Carlile drivers outside the Anchorage terminal.

Alaska's trucking industry still embodies a frontier spirit and Carlile Enterprises Incorporated sets a high standard among the pioneers: bold, innovative, reliable. Whether they are hauling hazardous materials, inventing new rigs to handle awkward loads or just delivering groceries throughout the state, Carlile's highly trained and motivated employees are guided by the company's mission statement:

To provide a dependable transportation service to the people and businesses of Alaska in a manner which ensures stable, profitable growth, a pride of employment and ownership, a positive public image and the respect of the industry.

"Our mission statement is based on years of experience, dating from the time when we had only two trucks," says co-owner Harry McDonald. "Now, with a large multi-purpose fleet, we have the expertise to back up our service commitments."

As an Alaskan-owned interstate carrier, Carlile is able to provide a seamless system for delivering goods using its own terminals in Anchorage, Fairbanks, Seward and Kenai and Seattle. Just recently, the firm bought interstate veteran K&W Transportation, enabling Carlile to offer their customers LTL (less-than-truckload) and truckload services between the Lower 48 and Alaska. Thanks to this acquisition, Carlile now has full interstate intermodal capabilities and interlines with all major motor carriers in the Lower 48. With one stop, customers can ship via land across the Alcan Highway or by sea five days a week through Carlile.

Many Alaskan truckers have come and gone over the years; it is the nature of the industry to be volatile and hard-pressed by the demands of economic fluctuations, weather, time and the shifting needs of customers. McDonald, along with brother John, joined later by owners Josh Stetson, Jeff Allen and recently Linda Leary, have made flexibility a hallmark of the company's service. They have placed a high premium on being able to respond to changing circumstances without sacrificing performance, safety or customer satisfaction. A tangible reflection of this can be seen in Carlile's diverse fleet. The company routinely utilizes tractors, fifth wheel hoists, gravity-feed hoppers, double drop lowboys, fixed box trucks, dollies, vans, curtain vans, several flatbed and lowboy types, bulk tankers, dry bulk trailers and refrigerated vans. This rolling stock can handle everything from pipe to pipe cleaners, and loads up to 180,000 pounds.

A high standard of achievement is made possible by the company's Alaskan origins. This team knows Alaska like few others, from the rain forest of southeast Alaska to the shores of the Arctic Ocean. But Carlile has built its industry leadership on consistent investment in its employees—their safety, their talents, their future. The company does not even consider hiring drivers who cannot demonstrate a high level of proficiency and responsibility. Once on board, training and other skill enhancements remain a high priority. Drug-screening policies are rigorously enforced and the safety of drivers, rigs and loads is a continual focus. This kind of teamwork has helped Carlile flourish where others have foundered.

Carlile is also a good corporate neighbor, a partner with Alaskans in building a strong economy. But this policy extends beyond the bottom line. The firm's owners have always supported a wide range of civic activities, a way of acknowledging the support of Alaskans in building Carlile's success over the years.

As McDonald explains, "Without the patronage of Alaskans, who have come to expect our best effort, we wouldn't be here."

In the village of Nuiqsut, children welcome the arrival of supplies delivered by Carlile.

Golden Valley Electric Association

Golden Valley Electric Association has a proud history of providing electric service to Interior Alaska where temperatures in summer soar to over 90 degrees and plunge to 50 below zero in the winter. A geographically diverse area, from fields to forests and marsh to mountains, makes operating this electric utility a dynamic challenge.

Yet, Golden Valley Electric Association (GVEA) maintains an average service reliability of 99.9 percent. Their diverse power supply, with four fuel sources, is only one reason why there has not been a rate increase since 1982. They have 200 megawatts of generation, 200 employees and over 2,000 miles of line to provide service throughout a service territory spanning 2,200 square miles. Although the customer base is 90 percent residential, GVEA serves large commercial customers ranging from oil refineries to retail shopping malls.

GVEA owns and operates a mine-mouth coal-fired plant in Healy, Alaska and an oil-fired plant adjacent to a North Pole, Alaska refinery. They also share in the output of a state-owned hydroelectric plant on the Kenai Peninsula. In addition, GVEA is the northern control for a 175 mile, 138 kV intertie connecting Alaska's two largest cities, Fairbanks and Anchorage. This intertie completes a Railbelt grid and enables the transfer of economy energy generated from natural gas in the Anchorage area.

By 1997, GVEA will operate and purchase power generated by a state-of-the-art, coal-fired power plant at Healy, Alaska. The power plant will provide 50 megawatts of competitively-priced electric power and will demonstrate innovative clean coal-burning technologies. Combined with low-sulfur Alaska coal, these new technologies will result in one of the cleanest coal-burning plants in the world. The construction of this 50 megawatt clean coal plant is a joint venture between the U.S. Department of Energy (DOE) and the State of Alaska. The project received a $117 million grant from the DOE under their Clean Coal Technology Program. Once proven, this new technology can be used to retrofit existing coal fired plants around the world.

General Manager Mike Kelly knows that computers can never replace the value of meeting customers face to face, but to meet customer expectations and the challenges of providing reliable electric service in Interior Alaska, GVEA's computerized dispatch command center is critical.

GVEA is a locally owned rural electric cooperative whose mission is to make electrical energy available to its members at the lowest cost consistent with sound economy, wise use of resources and good management. This corporate philosophy has seen GVEA through the increased military presence in the 1940s, statehood in the 1950s, the Good Friday earthquake and Fairbanks flood in the 1960s, the world oil crisis of the 1970s, and the growth from the Trans Alaska Pipeline in the 1980s. Today, GVEA is a progressive, stable utility planning for environmentally sound expansion to meet Interior Alaska's energy needs well into the future.

Tundra Times

Founded in 1962 by Inupiat artist Howard Rock, *Tundra Times* has been the voice for Alaska Native rights and social progress. The paper has received numerous state and national awards testifying to its professional credentials, including a Pulitzer nomination.

Though unschooled as a journalist, Rock set a high standard for reporting and political commentary as he rallied Natives across the state to unite against racism and economic oppression. His passion for justice under-girded articles and editorials on a wide number of subjects ranging from Native/state relations, protection of village land, subsistence rights and civil rights to health care and education. The first decade of Tun*dra Times* culminated in the Alaska Native Claims Settlement Act of 1971, a landmark bill that has literally transformed the face of Alaska. Though the work of many, passage of the bill was an elegant testament to Howard's vision of Native unity.

Tundra Times is recognized nationwide as the voice of the Alaska Native experience. Its mission has always been three-fold:

Toni Kahklen-Jones; chairperson, president and publisher of the Tundra Times.

• to provide a means for Natives to share information, analysis, inspiration, concerns and ideas with one another in a way that encourages unity while honoring cultural and individual diversity;
• to influence public policy in support of Native concerns; and
• to persist in the struggle against racial stereotyping, providing the general public with accurate information about Alaska Natives and their rich, thriving cultures.

Tundra Times is published biweekly and distributed to every corner of the state. The dreams and struggles of every one of Alaska's 86,000 Natives — urban and rural — are important to the paper's board and staff. The *Tundra Times* aims, through creative application of its journalistic resources, to make their lives better, to acknowledge their numerous achievements, to defend their rights to individual and collective self-determination.

In the years to come, the *Tundra Times* will go everywhere that Alaska Natives yearn to hear the truth spoken in a clear voice, and everywhere they need their wisdom, their dreams, their stories, to be clearly heard: from urban boardrooms to village schools; from village council meetings to legislative hearings; from fish camps to Congress; and from the homelands of all of Alaska's indigenous people — the Eskimos, Indians and Aleuts — to Alaska's largest Native villages: Anchorage, Fairbanks and Juneau.

In its fourth decade, *Tundra Times* is determined to become an indispensable information tool for Alaska's Native people, and for non-Natives committed to social and economic justice for all people.

Together, the board and staff of *Tundra Times* are committed to preserving their historic mission as:

"The Voice of Native Experience."

Markair

When December found a young village girl hospitalized in Anchorage with terminal cancer, she was asked what she most wanted for Christmas. She replied she most wanted to see her father, who had remained home in their small rural village. With the goodwill that marks it as a truly Alaskan company, Markair flew the girl's whole family to her bedside. On another occasion, a Kenai boy and his father were severely burned in a house fire and sent outside Alaska for treatment. When company officials learned the mother and another son were without funds, they offered to reunite the family at the distant burn center.

Being neighborly just comes naturally to Markair, founded in 1947. Though its horizons have expanded dramatically since then, Markair still calls Alaska home. The carrier provides service to 140 Alaskan communities, as well as nearly a score of cities in the Lower 48. Responding quickly to the shifting demands of a dynamic industry, Markair is the only carrier in the U.S. to offer complete Alaska-owned service from the Arctic Ocean to Washington D.C., from fabled wilderness fishing lodges to the nerve centers of American commerce, industry and government.

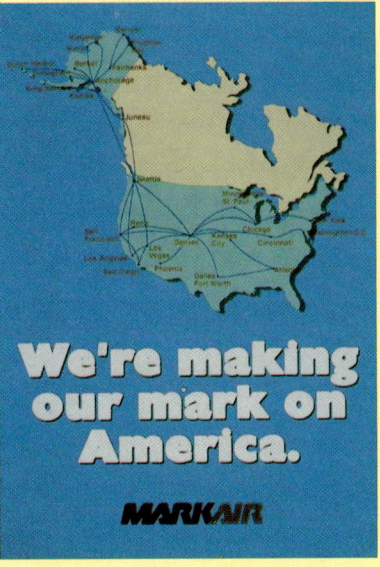

The father and son team of Neil and Mike Bergt know Alaska, and aviation, from the ground up. Neil started with the company as chief pilot in 1957 and parlayed a Bush flying career into a rapid rise through the ranks. He currently serves as chairman and CEO. Mike began as a station manager and pilot in rural Alaska in 1987 and has held positions of increasing responsibility since then. He is currently president and COO. Together, their vision is to bring affordable transportation to every Alaskan who needs and wants it, and they are proud to do it with a professional workforce of about 1500 employees, 1300 of whom are Alaskan residents.

Relying on a diverse fleet of modern aircraft manned by highly-trained crews, Markair is poised for another 50 years of neighborly service to Alaskans with a strategy that focuses on:
• continuing comprehensive service to rural Alaskan markets;
• providing the most cost-effective and timely service for business travelers;
• hosting a growing number of tourists to the splendor of Alaska; and
• maintaining affordability, reliability and safety in all markets.

"We're very confident about our role in the industry," says Mike Bergt. "We've kept pace and shown them what an Alaskan company can do."

PTI Communications

Upon their arrival in Alaska, new comers find a society and an economy as thriving, modern and sophisticated as any of its sister states. While Alaskans may make it look easy to prosper against the backdrop of the beautiful northern wilderness, that vast, often rugged landscape has presented many obstacles to progress.

For this reason, Alaskans have readily embraced the opportunities afforded by telecommunications and telecomputing technology. In fact, Alaskan firms have been leaders in developing the state's model telecommunications infrastructure with innovative applications for community and industry. One of those leaders is PTI Communications (PTI).

"We're proud of the fact that we've pioneered telephone systems in so many of the communities in the state," says Bernadette Murray, Vice President. "We're very proud of the fact that all of the communities we serve, we serve with not only the finest, but the most current technology. It's all digital switching, and many of the towns and cities we serve have fiber optic infrastructure."

A subsidiary of Pacific Telecom, Inc., of Vancouver, Washington, PTI has a long and proud homegrown heritage. PTI was formed by uniting Juneau/Douglas Telephone Co., (founded during the Gold Rush era of the late 1800s), Sitka Telephone (serving Southeast Alaska since the 1930s), Greatland Telephone (Ft. Wainwright) and Glacier State Telephone Co. (Kenai Peninsula and Kodiak Island). Today, many of PTI's 260 employees are veterans of the original predecessor companies.

Since the early 1980s, PTI has expanded its reach to serve 74 Alaskan communities, many of them remote, roadless towns and villages, with the most reliable communications available. Larger service areas include Juneau, Alaska's bustling state capital, surrounded by America's largest temperate rain forest, and the strategically critical Ft. Wainwright and Eielson AFB military installations, situated near Fairbanks, Alaska's second largest city.

"We serve 80,000 customer lines in 74 urban and rural Alaska communities, stretching from Prince of Wales Island in Southeast Alaska, to Kodiak Island, to Nulato in the Interior, to St. Paul Island in the Bering Sea," says Murray. "More than half of these towns had no local phone service before 1981. Since PTI's implementation of the original systems, most have grown considerably. It has been a pioneering effort in the fullest sense of the word."

Customer growth is positive for PTI, which has realized more than 50% growth in the last decade, averaging about 4% per annum.

"This kind of expansion, including large new installations like the 2100 lines at Eielson Air Force Base, has kept us on our toes and looking towards the future," says Murray. "Our customers have come to rely heavily on us for quality and reliability. They want clear, crisp transmission and reception, and prompt, efficient back up should part of the system falter. In fact, our customers demand, and we are proud to offer, service that is as robust and reliable as that found anywhere in the 'Lower 48.'"

PTI Communications provides local telecommunications service to over seventy-four Alaska communities including Juneau, the state capital.

Overcoming some of the most difficult logistics and terrain in the United States, PTI has extended local telecommunications service to over seventy-four Alaska communities. Over forty of these communities received their first-ever telephone service from systems PTI constructed in the early 1980s.

Alaska Marine Highway

A MAINSTAY OF COASTAL ALASKA'S ECONOMY

Funny thing about the Alaska Marine Highway System of state ferries, you won't find freight handlers on any of the eight ships in the fleet. There are no cargo holds in any of the vessels. In the tariffs published by the AMHS, you won't see any commodity rates for, say, representatives of the system. But it is also important to know that *inside the big commercial trucks and vans that go aboard ships at virtually every port* there are substantial loads of foodstuffs, industrial equipment, medical materials, furniture, mail, construction supplies, and countless other kinds of freight that are vital to the health and economic well and barge operations, and freight-moving ships, the Alaska Marine Highway System is one of the mainstays of coastal Alaska's economy. Especially between small communities, the ferries often provide the only regularly scheduled connection for delivering goods and services — goods and services such as eye clinic examination vans, portable X-ray mammography units, horse and livestock trailers, and Sitka Raptor Center's "Buddy" the bald eagle en route to school and nature events.

"And elephants," says Foster. "We haul elephants. In fact we've hauled whole circuses and carnivals."

"In December, we deliver Santa Claus to eleven villages."

"Deliver" is the key word at the Alaska Marine HIghway System, year-round. Whether it is 400,000-plus passenger

The Alaska Marine Highway's eight vessels cover some 3,500 miles of waterway, about the same distance as sailing form New York to London.

The M/V Bartlett passes through Alaska's pristine waters. The vessel joined the Marine Highway fleet in 1970 and continues to serve the Prince William Sound route.

shipments of frozen Alaska fish, or office supplies, or U.S. mail. Nevertheless, Alaska's state ferries carry tons of such goods, year-round.

Most observers, even Alaskans, think of the ferries in terms of hauling people — residents, visitors, school groups. Of course, people-moving is a prime objective, say being of coastal Alaska.

"We feel," says George Foster, traffic manager of the Alaska Marine Highway System, "that moving commercial goods is important to Alaska, therefore it's important to us. Commercial vehicles travel on most sailings."

It is no exaggeration to say that, along with air cargo, tug boardings annually or more than 107,000 vehicles carried on the ships, the AMHS delivers. In the process it returns more than $40 million to Alaska's state treasury and provides employment for more than 900 dedicated Alaskans.

Not bad for a water highway.

SHIP NUMBER NINE EXPECTED IN 1997

A brand new 380-foot fully ocean-going Alaska ferry vessel should be on line by 1997. The $85 million ship will be the first ocean certified passenger ship built in the U.S. since 1952. With a passenger capacity of 500, the ship will contain 80 cabins with 24 roomettes. It will sail three itineraries: Bellingham to and through Southeast Alaska to Skagway; Southeast Alaska to Southcentral via the Gulf of Alaska; plus Southcentral ports to Kodiak Island when the Tustumena is in annual overhaul.

Raw Materials and Production

Portage Glacier provides the icebergs in Portage Lake.
R.J. Hayes, photographer.

Ketchikan Pulp Company

A Ketchikan Sawmill employee double-checks the bar-coded finished lumber as it awaits shipment to domestic and export markets. Finished lumber from the Ketchikan Sawmill can be found in a variety of markets from studs used in the building of homes to the intricate and unquestionable beauty of oriental architecture.

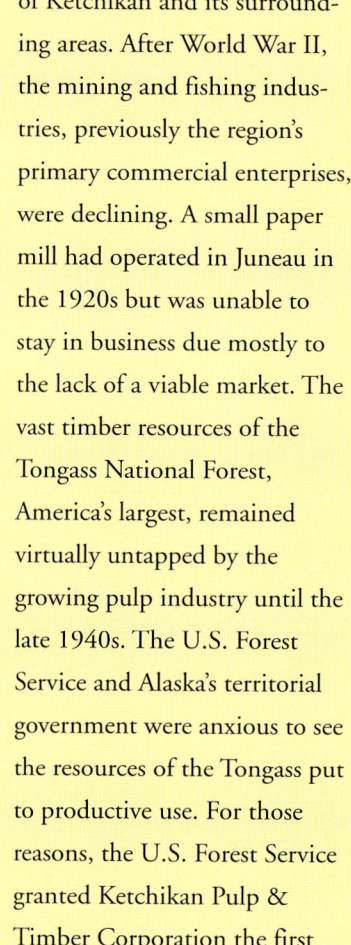

The finished pulp product "Tongacell" is loaded onto ocean-going freighters for export shipment to points around the world. Pulp destined for domestic markets is loaded into railcars and then barged to ports in the Northwest for shipment throughout the United States.

The Ketchikan Pulp Company in August of 1989.

WORKING WITH NATURE, WORKING WITH THE COMMUNITY

Since its founding in 1954, Ketchikan Pulp Company has become a major force in the economic life of Southeastern Alaska and, indeed, the entire state. It is the largest manufacturer in the State of Alaska and approximately 950 people are currently at work in the Company's various operations, making it one of the region's largest employers. Throughout its history, Ketchikan Pulp Company (KPC) has endeavored to lead in both environmental responsibility and community commitment.

A wholly-owned subsidiary of building products manufacturer and wood products innovator Louisiana-Pacific Corporation since 1976, KPC evolved 40 years ago as part of the federal government's goal to provide a stable economic base, year-round industry, and permanent jobs for the residents of Ketchikan and its surrounding areas. After World War II, the mining and fishing industries, previously the region's primary commercial enterprises, were declining. A small paper mill had operated in Juneau in the 1920s but was unable to stay in business due mostly to the lack of a viable market. The vast timber resources of the Tongass National Forest, America's largest, remained virtually untapped by the growing pulp industry until the late 1940s. The U.S. Forest Service and Alaska's territorial government were anxious to see the resources of the Tongass put to productive use. For those reasons, the U.S. Forest Service granted Ketchikan Pulp & Timber Corporation the first long-term timber sales contract for the Tongass in 1947.

The primary product of Ketchikan Pulp Company is dissolving sulfite pulp fiber. This fiber is processed into viscose for use in the manufacture of rayon, cellophane, cellulose sponge, and similar materials. The dissolving pulp process creates the highest grade of wood pulp produced so it is not surprising that the Company's origin came as a joint venture of American Viscose Corporation and Puget Sound Pulp & Timber. Construction on the Company's pulp mill at Ward Cove began in 1952 and, in just two years, what had been an undeveloped area north of town, became the site of the fully operational pulp mill. The impact on Ketchikan was immediate and profound. Homes were built for workers; a bond issue was passed for the construction of a new high school; road building and improvement projects were launched. In late 1954, the first pulp was exported and the Company's product (dubbed "Tongacell") soon gained a

worldwide reputation for quality.

Although little was known in the early 50s about environmental controls, those that were available had been built into the mill during initial construction. Environmental protection measures began with selection of the magnesium bisulfite pulping process which employs a chemical recovery system using evaporators and recovery boilers to recover over 90% of the chemicals used to cook wood chips. In 1971, a primary wastewater treatment plant was built. A three-year wastewater discharge-reduction program, started in 1976, was marked by the introduction of a biological treatment system. That system was expanded in 1989. Additional evaporation capacity was also installed which increased chemical recovery to above 96%. Air quality has always been equally important and the Company's woodwaste boilers were, and continue to be, frequently upgraded and improved to reduce emissions. KPC was the first to design and build an oil/railcar/bulk chemical cargo barge which met the requirements of the 1990 Oil Pollution Act as well as all government and Coast Guard safety standards. KPC's ongoing commitment to environmental awareness and sensitivity continues to be visible and encompasses every aspect of its operations (KPC's distribution of its *Environmental Handbook for Employees* reinforces its environmental concerns).

The acquisitions of new properties (Ketchikan Spruce Mills in 1967 and Annette Hemlock Mill in 1971) have helped to assure KPC's continued progress and success. A new computerized sawmill was built at Ward Cove for the production of sawn lumber from small logs rather than using those logs in the pulping process or processing them as cants. Named the Ketchikan Sawmill (KSM), its first load of lumber was shipped in June of 1989. The addition of KSM and its manufacturing of quality, high value products from logs previously used only for pulp fiber is the most recent example of KPC's commitment to diversifying and improving its operations.

Full scale timber harvesting operations began around 1954 near Hollis on Prince of Wales Island (POW). Today, Hollis is a thriving community. The cities of Thorne Bay and Coffman Cove, also located on POW, owe their beginnings to logging camps that operated in their areas. The existing road system on today's Prince of Wales Island is a direct benefit of the past and present timber harvesting activity; they supply a vital link between island communities, natural resources, and access for recreation and tourism. Today, KPC continues timber harvesting operations in these areas with a sorting and scaling yard located at Thorne Bay and timber harvesting camps at Coffman Cove, Polk Inlet, and Naukati.

About 10% of the Tongass National Forest will ever be harvested over a sustained, 100-year rotation and the remaining 90% is not scheduled for any harvesting activities. It is KPC's commitment to ensure harvesting operations are conducted in a manner that protects land, wildlife, and other resources. Before timber harvest begins, an Environmental Impact Statement (EIS) is completed. This process includes an opportunity for public input, a draft EIS offering a "no harvest" and other alternatives, and a final decision. Each harvest area is reviewed by Forest

The Ketchikan Pulp construction site in May of 1953.

Service geologists, fish and wildlife biologists, archaeologists, silvaculturists, landscape architects, forestry engineers, and professional foresters. These experts review each area to ensure that "buffer zones," erosion controls, and other harvest procedures are in place. Finally, a KPC forester reviews the harvest area to ensure that it can be harvested without any adverse affects on the web of biodiversity found in the Tongass.

Functioning as a vital part of the community has always been one of KPC's top priorities. The considerable annual stumpage payments made by KPC (averaging $13.3 million per year from 1989 through 1993) cover the federal government's cost to administer the long term sales contract and those same timber dollars benefit schools, construction of roads, and other projects throughout Alaska. KPC writes checks totaling $50 million a year to more than 300 local vendors and pays out an average of $40 million in wages in the region annually. KPC provides its employees with a full health care package and retirement program as well as profit and gain sharing programs. The Company is strongly committed to "safety first" policies and to maintaining a safe and injury-free workplace, offering safety-award payments and incentives to employees who meet or exceed KPC safety standards.

Conveyers carry the cut pulp product to the Finishing Room to be wrapped and baled in preparation for shipment to domestic and export markets.

Today, KPC continues to play a major role in the daily life of Ketchikan and the communities on Annette Island and Prince of Wales Island. More than 15,000 people have been employed by the Company during its 40-year history. Although there is some seasonal fluctuation in employee numbers, KPC still qualifies as Alaska's first year-round industry and provides an indirect contribution to the local labor market through stable, year-round employment in the service, longshoring, and transportation industries.

In its short 40 years, Ketchikan Pulp Company has forged a unique and solid bond with the residents, governments, and industries of the community, the region, and the state. In the process, KPC has changed the lives of thousands of people along with the very face of Ketchikan and the communities around it.

A CHANGING KETCHIKAN:
Four Decades of Development
In 1954, when KPC opened its pulp mill, Ketchikan, a town of approximately 5,500, shared the common problems of most of the island communities in the Southeastern region of the Territory of Alaska. It wasn't easy to get in and out of town as the air trip included seaplane travel to and from Annette Island which took some visitors aback. As in so many remote areas of the future state, fresh eggs, milk, and produce were hard to come by. Streets were unpaved or paved with wooden planks; what city sewers existed emptied directly into the Tongass Narrows.

Since those days, Ketchikan has grown from a small, isolated island town to a busy city of more than 13,000. Regular contact with the outside world is no longer the exception, thanks to the construction of a new jet airport and the introduction of a unique State ferry system called the Alaska Marine Highway. Most of the streets and roads are paved, and plans continue for a highway to link Ketchikan with

The Ketchikan Pulp building site at Ward Cove, before construction begins.

Raw product awaits processing in the Ketchikan Sawmill sort yard.

the rest of the world. Schools, libraries, and cultural opportunities abound. KPC is proud to have helped stimulate this development by providing employment for Ketchikan and a market for these and other urban amenities.

KPC PROPERTIES; MILLS AND MORE

Ward Cove Dissolving Pulp Plant (KPC)

This is where logs are barked, chipped, and fed to digesters. The resulting pulp is cooked, washed, screened and bleached before being formed into sheets, pressed, and wound into jumbo rolls. After rigorous quality checks, the pulp product is cut into bales, pressed to size, and wrapped for shipment.

The plant produces about 190,000 tons per year. Half is used for rayon staple, one-fourth for continuous-filament rayon, and the balance is devoted to the manufacture of cellophane, cellulose sponges, and other consumer dependent products.

TIMBER DIVISION

Working closely with the Forest Service, KPC's Timber Division is responsible for ensuring a steady supply of raw material (timber) to all of KPC's mills. Company operations currently include a sorting and scaling yard at Thorne Bay and harvest operations at Coffman Cove, Polk Inlet, and Naukati (Prince of Wales Island) and at Shelter Cove (Revilla Island). There are also numerous contract operations in many areas of Southeast Alaska. Timber harvested is transported to Thorne Bay where it is scaled, sorted, bundled, and rafted and then towed by tug to the pulpmill and saw mills.

ANNETTE HEMLOCK MILL (AHM)

Located at Metlakatla on Annette Island and operated by contract with the Metlakatla Indian Corporation and the Bureau of Indian Affairs, this mill handles the larger logs harvested in the forest. The end product, shipped to both foreign and domestic markets, is a semi-finished cant which can

The final stage of the production process is the conversion of pressed pulp into wound rolls weighing an average of 18 tons each.

be processed further to form such items as doors, windows, stair components, and even piano sound-boards.

KETCHIKAN SAWMILL (KSM)

This facility makes use of the smaller logs. The best are processed into high-quality, metric-sized lumber for the export market as well as a tight-grained cut-stock product used in domestic manufacturing plants. The lower-quality logs also supply the domestic market with studs. Largely computerized processing and sorting systems prepare the product for loading onto ships destined for the export markets and for shipment to domestic destinations. Bark removed at the sawmills is used to fuel the woodwaste power boilers at the pulp mill. All residual chips from the lower quality part of the log are used in the pulping process.

Petro Marine Services

The company's real growth began in 1984 when Dale Lindsey built a 3 million gallon bulk fuel plant at Dutch Harbor, the key port for fleets fishing the lucrative North Pacific Ocean and Bering Sea. This facility is the largest in our network of eleven strategically located facilities in Southcentral and Southwest Alaska.

PETRO MARINE SERVICES: A LOT BIGGER, BETTER AND STILL FOCUSED ON PROVIDING NORTHERN HOSPITALITY

Petro Marine Services is fueling an ever-growing share of coastal Alaska's market for petroleum products. Founded in 1936 as a small-town oil delivery service, today the company has expanded to a network of eleven strategically located Southcentral and Southwest Alaska locations. Petro Marine Services also is affiliated with the **Petro Star Refinery** in Valdez and **Forty Niner Transportation, Inc.**, a barge company plying the waters of much of Alaska's vast coastline.

The small, Seward-based operation owned by Dale Lindsey has become one of the state's major revenue-producing companies. "We are an Alaska-based company, more sensitive to Alaska's unique marketing requirements and idiosyncrasies," Lindsey says.

Petro Marine Services had its beginning in 1936 when Andy's Oil Delivery was founded. Andy's, named after founder Andy Novak, delivered heating oils to area businesses and residents. Lindsey joined Andy's as a truck driver in 1956 and purchased the company three years later.

"In one respect, it was a matter of being in the right place at the right time," says Lindsey. "Still, going into business for myself was the single most significant career milestone in my life. My grandfather, father and brother all worked for the Alaska Railroad, so becoming an entrepreneur was a major shift away from family tradition.

"I had to borrow the money to make the down payment, but I learned early on that indebtedness is a great motivator. I also came to understand the importance of accurately assessing risk and balancing this with perceived opportunity."

For the next twenty-five years the company, by then named **Harbor Enterprises, Inc.**, provided stable and profitable service to the Seward area. The firm's real growth curve, however, began in 1984, when Lindsey built a 3 million gallon bulk fuel plant at Dutch Harbor, the key port for fleets fishing the lucrative North Pacific Ocean and Bering Sea.

Lindsey named the facility **Petro Marine Services**, reflecting the company's primary function of marketing petroleum products to Alaska's fishing industry. Despite the marine focus, however, Lindsey noted the company caters to all customers who need petroleum products.

Within two years, Petro Marine expanded the Dutch Harbor operation to 6 million gallons, acquired a bulk plant in Kodiak, and rebuilt another in Nikiski. To fuel additional expansion, in 1992, the company acquired **Alaska Oil Sales** which operated facilities located in Kenai, Soldotna and Homer. **Terminal Oil Sales**, a long-time Homer-based distributor, was acquired in 1993 to further expand Petro Marine's presence on the western side of the Kenai Peninsula.

By 1987, Petro Marine was barging petroleum products to communities along the Southcentral coast, Kodiak Island, the Alaska Peninsula and the Aleutians. In 1988, the company chartered a second barge and extended its service to Prince William Sound, Bristol Bay and the Kuskokwim Delta. By 1993, the fleet had again been expanded, and today four barges operate under charter to Petro Marine by the subsidiary company, **Forty Niner Transportation, Inc.**

Marketing efforts to serve the fuel needs of Pacific Rim companies were begun in the mid-1980s, and today this focus has been expanded to include the Russian Far East. Although international marketing offers unique challenges, Lindsey said he views sales to the Pacific Rim as a new frontier offering tremendous opportunity.

The results of overall expansion have been dramatic. Company sales jumped from 6.2 million gallons in 1984 to 126.3 million gallons by 1993. During the same period, revenues increased from $6.1 million to $117.5 million. The revenue increase in 1985 alone amounted to an astronomical 330 percent. Revenues increased another 47 percent in 1986, 37 percent in 1987, 53

Dale Lindsey is owner and president of Harbor Enterprises, Inc., with headquarters in Seward. The company has a number of affiliates, but operates most of its facilities under the name Petro Marine Services.

percent in 1988 and an additional 21 percent in 1989 before leveling off in the early 1990s.

The company's major capital expansion during the mid-1980s is particularly noteworthy because the growth occurred during a severe economic downturn. The global oil price collapse of 1986 curtailed almost all development throughout Alaska.

The move into Dutch Harbor reflected a critical decision for Lindsey. Investing a significant amount of money to build a plant at such a remote port to serve a volatile market is a risk. Still, Lindsey says, "As an owner of two crab fishing vessels, I knew the area's potential. Also, I wanted to expand geographically and not be so dependent on the Seward market.

In 1992, the company acquired Alaska Oil Sales, which operated facilities in Kenai, Soldotna and Homer. The name, well known to customers on the Kenai Peninsula, today is used interchangeably with Petro Marine Services.

"I have always pushed for internal growth, but I also wanted to keep the business expanding through acquisitions," he said. "This dual expansion has increased our overall volume to the point where we could achieve significant benefits through purchasing power and other economies of scale."

Petro Marine Services' capital expansion program was carried out with a strong consideration for efficiency. In 1988, when sales from the five bulk plants shot above $68 million, the company had just forty-three employees. "It's significant to note that each employee's efforts — on average — generated more than $1.5 million in revenues," Lindsey said.

Petro Marine's shoreside plants are situated so that plants complement each other by providing convenient, consistent and efficient service to the predominantly marine clientele. Competition from other companies in some areas is intense, but Lindsey's philosophy is that competition makes Petro Marine a better company.

"Consistency is the bottom line for continued success," Lindsey says. "First and foremost, Petro Marine is a petroleum marketing company that is in the service business. While increasing volume has been our strategic goal, we also have focused on learning what customers expect in terms of products and services."

And that's a mission with no end.

"As a company, we constantly try to enhance our level of service by paying attention to details, the little things that win customer loyalty. The essence of successful marketing, whether marine or otherwise, is to consistently offer quality products and premium service at competitive prices."

Lindsey noted that the key is remembering that each and every customer — large and small — counts. "We may be large by Alaska standards, but customers will not be just another number with us," Lindsey said. "We still sell by the gallon and on a first-name basis."

Shoreside Petroleum, Inc., is an affiliated company offering a wide range of products in Seward. Our warehouses are kept well stocked to meet the needs of all customers.

Artic Slope Regional Corporation

Arctic Slope Regional Corporation draws on shareholders for many of its more than 2,700 employees, including Marie Ireland, a mapping and lands information technician in the corporation's Anchorage offices.

Arctic Slope Regional Corporation (ASRC) is a special, for-profit corporate body established for the benefit of the Inupiat Eskimos of Alaska's North Slope.

ASCR's uniqueness is based on the ancient spiritual value of protecting the land, the environment and the culture of its people. The corporation's mission is to conduct commercial, industrial and other economic activities to enhance Inupiat cultural and economic freedoms.

ASRC grew out of the land claims struggle of Alaska's indigenous peoples. The discovery of enormous oil reserves at Prudhoe Bay in 1969 added urgency to the demands of Inupiat and other Alaska Natives for aboriginal title to their lands. Clear title was needed to allow construction of the trans-Alaska Pipeline to bring North Slope oil to American consumers.

Working in alliance with other Alaska Natives, the Inupiat won passage of the Alaska Native Claims Settlement Act of 1971, granting Alaska Natives forty million acres of land and monetary payments in return for extinguishment of their aboriginal land claims. One of the key provisions of the settlement act was that Alaska's Native Peoples would not receive their land and monetary settlements individually, but through private regional and village corporations owned by the people. Accordingly, the Inupiat Eskimos formed Arctic Slope Regional Corporation in 1972. On behalf of its shareholders, ASRC took title to nearly five million acres of land in Alaska's Arctic and received some $22.5 million in compensation for other lands.

Over the years Barrow-based ASRC has grown and prospered, creating jobs and earning dividends for its shareholders — as well as the respect of the business community. In 1993, Arctic Slope Regional Corporation was ranked as the second-largest Alaska-owned business, grossing nearly $255 million in revenues, and employing 3,200 employees.

The corporation's core business strength lies in providing construction, support, contracting and oil field services to the petroleum industry. But the ASRC corporate family also includes subsidiaries with recognized excellence in engineering and architecture (ASCG Incorporated); petroleum refining (Petro Star, Inc.); civil construction (SKW/Eskimos, Inc.; Natchiq, Inc.; ASRC Contracting Company, Inc.); environmental clean-up (VRCA Environmental Services); waste management contracting (FSEC, Inc.); management services (Piquniq Management Corporation); telecommunications (Axis Communications; PMC Telecommunications); and tourism (Top of the World Hotel; Tundra Tours). ASRC is also seeking investment and expansion opportunities that complement its capabilities in resource development, con-

Arctic Slope Regional Corporation, headquartered in Barrow, is the second-largest Alaska-owned corporation, with a family of subsidiaries operating in oil field services, petroleum refining, engineering and architecture, environmental services, construction, communications and tourism.

struction, services and other areas of business.

ASRC also owns nearly five million acres of land, much of it near the largest known deposits of petroleum and

As a leader in oil field service and support for Alaska's petroleum industry, Arctic Slope Regional Corporation operates in North Slope, Cook Inlet and Kenai Peninsula — and is looking abroad to the Russian Far East and Pacific Rim.

natural gas in North America. The corporation has many of these lands available for exploration leasing.

Understanding the important role that resource development has played, and will continue to play in Alaska's economy, ASRC is looking to the future through its Western Arctic Coal project. The corporation is seeking a development partner to help produce and market its immense reserves of high-rank, low-sulfur coal located within ASRC lands forty miles south of Pt. Lay, overlooking the Chukchi Sea.

As a Native-owned enterprise, ASRC has developed expertise in working cooperatively with both industry and government. Through its technical subsidiary, ASCG Incorporated, ASRC has established successful working relationships with tribal Indian authorities and the U.S. Bureau of Indian Affairs in the western United States. Piquniq Management Corporation (PMC), jointly owned by ASRC and Ukpeagvik Inupiat Corporation, provides facilities management, supply and operations services to U.S. Defense Department facilities in the Arctic, Far East and Pacific Ocean regions. PMC is itself the 19th largest Alaska-owned business.

Arctic Slope Regional Corporation has expanded into overseas business activities as well. Corporate subsidiaries have provided technical inspection services to the oil industry in Indonesia, and have established joint ventures with indigenous Natives of the Russian Far East to develop their vast petroleum reserves. ASRC also provides communications and construction services to clients in the Russian Far East. The corporation is continually exploring other business possibilities, including construction of pipelines, refineries, telecommunication systems and insulated building systems in European and Pacific Rim markets.

Success in business has allowed ASRC to provide many special shareholder benefits over and above its regular shareholder dividends. These include the Elders Trust Fund to benefit older shareholders; the Arctic Education Foundation to provide scholarships and educational support to college students; and the Permanent Fund to create an endowment for shareholder services. ASRC also offers quiet financial support to many other charities, foundations, scholarships, and other philanthropic efforts in Alaska.

Thanks to ASRC, Alaska's Inupiat Eskimos have been able to enjoy the benefits of a modern economy without sacrificing their traditional lifestyle. The Inupiat still hunt, fish and take whales in much the same way their ancestors have since time immemorial. But they also have access to new jobs, better housing and a modern infrastructure in their communities.

With better educational and employment opportunities in their own region, young shareholders in the villages of the North Slope are no longer migrating away from home. The increased opportunities have strengthened Inupiat families and helped the traditional Inupiat culture to flourish.

Working successfully to fulfill its dual mission to serve both the economic and cultural needs of its Inupiat Eskimo shareholders, Arctic Slope Regional Corporation is continuing to post an admirable record of success — one that promises continued achievement into the twenty-first century.

With a full inventory of equipment and personnel uniquely adapted to operations in the harsh Arctic environment, Barrow-based Arctic Slope Regional Corporation provides unmatched experience to Alaska's petroleum industry.

Petro Star Incorporated

Petro Star Incorporated is a company with deep Alaskan roots and broad horizons. Owned by people born and raised in the state, Petro Star Inc. was formed in 1984 to provide an important service in an overlooked niche: production and distribution of light fuels critical for heating homes and businesses.

Both the company's refineries, one in North Pole (near Fairbanks), and one in Valdez, draw their crude oil stream directly from the trans-Alaska pipeline. The 10,000 barrel-per-day facility in North Pole produces kerosene, diesel and jet fuel for Interior markets. The 30,000 barrel-per-day refinery in Valdez manufactures jet fuel, marine diesel and heating fuel for private, commercial and military customers, primarily in Southcentral Alaska.

Both facilities are models of efficiency. Their small scale keeps overhead costs down and productivity high. The entire operation in North Pole requires only seven personnel. Cross-training in refinery operations, welding, engineering, oil field construction and chemistry contributes significantly to the efficiency of the facility. The larger refinery in Valdez is a modern, fully-automated plant operated every day of the year by twenty-four highly-trained employees.

The different ownership and management structures of the two refineries are indicative

Chairman/CEO, Stephen Lewis (seated); President/COO, Walt Schlotfeldt.

of the flexibility and creativity that Petro Star brings to its corporate mission. Sole ownership of the North Pole refinery made sense for the capacity of the plant and the market demand. In Valdez, circumstances favored a joint venture with Harbor Enterprises Inc. and Alaska Refining Inc., which is owned by Neil Bergt, who also owns MarkAir, the state's largest air carrier. Both of these partners either consume or distribute large quantities of fuel and were searching for a steady and cost-effective source of product. The partnership has proven successful not only for the owners, but other customers in the marketplace as well.

Since the inception of the refineries, through careful planning and acquisition, Petro Star has gradually expanded its market niche in Alaska and begun analyzing opportunities overseas for selling not only refined oil products but technical expertise as well. Analysis of new business opportunities indicates a growing demand for value-added manufacturing know-how for natural resources in developing nations. Petro Star's experience in assembling and operating safe, efficient and relatively small-scale refineries is highly marketable in areas where new oil discoveries are slated for production. Initially, the company has targeted China, Russia and Indonesia for closer examination of their potential as markets for Petro Star's fuels and related services.

Co-founder and chairman, Stephen Lewis, describes the refineries themselves as the heart of the corporation, and Petro Star's employees as the brains and nerves of the operation. "There's a certain amount of risk inherent in the refining industry. Every day, we ask our people to assume that risk—and they do it," says Lewis. He gives them high marks for loyalty and dedication, noting proudly that every refinery worker who started with the company is still

Petro Star Valdez Refinery.

On-site laboratory facilities for quality assurance.

on the job, an enviable record for any company in any industry. He also cites their high level of technical capability.

"In essence, we don't pay them for what they do every day. We pay them for those extremely rare and unforeseen occasions when the machinery falls short of expectations, when there's vulnerability or failure in the highly complex and mechanized systems which momentarily put the plant, the product and the people in jeopardy. Then we look to our crew to fill the breach. And they do, every time."

This high level of performance has not only enabled a profitable operation, but one that consistently meets or exceeds tough environmental standards. The company has always worked closely with state regulators and won high praise from the Alaska Department of Environmental Conservation.

Also important to Petro Star's success is the quality of its products, which all undergo thorough testing in state-of-the art laboratories to assure a consistently high standard. Of particular concern to many of the company's customers, Petro Star has developed a line of fuels with one of the lowest pour points available in the market, allowing their use even in the Arctic and sub-Arctic conditions that predominate in Alaska and other northern regions for much of the year.

In addition to the refineries, other subsidiaries carry out the important function of distributing increasingly diverse products to their urban and rural destinations. Alaska Lube and Fuel imports a range of lubricating oils to the state, repackages them and distributes the finished product to industrial clients throughout the state. In the Anchorage area, Alaska Lube and Fuel also sells gasoline, jet fuels and diesel manufactured at Petro Star's refineries. In addition to product, the company also provides technical assistance to customers in proper product handling.

Another key subsidiary of Petro Star is Sourdough Fuel, the oldest and largest fuel distributor in the Interior of Alaska. Acquired in 1986, the origins of the company date to the gold rush of 1898 when a venerable Alaskan known as "Sourdough Ellis" supplied miners in the region. Eventually, the Schlotfeldt Family of Fairbanks assumed control of the firm and developed it into a first-class business which provided a perfect addition to Petro Star's strategic development. In fact, Walt Schlotfeldt is now Petro Star's president.

"It's been very gratifying to see Petro Star grow over the years," Schlotfeldt says. "We feel we've captured just the right combination of quality service that you'd expect from a locally-owned enterprise, and progressive, forward-looking philoso-

Petro Star Inc. North Pole Refinery.

phy that will take us overseas into new areas. Alaska is our home and will always be our core market. And, there are whole new world markets to explore."

Echo Bay Mines Alaska

Echo Bay Alaska is part of Echo Bay Mines, Ltd., the fourth largest gold mining company in North America. The company, which operates four gold-mining properties in the Canadian Arctic, Nevada and Washington state, has demonstrated a commitment to resource development and environmental concern.

In Alaska, two properties, the Alaska-Juneau Mine four miles from Juneau and the Kensington Mine about 22 air miles from Juneau on Lynn Canal, are in the environmental permitting stages and under development.

With the reopening of the A-J Mine, Echo Bay estimates 22,500 tons per day of low-grade ore will be mined underground to produce 367,000 ounces of refined gold annually. The A-J project will employ about 450 people when it is fully operational. The company is committed to local hire and has been working with the University of Alaska Southeast's Institute of Mining Technology in Juneau to establish a training and safety program for miners.

Reopening the A-J mine involves restoration of old underground workings from the Alaska-Juneau Gold Mining Company, first established in 1897. New workings, the development of a new main access to the mine near sea level, and the development of underground and surface milling and support facilities will occur once the environmental permitting and development phases of the project are complete.

One of the unique aspects of the project plan is the

Architectural plans for A-J project.

establishment of a mill, underground within the mine. By milling and crushing the ore underground and completing its initial treatment there, the noise and dust generated from these activities will be contained.

The surface facility and docking area that are being planned for construction have also taken into consideration environmental and other impacts on Juneau residents. A tourist center that will provide information on mining and mining history is also planned.

Echo Bay is committed to protecting the environment in the conduct of all its business. The company, both in Alaska

Kensington Mine.

City of Juneau.

and elsewhere, maintains an active, self-monitoring program to ensure the highest standards.

The Kensington Project, near Berners Bay on the Lynn Canal between Juneau and Haines, is a joint venture between Echo Bay and Coeur-Alaska, Inc. For the past several years the project has conducted extensive underground exploration at the Kensington site to identify gold deposits and has been involved in the environmental permitting process.

The Kensington will mine approximately 4,000 tons of ore per day and produce 190,00 ounces of gold per year. The site to be developed, about 275 acres, will include a marine terminal, storage, housing, administrative and maintenance areas, a heliport, a power plant and the underground working. The project is expected to employ about 340 people.

Echo Bay's high standards of environmental monitoring and protection and our commitment to safety is a primary feature of our Alaska projects.

Sheep Creek Monitoring.

Tesoro Alaska Petroleum Company

Tesoro Alaska Petroleum Company's Kenai refinery began operations in 1969 with an initial production capacity of 17,500 barrels per day of crude oil. Since its inception, the refinery has been expanded to a capacity of 72,000 barrels per day to service Alaska's growing economy.

Marking 25 years in partnership with the State of Alaska, Tesoro Alaska Petroleum Company celebrates a relationship rich in its past, innovative and active in its present and visionary for its future. Having taken a leading role in developing and marketing Alaska's resources, Tesoro Alaska continues to be the primary supplier of petroleum products in Alaska as well as an export leader for the State.

From providing the State's first made-in-Alaska gasoline almost two decades ago, to plans for launching a state-of-the-art vacuum distillation unit to enhance the refinery's overall product mix, Tesoro Alaska has become an integral part of the State's economy with customers ranging from the individual automobile owner, to large commercial enterprises, electric utilities, contractors, schools, governmental agencies and military installations.

Founded in July 1969, Tesoro Alaska Petroleum Company was established to refine Alaskan crude oil and market finished products for use by Alaskans. Tesoro Alaska would open its new Kenai refinery several months later, staffed by only 17 employees. The new facility came on-line with the capacity to process 17,500 barrels of Cook Inlet crude oil per day. These relatively modest beginnings were the first steps toward correcting the irony that a state with abundant new oil reserves was paying some of the nation's highest prices for refined petroleum products.

Starting in 1973, Tesoro embarked on several major upgrades and expansions at the refinery, which ultimately resulted in the Company investing hundreds of millions of dollars in the refinery. The main benefits derived from the 1975 expansion included the ability of the refinery to produce 252,000 gallons per day of all-made-in-Alaska gasoline. Also in that same year, construction of a 70-mile long 10-inch diameter pipeline from the Kenai refinery across the northern end of the Kenai Peninsula and under Cook Inlet to the Port of Anchorage was completed. Tesoro's pipeline is designed to carry a variety of finished products including jet fuel, diesel and gasoline to a tank farm and distribution center in Anchorage.

With the advent of world class oil development at Alaska's North Slope, the State's economy began to grow dramatically. In concert with Alaska's growth during the 1980s, Tesoro Alaska substantially modified its plant to accommodate a shift in feedstock supply from the light Cook Inlet crude oil to the heavier North Slope crude oil. In conjunction with this expansion, Tesoro processed the first cargo of Alaska North Slope crude loaded at the Port of Valdez into the very first gallon of gasoline manufactured from Alaska North Slope crude and sold in Alaska.

Expansion and moderniza-

Tesoro holds an exclusive license agreement for all 7-Eleven convenience stores within Alaska, and currently markets gasoline from more than thirty of these stores in three major areas of the state.

Over ninety independently owned branded and unbranded dealers and jobbers sell Tesoro gasoline throughout Alaska.

tion continued at the Kenai refinery with a near capacity-doubling expansion of the gasoline-producing reformer, the construction of a new hydrocracker unit to produce more jet fuel and gasoline blendstocks and an isomerization unit which increases the octane rating of gasoline components without using lead.

Moving into the nineties, Tesoro Alaska's technology continues to find ways to meet the changing demands of a fluctuating market, as evidenced by the construction of a vacuum distillation unit, mentioned earlier. This $24 million investment will enable the refinery to continue to substantially reduce the production of residual fuel oil and enhance the value of the refinery's overall product mix.

As the refinery was expanded and upgraded, Tesoro's network of service station retailers also grew. Tesoro holds an exclusive license agreement for all 7-Eleven convenience stores in Alaska and markets gasoline through more than 30 of these stores in three major areas of the State. The Company also markets its gasoline at wholesale through more than 90 branded and unbranded dealers and jobbers throughout Alaska.

An important aspect of Tesoro's continuing success is its commitment to environmental sensitivity. In the process of upgrading those service stations which sell refined products under its distinctive banner, the Company strives to maintain strict compliance with laws regulating underground storage tanks and other industry-related concerns.

Product quality is another area in which Tesoro Alaska can firmly stand behind its marketing claims. "Our gasoline was tested by an independent, nationally recognized laboratory and determined to be the cleanest burning gasoline produced in Alaska and one of the cleanest burning fuels in the nation," stated Lou Thomason, Vice President of Tesoro Alaska marketing, who further stated, "Results like these are important to Tesoro because we strive to be a good corporate citizen as well as a successful company."

Tesoro has maintained a strong market share in Alaska despite the fact that it operates in an extremely competitive industry. This success enables Tesoro's more than 540 employees in Alaska, who generate a $20 million payroll, to make a substantial contribution to the State's economy. To ensure its future success, Tesoro's senior management is continuously improving its Alaskan refining and marketing processes. Tesoro's strategically located base

This Company-owned truck rack loading facility is located in Anchorage, Alaska and offers state-of-the-art servicing to Tesoro customers.

of operations uniquely positions the Company to seek new markets in the fast growing Pacific Rim area, a vision which we hope will further strengthen Tesoro and provide benefits to the State of Alaska.

NANA Regional Corporation

Alaska's indigenous peoples have struggled with both cultural and technological change in the last 100 years. The Inupiat Eskimos of Alaska's northwest coast have taken the lead in attempting to manage that change. As shareholders of NANA Corp., they have nurtured a diverse and profitable family of enterprises. In fact, the company's work in mining and oilfield support services has made it an Alaskan leader in those industries.

Most importantly for its Native shareholders, NANA has attained its stature without sacrificing traditional Inupiat lands and values. The corporation's philosophy and operations are nurtured by ancient cultural traditions whose origins are concealed by the mists of time. The company prides itself on successfully incorporating those traditional values with modern management concepts that have been a source of inspiration and direction to some of the world's largest and most successful corporations. Chairperson Christina Westlake and President Charlie Curtis describe it this way in NANA's 1993 Annual Report:

"NANA has embraced the Continuous Improvement Process for creating a form of management that draws on every employee's knowledge and abilities. This philosophy is based on cooperation and consensus building, which is the same philosophy that the Inupiaq people have used for thousands of years in order for our culture to survive. This approach mirrors our Inupiat Ilitqusiat values."

NANA's birth was the culmination of a long and difficult process. The dawn of this century was marked by the arrival of whaling and trading vessels on the remote coasts of Arctic Alaska. The upheaval engendered by this development severely compromised the health and social well-being of Inupiat communities and created serious social, cultural and economic conflicts. However, the people of the region surrounding Kotzebue Sound joined with indigenous peoples across Alaska to help control their destiny. After years of litigation and lobbying, they secured passage of the Alaska Native Claims Settlement Act of 1971. This landmark legislation recognized Native title to most of the state, allowed them to retain 44 million acres and paid

The Red Dog mine is a partnership of NANA and Cominco Ltd. of Canada to extract high grade zinc from Native land in the upper Wulik River drainage.

$962.5 million as compensation for lands lost. One of twelve Native regional corporations in Alaska, NANA was formed to implement the settlement in a 36,000 square mile area, with residents of Kotzebue, Kiana, Kivalina, Deering, Buckland, Noatak, Shungnak, Kobuk, Ambler, Noorvik, and Selawik as shareholders.

Initially capitalized with its share of the settlement fund, NANA has grown to a company with revenues exceeding $35 million per year and assets of more than $75 million, and a mission statement that proudly declares in English and Inupiat that the company's purpose is "To protect our land and culture and provide shareholder jobs while maintaining profitability."

Early on, NANA developed a successful model by entering the oil field services arena, providing a variety of capabilities for industrial application, from oil drilling to remote camp catering and security in the North Slope oil fields. Those endeavors have not only proved profitable, but have also advanced the goals of shareholder training and employment while allowing many shareholders the opportunity to fulfill important family and cultural obligations during subsistence hunting and fishing seasons.

After developing a successful business track record

in several ventures, NANA's shareholders rose to a new challenge: the development of the Red Dog mine on its own land. Red Dog is a partnership of NANA and Cominco Ltd. of Canada to extract high grade zinc from Native land in the upper Wulik River drainage. Developing the NANA-Cominco relationship was a long and sometimes difficult process, requiring much discussion and some accommodation by both parties. Red

In return, NANA receives a share of mineral profits. The agreement calls for a comprehensive shareholder hire program to insure NANA shareholders are employed at the mine. A joint committee reviews and approves operations activities, and an employment committee helps guide the effort to hire, train and promote NANA shareholders. NANA and its subsidiaries also provide drilling, catering and other subcontract services on

NANA entered the oil field services arena, providing a variety of capabilities for industrial application, from oil drilling to remote camp catering and security in the North Slope oil fields.

Whatever avenues NANA pursues for generating revenues, its approach to management always applies the same progressive leadership that combines traditional values and common sense development strategies in a way that has made it a standout in Alaska's business community. "We believe that we must have a vision for NANA," Curtis says. "We must all remember that vision without action is a dream, action without vision is passing the time away, but vision with action can change the world! Without our vision for NANA, we would not have been able to open the Red Dog Mine. It required our Elders, leaders and shareholders all working together on the vision of having shareholder jobs while preserving our culture. Everyone took on responsibility and accountability for doing his or her own part in making the vision become reality."

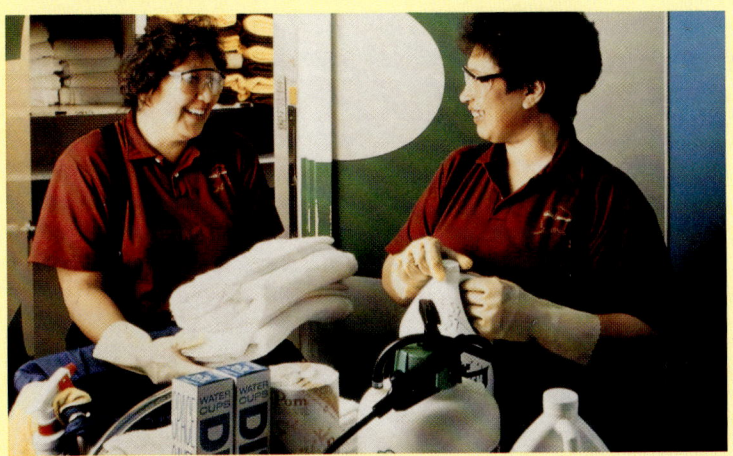

NANA shareholders Angie Larkin, left, and Barbara McGee enjoy a laugh as they replenish their housekeeping supplies for NANA-Marriott at Prudhoe Bay. NANA's joint venture with the Marriott Corporation provides housekeeping, food services and maintenance services at remote sites and Anchorage cafeterias.

Dog has become a much-studied model with applicability to other areas of the world.

The partners developed a highly progressive agreement in 1982 which granted Cominco the rights to build and operate the mine and market the metals.

the project. One of the most innovative aspects of the agreement is its provisions for traditional subsistence activities of the Inupiat. Relying on the advice of residents of Kivalina and Noatak, the closest communities to the mine, NANA has

significant authority to protect hunting, fishing and other subsistence resources.

With Red Dog, NANA again proved itself a truly Alaskan leader and is now poised for the future, in which further natural resource development will likely play a key part. Against this day, NANA has developed an active land management program covering its two million acres of land. Resource inventories are conducted and updated, and plans developed within the framework of goals dictated by shareholders. While Red Dog will remain the pre-eminent resource project for some time to come, other promising mineral deposits as well as oil and gas prospects have been identified. Mineral potential includes gold, jade, coal and copper.

With this kind of steady determination, it is no wonder that in barely two decades, NANA has written one of Alaska's, and America's, most remarkable corporate success stories.

Sealaska Corporation

Sealaska Corporation's history is carved in the landscape of Southeast Alaska. From time immemorial, Southeast Alaska Natives have lived along the forested shorelines of the North Pacific and its inland waterways. Their languages, traditions and culture are rooted here.

As modern society impacted the existence of Southeast's indigenous people, their resiliency and ability to adapt to their surroundings proved to be the determining factors in the survival of their culture. For many years, Native leaders fought to get the United States Government to recognize their aboriginal rights to Alaska lands.

The long struggle resulted in the 1971 passage of ANCSA — the Alaska Native Claims Settlement Act. This Act made it possible for Natives to keep part of their land and to be compensated for the land that they lost. When ANCSA passed — Sealaska Corporation was born.

ANCSA was shaped around the Native tradition that land was owned collectively by clans. As a result, the Tlingit, Haida and Tsimshian peoples of the Southeastern Panhandle now own their land as shareholders of the largest ANCSA corporation. The settlement act was the culmination of the aboriginal people's dream that their children and grandchildren would own land now — and forever.

Sealaska oversees 300,000 acres of land located within the Tongass National Forest.

In the formation of the corporation, these Natives recognized the special meaning of their heritage. Sealaska's corporate philosophy includes words rarely used by traditional American businesses. The importance of those words is clear: "... to support and preserve the economic, cultural and social values of its shareholders ..."

It is for those reasons that Sealaska set out on its unique path to use a portion of its business revenue to provide the means to help keep Native heritage alive. To do this, they created the Sealaska Heritage Foundation.

The Sealaska Heritage Foundation helps make possible Native scholarships, language and cultural studies, tribal archive collection and preservation, the Naa Kahidi Theater, and many other programs designed to perpetuate Native culture. Sealaska Corporation also speaks out for Alaska Natives on important cultural, social and economic issues.

In addition to protecting Native culture, Sealaska is charged with overseeing the most important part of the ANCSA settlement — its land. That is why the following segment of Sealaska's mission statement is so important: "Retain control and ownership of Sealaska's ANCSA lands in perpetuity for the original shareholders, their heirs, and their descendants."

Of course, how that policy is translated into action is the ultimate test. In Sealaska's case, they have cemeteries, historical sites and subsistence lands; they have land that is prized for its timber; and a wealth of subsurface lands with mineral potential. In all, the corporation owns more than 330,000 acres of surface land, 600,000 acres of subsurface rights, and approximately 80 historic and cemetery sites in Southeast Alaska.

Sealaska plays a unique role in the management of its land. Not only does it seek to maximize its economic opportunities as it pursues timber and minerals business opportunities, it must also safeguard the unique ecosystem in which its shareholders live.

For several years, most of the corporation's revenues came from a wholly-owned seafood company and a major building products business. But both were sold when it became apparent that prospects for the future were slowing.

As this occurred, Sealaska Timber Corporation, a timber harvesting and marketing subsidiary, was gaining strength. Today, it is the corporation's primary source of income, while its investment portfolio provides an important secondary source of income.

On the horizon is the minerals potential of Sealaska's extensive subsurface land holdings. The corporation expects to have one or two mining operations underway before the end of the 1990s. In addition to resource development, the corporation continues to review businesses for possible acquisition which will allow for more diversification and increase shareholder job opportunities.

In purely business terms, Sealaska is a profitable corporation. However, its real purpose is to ensure the long-term survival of Alaska Native society — a goal far more important than profit.

Sealaska's timber operations provide many employment opportunities for its shareholders.

Celebration, a biennial dance gathering, is one of many cultural events supported by both Sealaska and the Heritage Foundation.

Sealaska Timber Corporation

Sealaska Timber Corporation was founded in 1979 to provide timber development and marketing services to Sealaska Corporation and the Village and Urban Native Corporations in the Southeast Alaska region. Today, Sealaska Timber Corporation (STC) markets forest products from Washington State, British Columbia, Southeast Alaska and Southcentral Alaska. STC now markets over 200 million board feet per year of these products through its own multi-level distribution system to Pacific Rim Markets including Japan, The Republic of Korea, The Republic of China (Taiwan) and Canada as well as in Alaska and Washington State.

Old growth forest in Tongass National Forest, Ketchikan, Alaska.

The growth and success in STC's marketing program can be attributed to consistently attaining highest value by delivering both products and services that meet customer needs. Timber is sorted to strict quality control standards, which have been developed for specific markets and is then shipped by STC to the customer's desired port of discharge. Close working relationships with both suppliers and buyers are maintained to ensure timely shipment and up-to-date market knowledge.

STC is an Alaskan business, providing substantial economic benefit to local economies. More than 500 direct and indirect jobs are generated due to timber operations alone. It is the state's largest exporter of round logs and is well known for its timber harvesting and marketing. Less widely known is that STC works with timber owners from as far west as Southcentral Alaska and as far south as Puget Sound, Washington.

An essential part of STC's program for development of timber resources is an aggressive forest management program. Sealaska relies on nature in many area for reforestation but uses hand planting to replace trees in areas where reforestation is hampered or to protect water quality. Precommercial thinning, fertilization and grass seeding projects are also underway as part of silviculture management. Precommercial thinning can be used to control species mix, increase productivity and shorten the rotation age of second-growth forests.

Sealaska Timber Corporation's regeneration practices ensure healthy, productive, timbered lands.

Forest products marketed by STC include Alaskan Western Hemlock, Sitka Spruce, Western Red Cedar and Yellow Cedar logs, Douglas Fir, Western Hemlock, White Spruce and other species of logs and cants, flitches and finished lumber products cut from Alaskan Western Hemlock and Sitka Spruce. STC entered the processed products sector of the forest products industry in 1990 by purchasing lumber from other parties and reselling them into its existing distribution system. In 1991, STC began to purchase both logs and standing timber from either the Forest Service or other private owners that had purchased timber from the public source. These logs then underwent at least primary manufacturing requirements prior to shipment, mainly to Asian markets.

Future plans call for further entry into the processing industry by continuing to add value as well as to further geographic log sourcing within Alaska and Washington State.

Goldbelt, Incorporated

A STRONG CULTURE, A RICH HERITAGE

Nestled in Southeast Alaska against the rainforest and a towering backdrop of mountains lies Alaska's capital city of Juneau, home to Goldbelt, Incorporated. The name itself conjures up images of gold and mining activity. Actually, the name is derived from an early-day designation of entire gold mining areas first discovered by Richard Harris and Joe Juneau. Gold mines extended throughout the region and, at the time, were collectively known as "The Juneau Gold Belt."

Like the early gold seekers, the present day management of Goldbelt is continually seeking golden opportunities to benefit its shareholders.

Goldbelt, Inc. was organized as a for-profit corporation in 1973, under the terms of the Alaska Native Claims Settlement Act of 1971. Its shareholders are primarily the Tlingit and Haida Indians. These Indians are the aboriginal people of the region and are people of the forest and sea. Originally, the people subsisted upon the land and the water. Now, through their corporation, they are wisely using the resources to make profits which benefit the people as shareholders.

Goldbelt's shareholders number more than 2,800, making it one of the largest businesses operating in Juneau. Goldbelt is a significant economic force in Southeast Alaska.

In its first decade, Goldbelt focused its efforts on harvesting of timber and development of its real estate. It also took advantage of the region's natural beauty and entered the tourism industry. More recently, Goldbelt has been forging alliances and partnerships to develop mining, transportation and recreational land use activities.

As Goldbelt enters the second millennium, it seeks new opportunities that can make "a significant and positive difference in the lives of its shareholders." Goldbelt is seeking business partners and new growth ventures as it forges ahead.

Our elders are our most cherished resource. At Goldbelt, we are working hard to provide elders with recognition and benefits.

Just as important as our elders are our youth, the future of our corporation. This child takes part in a bi-annual Celebration; an event held in Juneau, Alaska, where Natives from all over "celebrate" their unique heritage.

Seafood Industry

St. George Island, one of the remote Pribilof Islands.
Alaska Division of Tourism.

Alaska Seafood Marketing Institute

The Bering Sea, the Gulf of Alaska, and the North Pacific Ocean hold treasures worth billions of dollars. Unlike sunken, buried, or hidden riches that have a one-time value when discovered, this wealth may be reclaimed each year.

From these rich, clear, icy waters off Alaska's coast, commercial fishermen annually harvest over five billion pounds of seafood. Alaska's annual seafood catch is valued at $3 billion. Alaska's portion accounts for over 50 percent of the total American seafood catch and includes 95 percent of all salmon in North America.

Those catching and selling fish compete in a global marketplace. To ensure Alaska seafood remains competitive in national and international markets, the Alaska legislature in 1981 created the Alaska Seafood Marketing Institute (ASMI).

ASMI promotes Alaska seafood generically without regard to brand names. It also helps market Alaska seafood products, advocates high seafood quality and provides educational material to fishermen and processors regarding proper handling and storage of seafood.

ASMI is funded by a combination of industry, state and federal sources. This innovative partnership of government and private industry is guided by a 25-member board of directors representing commercial

Roger Jensen hooks a pot full of opilio crab as it breaks the surface of the Bering Sea.

The salmon seiner "Paragon" with its nets out, fishing off of Baranof Island.

fishermen, large and small processing firms and the public. The members are appointed by Alaska's governor.

ASMI's responsibility is significant because fishing is so vital to Alaska. The seafood industry is Alaska's largest private-sector employer, directly providing 70,000 summer and 35,000 year-round jobs. Seafood industry taxes account for more state income than all other non-oil and gas resource industry income combined. Each year the state earns about $87 million from the seafood industry, and local governments earn even more in property and sales taxes on the industry.

The size of ASMI's responsibility is matched by the size of the Alaska fishing grounds. Travel America's borders between Seattle, Los Angeles, New Orleans, New

York, and Seattle once and you would cover about 6,000 miles. Make the same trip five times and you still will not have traveled as many miles as Alaska's 34,000 mile shoreline.

The rivers, streams, bays and fjords along Alaska's shoreline support a rich

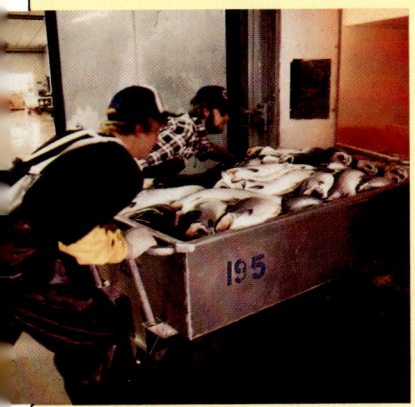

Plant workers load fresh Alaska salmon into cold storage freezers.

abundance of marine life, including five species of wild Pacific salmon, crab, halibut, rockfish, cod, pollock, sablefish, herring, shrimp, cultured oysters and abalone. Alaska's clean waters help develop this seafood with lean flesh, firm texture, rich color and superior flavor. ASMI tells consumers and retailers around the world how Alaska's waters produce seafood distinguished from all others.

The U.S. market promotions, funded totally by the industry, are aimed at consumers, wholesalers, and retailers. ASMI conducts joint promotions for Alaska seafood with grocery stores and restaurants targeting the fall and Lent seasons each year The message is carried through television, radio and print advertising and promotional material distribution.

The Quality Program at ASMI is designed to unite fishermen, processors, distributors and resource managers into an effective alliance. The program works to educate the industry about proper handling techniques for all Alaska seafood throughout the distribution chain.

ASMI's international marketing program promotes Alaska seafood in Japan, Korea, Australia, France, Netherlands, Ireland and the United Kingdom. In each market, ASMI is represented by a national trade liaison who does everything from finding suppliers to planning promotional campaigns.

Past campaigns have proven successful. Generic regional television advertising combined with in-store campaigns in Japan boosted Alaska salmon sales an average of 173 percent. Promotions in the United Kingdom helped increase per capita canned salmon consumption from 12 ounces to 21 ounces, and Alaska's share of U.K. canned salmon sales rose from 44 to 52 percent.

Alaska seafood benefits from the worldwide trend toward health and fitness

ASMI promotional efforts include recipe development and publicity.

because of its natural low-fat and high-protein qualities. Before ASMI's creation, there was not a coordinated effort to market Alaska's seafood. The Alaska King Crab Marketing and Control Board, the Canned Salmon Institute, the Halibut Association of North America, and the Alaska Seafood Foundation promoted their products, but none shared common goals and objectives.

Since 1981, ASMI has proven to be an integral part of Alaska's fishing industry. In the future, its role will become even more important because of increasing international competition. Expanded fishing efforts and the emerging salmon production from countries like Norway, Scotland and Chile will continue to challenge traditional Alaska salmon markets.

Historically, Alaska's development has been closely tied to the sea. Today, modern techniques and scientific research have increased the production, harvest and conservation of this valuable American commodity. ASMI works on a world stage for high stakes to ensure Alaska's healthy, renewable seafood resource remains a vital part of the state's future.

Ocean Beauty Seafoods, Inc.

M/V OCEAN PRIDE.

AT HOME IN ALASKA, KNOWN AROUND THE WORLD

Ocean Beauty Seafoods is one of the oldest firms of its kind operating in Alaska. Founded in Seattle in 1910, the company began its Alaska operations in the 1930's, under the name Washington Fish & Oyster Company. Ocean Beauty currently operates four on-shore processing plants in Kodiak, Petersburg, Cordova and Naknek, and one offshore processing vessel, plus support operations and offices in Ketchikan, Dutch Harbor, and St. Paul in the Pribilof Islands.

Ocean Beauty's largest and oldest Alaska facility, in Kodiak, occupies the site of Kodiak's first cannery, opened in 1911. The plant survived the 1964 Good Friday earthquake, and Ocean Beauty took ownership in the late 60's. This year-round facility employs more than 280 workers at peak season, processing all species from Alaska's central gulf, including pollack and various bottom fish; cod, herring, frozen & canned salmon, and crab. As a caring and conscientious corporate citizen of Kodiak, the company is active within both the fishing industry and the community, participating in fisheries organizations, sponsoring sports teams and offering a high-school scholarship program.

The plant in Petersburg is the second-oldest of Ocean Beauty's Alaska facilities, with one of its original buildings dating from 1925, although the company did not purchase the facility until 1984. This plant has been extensively rebuilt and expanded, and now boasts both canning and freezing capacity for all Southeast Alaska seafood species: salmon, herring, black cod, halibut, and crab. Ocean Beauty is a major area employer, particularly during peak salmon season, when it offers more than 160 jobs to local and seasonal workers alike. Here, too, community involvement is reflected in the sponsorship of Little League and school sports teams and high-school clubs, plus the award of two $1,000 college scholarships each year to Petersburg high-school graduates.

Bristol Bay gillnet boats today.

Bristol Bay gillnet boats. Circa 1940.

The Ocean Beauty plant in Cordova, on Prince William Sound, was built in 1978, and was the city's largest employer in 1993. At peak production each year, more than 190 workers process canned and frozen salmon. During the course of the year, the Cordova plant produces the famous Copper River sockeye salmon, as well as halibut, herring, crab, and black & Pacific cod. Active community participation involves sponsoring sports teams, clubs, and scholarships.

Ocean Beauty's Naknek facility is its only purely seasonal operation. Acquired in 1988, it is located on the Naknek River in Bristol Bay. The village is iced in for eight months of the year, but each May the Naknek operation opens for the herring season, then handles abundant amounts of salmon during the dynamic Bristol Bay salmon fishing season from June to August. Each year, two graduating seniors from King Salmon High School are the recipients of Ocean Beauty-sponsored college scholarships.

One of the most modern and efficient ships in the Alaska processing fleet, the *Ocean Pride* was launched in 1989. Over 230 feet long and 57 feet wide, it has bunkspace for more than 140 crew members. The ship's mainstay is the Bering Sea crab fishery out of Dutch Harbor and the Pribilofs, but it also it travels throughout Alaskan waters from far-north Norton Sound to Southeast, processing herring, cod, salmon, and several King, Opilio, and Bairdi crab.

The huge quantity and variety of seafood produced from Alaska waters is sold by Ocean Beauty's experienced sales staff throughout the United States, Europe and Asia, in fresh, frozen, canned, and value-added form. Unique among traditional "production only" oriented seafood companies, Ocean Beauty has over 40 distribution outlets, from Washington to Utah to Tokyo, allowing the company to reach directly to customers and, ultimately, to consumers. Ocean Beauty's size, strength, scope, and worldwide sales and distribution have made it a world leader in the seafood industry.

Ocean Beauty is proud of its long and productive history in the 49th state, and of its role as a responsible and responsive member of all the Alaskan communities in which the company operates.

Fishing boats in Harbor — Petersburg.

Taku Smokeries

It's rather amazing, looking today at Taku Smokeries' large, modern, bustling seafood processing plant on the Juneau waterfront, to associate the company with its modest beginnings. The firm, which now processes nearly five million pounds of salmon a year for local, U.S., and foreign markets, had its start in company president Sandro Lane's garage.

In 1983, Lane, then a fisheries biologist, had been working on his own for several years to perfect a personal recipe for making lox (mild-cured smoked salmon). During that time he had produced the lox for family and friends and there is no question that they rated it highly. Lane recalls, "By 1983, I had requests in hand for more than 1,200 pounds of gourmet gift packs."

"Maybe," he thought, "This recipe is good enough to sell commercially."

Lane launched Taku Smokeries at his Mendenhall Valley home by converting his garage into a processing plant. Financing came from a $30,000 loan from his mother. The following year, 1984, Taku smoked about 7,000 pounds of fish and grossed $48,000.

Sandro Lane worked for several years to perfect his personal recipe for lox. Lane's business has grown from filling requests for family and friends to supplying cruiseships, running a retail store in Juneau, controlling a burgeoning catalog mail order business, and shipping products to restaurants and wholesalers in every state in the U.S. and around the world.

The years that followed were busy one. Lane did everything: fish buying, processing and smoking, sales, accounting, the works. Then as now, quality was everything at Taku Smokeries — in fish handling, cleanliness, packaging, and presentation.

His sales techniques proved imaginative. For instance, he determined that Alaska-bound cruiseships served substantial amounts of lox to their hundreds of thousands of passengers. But the ships' Italian catering executives could not believe that an Alaskan product, though less costly than the lox they had to import, could meet their demanding requirements.

In his sales negotiations, Lane's childhood years came into play. He was born in Italy, in 1952, to American parents. His father served in corporate and U.S. chamber of commerce positions, helping to rebuild Italy's shattered, post-war economy. As a result, young Sandro conversed as comfortably in Italian as in English.

Speaking the fluent Italian of those years, Lane convinced the cruiseship chefs to set up tests — his Taku Smokeries lox against the European products they had been using. Taku Smokeries prevailed, and supplying the cruiseship industry has been a major continuing element of the company's growth through two major relocations and an extensive plant expansion.

The first relocation occurred in 1986, when Lane moved out of his former garage site. Financed by a loan from the federal Small Business Administration, he moved into a 3,200-square-foot warehouse in the Juneau's Lemon Creek industrial district. The decision to move was a tough one. He remembers thinking, "This decision could be the biggest mistake of my life." It turned out to be one of his best.

The crew of the retail store caters to the tourists and locals that wander the streets of historic downtown Juneau.

At that time, he also doubled his work force by hiring one other person in addition to himself. By 1991, Taku had fifty employees working full- or part-time at the Lemon Creek site and was processing just under a million pounds of seafood; including additional products such as halibut, fresh and frozen salmon, and crab. But it was apparent that Taku Smokeries had again reached the limits of its plant capacity; a larger facility was necessary if the company was to continue growing.

Lane's choice for a new site was a freight warehouse on three acres of waterfront property just south of Juneau's cruiseship docks. He saw in the warehouse an ideal location where he could receive raw fish direct from boats and buyers and from which he could dispose of what remained after processing.

It was at this point, in order to fully finance the expansion that the new location allowed, that Lane took on a financially strong partner in the person of Giorgio Gallizio, head of a global marine catering enterprise that operated dining rooms and food services aboard cruise vessels and other ships worldwide. Lane had known and worked closely with Gallizio since the earliest days of supplying lox to Alaska-bound ships.

The arrangement was that Gallizio would purchase the property and lease it back to Taku Smokeries. This allowed for a major remodeling of the former freight-handling structure, including the addition of a second floor, installation of blast freezers and the addition of cold storage capacity to store up to a million pounds of fish.

Today, Taku Smokeries employs more than 120 men and women full- or part-time, a substantial work force by Alaskan standards and a source of considerable satisfaction to Lane. "These employees process and ship products to restaurants and wholesalers in every state in the U.S.; plus Japan, Europe and even South America," explains Lane.

A burgeoning catalog mail order business is also located on site, more than 30 percent of its customers being repeat purchasers who first tasted Taku Smokeries products on an Alaska vacation. The company's principal direct-sales outlet is a streetfront operation in Juneau's tourist and historic district.

In recent times, a whole new operation has developed adjacent to the terraced plaza at the plant site. Recognizing the location's enormous tourism and local potential, Giorgio Gallizio has added, and manages, a quality Italian and seafood restaurant and lounge there. The two — Lane and Gallizio — see great promise in the years ahead for both enterprises.

Not bad, many a local observer has noted, for an outfit that started in a converted garage.

Quality is everything at Taku Smokeries. Sandro Lane insists on the freshest seafood available. Taku Smokeries' location on three acres of waterfront property is ideal for receiving raw fish directly from boats and buyers.

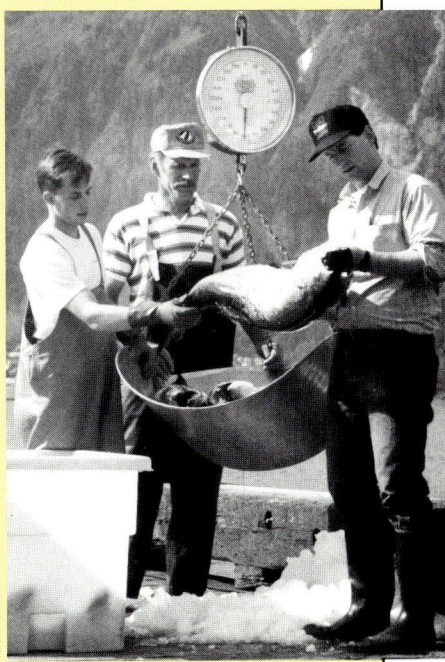

Sandro Lane, right, president of Taku Smokeries, inspects a fresh King salmon.

Maserculiq Incorporated

The Alaskan Congressional delegation heaves a sigh of relief when they reflect on the fact that the Alaska Native Claims Settlement Act of 1971 gave birth to at least one Village Corporation like Maserculiq Incorporated.

Established in 1971 in the community of Marshall, Alaska, Maserculiq Inc. has met the challenge of ANCSA. Through conservative investments in the local economy, "Mas Inc." has promoted economic development throughout the community while sustaining steady growth in retained earnings. Its diverse business activities include property management, operation of the local fuel storage and sales facility, a grocery store, and operation of a community fish processing plant. Land and resource development, tourism, and general contracting services are currently under development.

Maserculiq Inc. is an exception among Alaska's many village corporations. They have successfully maintained the unique balance between running a successful small business with the peculiarities of the ANCSA corporation system. Credit must be given to the board of five directors with sound business sense and a commitment to economic development in the region. The board has provided consistency in establishing corporate goals and the stability and vision necessary for future growth and success.

The anchor of Mas Inc. operations is the Marshall-based fish processing plant operated by the wholly-owned subsidiary Maserculiq Fish Processors Inc.

The corporate name, "Maserculiq" is Yupik Eskimo for "red fish," a reference to the tremendous salmon resource which migrates through the Yukon River community each season. Many of the corporation's shareholders are commercial fishermen and the investment in the industry has provided an economic benefit to both community and corporation.

The Yukon River drainage supports the finest run of King salmon, also known as Chinook, in Alaska. World-renowned for its rich flavor and high oil content, the Yukon King salmon is often called the world's finest salmon. Commercial salmon harvests over the 2,300 miles of Yukon River, a drainage of over 330,000 square miles, in recent years has averaged 107,000 Chinook (King), 640,000 summer chum, 150,000 fall chum, and 60,000 coho (silver) salmon.

Mas Inc. is intricately involved in the Yukon fishery

Maserculiq Inc. Board President and commercial fisherman, Tommy A. Andrew with a fellow fisherman after delivering their fish at the corporations plant in Marshall.

The corporate name "Maserculiq" is Yupik Eskimo for "red fish," a reference to the tremendous salmon resource which migrates through the Yukon River community each season.

both economically and culturally. The Corporation is at the forefront of efforts to promote the highest quality salmon in Alaska and has implemented quality control standards unique to the fishery.

Future goals include market diversification with efforts directed toward global distribution of Yukon King. Maserculiq Fish Processors is positioned to supply the world with the highest quality salmon at very competitive prices. The corporation is poised for dynamic growth in an industry which promotes the finest qualities of the great State of Alaska.

Business and Professional Services

Lighthouse near Sitka.
Alaska Division of Tourism.

Alaska USA Federal Credit Union

Alaska USA Federal Credit Union has been providing service to members for over 45 years. Since it was established in 1948, the credit union's goal has been to provide its members with consumer financial services as economically, conveniently and professionally as possible. In keeping with that goal, Alaska USA was among the first credit unions in the nation to offer share draft (checking) accounts and was the first federal credit union to close a 30-year mortgage loan. Today the credit union offers seven types of savings and investment accounts, three types of low-cost checking accounts, a wide array of affordable consumer and real estate loans, a competitively priced Visa credit card program, and free automated teller machine (ATM), point-of-sale (POS) and Visa Check Card service.

Alaska USA provides service to members worldwide through an extensive Member Service Network consisting of 19 branches in Alaska and Washington; the Alaska Option Network, which provides ATM and POS access worldwide; and the Member Service Center, which provides toll-free telephone access to virtually all credit union services 16 hours a day, seven days a week.

Alaska USA was chartered as the Alaskan Air Depot Federal Credit Union at Fort Richardson, Alaska, to serve the Depot's civilian employees. The charter was issued by the Bureau of Federal Credit Unions, which was responsible for administering the Federal Credit Union Act. This act, passed by Congress in 1934 during the depths of the Depression, was intended to provide working-class Americans with credit "for provident and productive purposes" and to assist in the nation's economic recovery.

It was also during the Depression that the federal government encouraged the settlement of Alaska. This brought many new residents to the state, and later, during World War II, there was an influx of military personnel and civilian workers as a result of Alaska's strategic importance in the Pacific war theater. The strategic importance continued after World War II, as the Cold War required a strong military presence in Alaska.

During this settlement period, established residents and many new federal employees and others who arrived from the "Lower 48" had a need for consumer credit. This need was not being fully satisfied by local financial institutions. The 15 founding members of Alaska USA recognized that a credit union, a not-for-profit financial cooperative, could satisfy those credit needs, as well as provide other financial benefits. Members pooled their savings and extended credit to one another while volunteering their time to operate the credit union. All members shared equally in the benefits of the credit union and collectively improved their standard of living.

Alaska USA's headquarters building in Anchorage houses the executive, operations and administrative staffs, as well as a branch office.

In the 1960s Alaska USA operated in an office provided by Elmendorf Air Force Base.

The idea of "people helping people" is a basic principle upon which the credit union operates and is an integral part of the frontier spirit that is shared by many Alaskans. This spirit is reflected in the credit union's commitment to the communities it serves, as well as its commitment to members. Each year, the credit union contributes to charitable organizations that address basic human needs and services that help people improve the quality of their daily lives. In addition, Alaska USA participates in the annual United Way campaign, local community food drives, and the Christmas in May program, a community effort of volunteers who, working with donated building supplies, improve the homes of qualifying low-income families. Alaska USA's employees also demonstrate this spirit by volunteering time to participate in fund-raising events to benefit a variety of charities and through their personal contributions to United Way.

Since its earliest years of service, the benefits of membership in Alaska USA have attracted the attention of consumers. The growing demand for credit union service from Alaska USA resulted in an increasing number of requests over the years for groups to be eligible to join the credit union.

In 1953, after the separation of Elmendorf Air Force Base and Fort Richardson, the credit union was renamed Elmendorf AFB Federal Credit Union. Shortly thereafter, it received authority to serve military officers and noncommissioned officers on the base. In 1958, all military and civilian personnel on Elmendorf AFB

Alaska USA's Board of Directors: Seated, left to right: Anna Hick, 2nd Vice Chairman; James A. Fena, Chairman; Leslie E. Dennis, Jr., 1st Vice Chairman; Darrel E. Cavender. Standing, left to right: Boyd S. Bennett, Secretary-Treasurer; William W. Dawson; Forrest (Woody) L. Hayes.

William B. Eckhardt, President (right), Robert A. Rylander, Executive Vice President.

Alaska USA's Member Service Center processes over 2.3 million member service requests annually.

became eligible for membership and, in 1964, membership was extended to personnel assigned to 24 remote Air Force stations in Alaska.

In 1970, the credit union's field of membership was amended to include all personnel assigned to Naval Station Adak, located near the tip of the Aleutian Island chain. To reflect its service to the military throughout Alaska, the credit union's name was changed in 1972 to Alaska Command Federal Credit Union.

As the credit union's branch office system began to expand statewide during the 1970s, it became apparent that an effective method was required to service members who were transferred from Alaska to locations in the continental United States and overseas. Accordingly, in 1973, the credit union's Member Service Center was established in Denver, Colorado, to provide members with mail and toll-free telephone processing of their service and transaction requests.

Extension of service to new civilian employer groups began during the construction of the trans-Alaska Pipeline, after service to Alyeska Pipeline Service Company and its subcontractors was authorized in 1974. In four years, more than 20,000 technicians, welders, truck drivers, and other personnel in this massive project opened member accounts. Like their military counterparts, many of these individuals retained memberships after moving on to other projects around the world, or returning to their homes in Alaska or the continental United States.

During this same period, the credit union's field of membership was expanded to Alaska Native Eskimos, Indians and Aleuts who were shareholders in 10 of the regional Native Corporations established under the 1971 Alaska Native Claims Settlement Act. This extension of service fulfilled a federal regulatory mission established in 1972 by the National Credit Union Administration (NCUA) to bring credit union service to Alaska Natives. The authority for Alaska USA to serve these Native Alaskans was to expire in 1978, but was twice extended by the NCUA and once by Congress before being made permanent by Public Law 97-110.

To reflect its growing field of membership and service to military, pipeline, and Alaska Native members within the state of Alaska and around the world, the credit union changed its name in 1975 to Alaska USA Federal Credit Union.

As Alaska USA expanded its Member Service Network and developed new services, it became an attractive merger partner for smaller credit unions that could no longer effectively compete within Alaska's financial services community. In 1979, the credit union accepted a merger proposal from USARAL Federal Credit Union (U.S. Army) and subsequently completed mergers with Union-Collier Federal Credit Union (oil industry), Mt. Edgecumbe Federal Credit Union (city, state and federal government), Alaska Coast Guard Federal Credit Union (17th Coast Guard District), and Wien Federal Credit Union (airline industry).

In 1981, Alaska USA was selected by the Department of Defense and NCUA as the credit union to serve U.S. military personnel at Clark Air Base in the Philippines. Service was provided to over 10,000 active duty and retired military personnel until the closure of the base as a result of the eruption of Mount Pinatabo in 1991.

Alaska USA members have access to their accounts 24 hours a day at over 160,000 ATMs.

In 1983, the 15,000 members of Whidbey Federal Credit Union (U.S. Navy) at Oak Harbor, Washington, voted to merge with Alaska USA. This merger provided the credit union with two offices in Washington state and led to the relocation of the Member Service Center from Denver to Oak Harbor the following year.

The decade of the 1980s brought change as NCUA authorized credit union membership for occupational and associational groups around the country that were without credit union service. This new policy resulted in Alaska USA extending service to more than 4,000 employer and associational groups that requested inclusion in the credit union's field of membership.

In 1987, after establishing a branch in Seattle, Washington, Alaska USA was once again selected as a merger partner, this time by Sound Credit Union and BluCo Federal Credit Union, both located in Seattle. These mergers resulted in 9,000 new members in the Pacific Northwest.

Today, Alaska USA is the nation's seventh largest federal credit union in terms of membership, serving over 185,000 members from diverse civilian and military groups with varying financial needs.

In support of its member service objectives, the credit union established Alaska Option Services Corporation in 1983. This shared EFT network, which Alaska USA manages and operates as the majority stockholder, provides account access worldwide 24 hours a day. In 1986, the credit union established Alaska USA Insurance, Inc., a wholly-owned subsidiary which has nearly 48,000 policies in force. In 1992, Alaska USA established Alaska Home Mortgage, Inc., another wholly-owned subsidiary which originated and closed over 1,000 mortgages during its first 18 months of operation.

To ensure reliable, timely and cost-effective service delivery, Alaska USA owns and operates its own data processing system and maintains its own operations, programming, and

The credit union owns, operates and maintains its data processing system to ensure reliable and responsive service.

maintenance staff. The data processing system supports nearly 250,000 deposit accounts and 90,000 loan accounts, processing over 35 million member transactions each year.

At year end 1993, Alaska USA reported over $1.4 billion in assets, making the credit union the state's second largest financial institution. Total member deposits of $1.01 billion and loans of $554 million also represented record levels for the credit union. Since being chartered in 1948, Alaska USA has granted 1.2 million loans to members totaling $5.3 billion. In addition, the sound financial performance of the credit union has been acknowledged by the "SUPERIOR" rating received from IDC Financial Publishing, Inc., one of the nation's most prominent firms rating the performance of financial institutions.

As a leader within the credit union industry, Alaska USA is recognized nationally for its operational expertise, service innovations and quality of service.

The credit union's services and their delivery have changed over the years in response to the membership's changing needs. However, since 1948, the credit union's commitment to its cooperative principles and the purpose for which it was chartered have been maintained. Alaska USA continues to satisfy the financial needs of members from all walks of life and levels of income, providing them with the opportunity to be financially successful and to improve their standard of living.

Alaska Option Services Corporation

In 1983, eight credit unions and two banks formed the Alaska Option Services Corporation, initially to estab-lish and operate a shared auto-mated teller machine (ATM) network. Operated under management contract by its majority shareholder, Alaska USA Federal Credit Union, the Network provides electronic switching and settlement of financial transactions among its member financial institutions, thus making it possible for a debit cardholder of one member institution to use another member institution's ATM.

Initially, ten institutions offered service through 21 ATMs in Alaska. Within a few short years, all of Alaska's major financial institutions had joined the founding Alaska Option institutions in providing shared ATM service to Alaskans throughout the state. Today, 24 financial institutions belong to the Alaska Option Network. The Network supports over 180 ATMs in 26 Alaska communities. These financial institutions have combined assets of over $6 billion, which is 97 percent of the total assets of all financial institutions in Alaska. These institutions provide service to over 280,000 debit cardholders who conduct over 10 million transactions each year.

Since it was established in 1983, access to the Network has expanded worldwide. Through a variety of regional and national network affiliations, Alaska Option member institutions can provide their cardholders access to the PLUS, Visa, CIRRUS, and MasterCard international networks, as well as the ACCEL and Exchange regional networks in the Pacific Northwest. These networks provide immediate account access through thousands of ATMs around the world. In addition, Discover and American Express cardholders, as well as cardholders worldwide that are affiliated with the networks mentioned above, can use most ATMs in the Alaska Option system.

ATMs are only part of the Alaska Option story. In 1987, together with Carrs Quality Centers and their commercial

Robert A. Rylander, Chairman (seated), Richard D. Barnhart, President.

Alaska Option provides in-house card production service for its Member Institutions, producing over 100,000 cards annually.

bank, Alaska Option developed a debit point of sale (POS) system that allows cardholders to pay for purchases at Carrs with their debit cards. Response to this new system in Alaska was overwhelming, with over 125,000 POS transactions processed in the first 90 days.

Since then, similar POS service has been extended to over 85 Alaska merchants in 29 communities throughout the state who operate 550 terminals in 219 locations. Today, Alaskans perform over 145,000 POS transactions every month and the use continues to grow.

In the future, POS service will be extended worldwide so Alaskans can use their cards while traveling to purchase goods and services at thousands of merchant locations throughout the nation and around the world.

In 1993, Alaska Option participated with the State of Alaska and various Alaska financial institutions to automate, for the first time, the State's Permanent Fund Dividend distribution process. Alaskans can now choose to have their Permanent Fund Dividend deposited directly to an account at the financial institution of their choice. Over 37 percent of Alaskans chose to participate in the first year of this convenient program. During the month of October 1993, when dividends were first deposited directly into Alaskans' accounts, cardholders conducted more than one million ATM and POS transactions.

Alaska Option continues to be operated for the mutual benefit of its member institutions and their cardholders. Alaska Option is an excellent example of the benefits of cooperation and is truly a story of shared success.

ALASKA OPTION MEMBER FINANCIAL INSTITUTIONS

Shareholders:
Alaska USA FCU
Alaskan FCU
Denali FCU
FedAlaska FCU
Fort Wainwright FCU
Frontier State CU
Matanuska Valley FCU
National Bank of Alaska

Other Member Institutions:
AK District Engineers FCU
AK Federal Savings & Loan
AK State Employees FCU
Atlantic FCU
Bank of America, N.A.
Denali State Bank
Eielson FCU
First Bank
First National Bank
Greenwood Trust (Discover)
Key Bank of Alaska
Mt. Kinley Bank
North Country FCU
Northern Schools FCU
Northrim Bank
RAA FCU

ASCG Incorporated

Arctic Slope Consulting Group was born in the Inupiat Eskimo village of Barrow, America's northernmost community, in 1978. Since then the firm has achieved a global reputation for the highest quality performance in engineering, architectural and surveying services. With revenues in excess of $35 million per year and consistently high national ranking by Engineering News Record, ASCG is a stable, growing firm eager to explore new opportunities in Alaska and around the world.

With clients ranging from Alyeska Pipeline Service Co. and the Port of Portland to the U.S. Dept. of Energy and the U.S. Navy, ASCG is pleased to offer a strong, interdisciplinary matrix of design professionals with comprehensive experience. That experience encompasses a wide range of project types, including power, port, water/wastewater, transportation and other public facilities, commercial and professional buildings, economic feasibility analysis, environmental assessment, monitoring and remediation design, lead-based paint testing, master plans and pipelines. Since team members have worked together on numerous projects, they organize quickly and perform efficiently on new undertakings. The origins and operations of ASCG tell a remarkable story, beginning with passage of the Alaska Native Claims Settlement Act of 1971. The act created the Arctic Slope Regional Corporation (ASRC) and twelve other Native corporations, wholly owned, managed and operated by its 6,500 Inupiat shareholders. ASRC has become an economic powerhouse with a family of equally successful subsidiaries, including Arctic Slope Consulting Group.

Prudent management, excellent acquisitions and top-notch performance by its staff have made ASCG the largest Native-owned architecture and engineering firm in America, with three hundred employees and five offices located in Barrow, Anchorage, Portland, Phoenix and Albuquerque. Ironically, the company is so successful, it does not even qualify for the minority enterprise points offered on many of its projects.

In addition to these bottom-line considerations, ASCG is a model firm in other ways, too. With a growing clientele among Indian tribes throughout the nation, ASCG places a high value on the commitment, communication and corporate sensitivity necessary to work successfully in cross-cultural environments.

"We're extremely proud of our own corporate heritage as an Inupiat enterprise," says Robert Hilton, ASCG president. "It is also gratifying that tribes throughout the country have come to trust and rely on us for the service we provide. Sometimes they come to us to find out what makes us tick, to see how we've built on the combined strengths of Inupiat and American corporate values. It is important to remember that part of ASCG's mission is to 'appreciate and honor' our client's values by blending their respective culture, lifestyles and artistries into the contemporary structures we build. Our goal is to balance each client's culture and spiritual values with their physical environment."

"Our design professionals are prepared to listen, see and learn of the various cultural, spiritual and physical require-

ASCG's technicians provide quality inspection and corrosion detection services to the trans-Alaska Pipeline and petroleum production and transportation operations.

ASCG provides civil, structural, mechanical/piping, transportation, utility and water/waste water engineering to a wide spectrum of private and public clients.

ments and incorporate them into culturally sensitive plans," says Hilton, noting that ASCG has developed long-term relationships with the Gila River Indian Community, Pasqua Yaqui Housing Authority, Acomita Indian Reservation, Yakima Indian Nation, Navajo Nation, and others. "Likewise, the other members of our team take great care in respecting the land and communities in which they work."

With a substantial portion of its business in oilfield activities, ASCG helps fulfill its parent company's strategic aim of being a vertically integrated oil well-to-gas pump participant in Alaska's oil industry, a leader in environmentally responsible development of the state's natural wealth.

"No one knows the Arctic the way we do," says Hilton. "And it isn't mere coincidence that the people who are most concerned about ecologically sound approaches to development are our shareholders, many of whom rely heavily on the bounty of land and sea as a matter of cultural choice."

This strong sense of stewardship as well as economic opportunity led to two important ASCG acquisitions. Oceantech Ltd., a prominent industrial firm in Alaska since the 1950s, substantially augmented ASCG's surveying and other oilfield engineering capabilities, while Arctic Slope Inspection Services added a proven component in the area of quality assurance/quality control inspection and testing with oilfields as well as many other applications.

"No matter what needs inspecting—high pressure vessels, pipelines, cranes, bridges, storage tanks, railroad or semi-truck tankers, we can certify its integrity, or, when necessary, flag problems promptly before the cost of fixing them becomes exorbitant," says Hilton. "We have superior technology and very experienced personnel."

To the capabilities offered by these acquisitions, ASCG has developed a wide range of expertise in design and engineering as well as a host of scientific disciplines associated with developing, maintaining and mitigating the impacts of the commercial and industrial infrastructure of the state and the nation.

In fact, it is worthy of note that in addition to many industrial clients, ASCG has been highly commended for numerous local, state and federal government projects, from the Arctic to the American Southwest, from the Bureau of Land Management, the Port of Anchorage and the Bureau of Indian Affairs to the U.S. Army Corps of Engineers and the Coast Guard.

"One of our most significant and satisfying projects is our work with the North Slope Borough, our hometown municipality, to develop water and sewer systems for all North Slope villages. We feel it's an excellent example of local self-governance and enterprise working together for our people," says Hilton.

Whether the project is local or global in scope, Arctic Slope Consulting Services brings the same level of excellence in service to all of its clients. Built on a strong foundation of cultural pride and integrity, ASCG enters the next century prepared for new challenges and opportunities.

ASCG uses traditional and state-of-the-art technology to perform topographic, site selection, construction, hydrographic, cadastral and aerial photogrammetric control surveys for both onshore and offshore projects.

ASCG architectural design services include those for diverse environments.

Coffman Engineers

The Oil and Gas Platform in Cook Inlet, Alaska is an example of multi-discipline engineering for 64-person living quarters.

The work of engineers is everywhere and vital to the backbone of civilization, yet many people don't realize the varied skills that make up the field, nor the diversity of talent needed to design, build and operate our most mundane, and most unusual, buildings, structures and related systems. In fact, engineering is comprised of an array of related disciplines, many of which Coffman Engineers Inc. of Anchorage and Seattle has gathered under one roof into a multi-disciplined firm which can field a team to match virtually any client need. Their multi-disciplined staff includes structural, civil, mechanical, electrical and corrosion control engineering.

"Very seldom does a project require the expertise of only one or two engineering disciplines. Yet that's what most firms offer," notes Harold Hollis, vice president and general manager of Coffman-Anchorage. "We offer not only the diversity of expertise, but also the management ability to hold that talent together and manage it cost-effectively for the maximum benefit of our clients.

In part, this is accomplished by offering prime design services for commercial, industrial, institutional and defense systems and facilities. This allows Coffman's engineers to apply their capabilities early in the project to insure consistency, quality and timeliness.

"That's where we shine," says Hollis. "We do a lot of prime design and it gives our clients peace of mind. They stay involved during that creative, conceptual process, which gives them a greater sense of ownership, but at the same time they gain confidence in us so that as the project proceeds they're comfortable with our professional judgment as well as our commitment to their needs. For that reason, many clients repeatedly retain us to provide project and construction management of their projects."

Another facet in which Coffman's team approach is applied is through the architectural community. "As sub consultants, our team works closely with architectural clients to successfully complete their projects," Hollis says.

Though its clients and projects run a lengthy gamut, Coffman is especially proud of its accomplishments in three main areas:

• **Arctic Cold Weather Design–** In this area, Coffman is a leader in the number and quality of projects, most completed under arduous or extreme conditions in remote areas. Coffman's accomplishments in designing and overseeing installation of water and sewer systems, power generation facilities, living quarters, oil and gas facilities and other projects flow from a wealth of experience in coping effectively with ice, snow, wind, permafrost and other harsh climatic conditions. Coffman's accomplishments in this area range from the $68 million Kuparuk Industrial Center on Alaska's North Slope to a comprehensive water and sewer project for the village of Emmonak. For the award-winning Kuparuk project, Coffman provided civil, structural, mechanical and electrical engineering for the oil field service base, as well as

Annual corrosion and multi-discipline engineering is being performed for Alaska's largest port facility, the Port of Anchorage.

The new State of Alaska Courthouse Expansion Project involves structural engineering for a 206,000 square foot, seismically enhanced facility and includes a full basement and underground tunnel.

complete project and construction management for the 140,000 square foot complex used to house and support up to 600 workers. Even more unique in scope, but no less technically demanding, the Emmonak project entailed environmental, civil, structural, mechanical and electrical design and construction management of an innovative system to handle water and sewer needs in the village of 750 residents. This was another award-winning effort by Coffman, actually one of many laurels the firm has received through the years.

• **Seismic Area Design**– Although cold and wind are the elements most often associated with threats to structural integrity in the north, earthquakes are an ever-present source of danger which can manifest with little or no warning at any time. At Coffman, the safety of their clients and the structural integrity of their facilities are paramount. The firm's performance is based on many years of experience, as well as a top notch cadre of experts. An excellent example of Coffman's work in this arena is the structural engineering for a new, six-story state courthouse building in Anchorage, incorporating specialized, state-of-the-art design technology on a site of known seismic vulnerability. Utilizing rigorous design criteria, and their own vast experience in conjunction with the Stanford University Earthquake Engineering Center, Coffman's team of experts developed an innovative steel frame design for the building to satisfy seismic concerns.

• **Corrosion Control and Prevention**– The inroads of cold and earth movement can be abrupt and painfully obvious. The silent parasite that plagues many facilities is corrosion from adverse combinations of air, water, fuel and industrial fluids and soil. Because of both cost and regulatory issues, Coffman's recognized expertise in this area assures careful analysis and custom-designed strategies to protect facilities, both old and new. Projects in this area range from relatively small residential and commercial efforts to large-scale industrial undertakings. One of the most noteworthy is the ongoing work performed for the Port of Anchorage, whose dock and cargo handling system is subjected year round to the simultaneous rigors of saltwater, tidal activity and native soil attacks.

"We've worked in many environments, and our expertise covers a wide range of technical situations. But nowhere are our services more critical, and our successes more evident, than here in the north," says Hollis. "Here, some of the toughest technical challenges imaginable are confronted, and consistently overcome, by our team. We're very proud of our accomplishments in providing facilities in Alaska that are highly functional, reliable and long-lasting. Equally important as we look to the future is our professional integrity and our philosophy of providing superior service, complete satisfaction, and the peace of mind that comes with our experience."

A complete heating and ventilation system renovation was finished for a 370,000 square foot high school in Anchorage.

National Bank of Alaska

Since its founding in 1916, National Bank of Alaska has safeguarded much of Alaska's wealth through seasonal booms and busts, the fortunes of war and territorial growing pains. The bank has continued to grow as well, matching the pace of the young state in its quest for economic expansion.

For decades, NBA has been a major player providing analysis, counsel, capital and a wide array of related financial support services to Alaska's premier industries of mining, fisheries, timber, oil and gas, tourism, and transportation. With its statewide network of over fifty branches, NBA has a long tradition of supporting business development both in urban and rural areas of the state. The bank is also proud of its long tradition of service to its retail customers.

"We're still the same solid reliable bank we've always been," notes President Richard Strutz. "However, we've done a lot of fine tuning in our service strategy to respond to our customers' needs for convenient services."

He cites a few key examples:

- Thousands of Alaskans have taken advantage of Loan by Phone, a program that allows application for loans and Visa cards by phone. This convenient service allows customers access to NBA loan officers from the comfort of their home or office, saving them valuable time.
- Also made possible by phone and computer technology, NBA's automated account information system gives customers access to checking and savings account information 24-hours a day, seven days a week.
- Smart Start is a seminar program that introduces low and moderate income borrowers to the home buying process. The combination of personal contact and professionally-designed instructional materials dignifies and empowers participants and allows them to progress and ask questions at their own pace in a relaxed, informal setting. This new initiative has been well received by the target audience.
- Another popular program is Carefree Checking, which affords checking account services for a flat monthly fee instead of more cumbersome per check charges.
- Anticipating the needs of Alaskans as economic change continues to sweep the world, a new Investment Center offers mutual fund investment and related services based on NBA's decades of experience in financial markets.
- Individuals and dealers have enjoyed the services offered by Northland Credit, a wholly-owned subsidiary of NBA, including competitive products, quick loan approval and convenient hours.

While Alaska's newspaper headlines often voice economic

In addition to traditional banking services, NBA offers investment services tailored to customers' investment needs and tolerance for risk.

Under the leadership of President Richard Strutz (left) and Chairman of the Board Edward Rasmuson, National Bank of Alaska continues to focus on offering convenient delivery of banking services.

Throughout the state, NBA customers use touchtone phones to pay bills and access their account information. Loan by Phone, a recent addition, allows customers to speak directly to a loan officer to apply for a loan by phone.

complaints, National Bank of Alaska's consistent, record-breaking profitability has been built on faith in an economy that is fundamentally strong and bursting with potential. Bank officers closely track trends in business and development locally, nationally and globally. This enables them to develop sound investment policies for bank assets and sound advice for customers.

As a family-owned enterprise, NBA regards Alaska as home and Alaskans as neighbors; and in the north country, neighbors look out for each other. The bank's nearly 1,200 employees do this in numerous ways, both formally and informally. One good example is an outreach program in rural areas. Community agents in several target villages which don't have branch service provide liaison between local residents and bank personnel. They offer information on financial services and track down answers to questions posed by residents. Complementing efforts of the local agents, community advisory boards have long been used throughout the state and in Seattle to help bank managers take the pulse of customer needs and trends.

"From our humble beginnings in Skagway during the Gold Rush era, we have always considered ourselves a hometown bank," says Strutz. "Our community agents and advisory boards help us keep in touch with customers around the state."

National Bank of Alaska's careful stewardship of customer assets, prudent investment policies and community spirit have made it Alaska's premier bank. This is reflected in stable earnings over many years, as well as in the clout that enabled it to acquire other institutions who lacked the strength to adapt to economic changes in the mid-1980s.

Recent statistics show the strong performance which has become an NBA tradition. In 1994, the bank earned $37.5 million, an increase of about 5 percent over the previous record of $35.6 million set the year before. Deposits reached $1.75 billion compared to the $1.61 million in 1993.

National Bank of Alaska has grown in 78 years to a large network of financial professionals dedicated to the state's future. Still a key player in that network is bank chairman Edward Rasmuson, grandson of Judge E. A. Rasmuson, a Swedish immigrant who was elected to the board of directors in 1918. When the judge stepped down in 1943, his son Elmer took the helm until his own retirement in 1989.

A lot has changed since the early days of NBA's history. For example, gold is no longer the chief medium of exchange used by bank tellers. Fame and fortune have come and gone for

In several rural villages, NBA community agents provide information about banking services and serve as liaisons between the bank and local residents.

many. Indeed, many fortune-seekers have come and gone. Through-out the swings of fortune over the years, National Bank of Alaska has not only survived sometimes tumultous change, but has thrived, casting its lot with the hardy souls who have chosen to make their permanent homes in America's far north.

Adams Morgenthaler and Company

VALUE BY ENGINEERING DESIGN

The sign out front says "Adams, Morgenthaler and Company... Value Added Engineering Services." More than a catchy slogan, the words reflect the company's vision of itself.

A case in point is the engineering firm's heating, ventilation and air conditioning work on the new $40 million state courthouse in downtown Anchorage.

"We were initially asked to consider using air conditioning concepts which called for a traditional mechanical refrigerant chiller," recalls Boyd Morgenthaler, a principal of Adams, Morgenthaler and Company (AMC). "But in our fee proposal we suggested an innovative use of a design which would circulate cold well water instead. We proved the concept for this job and won the approval from the project manager."

That innovative approach to a standard design component is typical of Adams, Morgenthaler and Company's value added approach — giving the client more than they anticipate. And in this case, the firm's innovative approach to the courthouse building's cooling and ventilation system will save the state some $200,000 in initial hardware costs, save some $60,000 per year in reduced electrical operating expenses, and save considerable maintenance labor expenses. A bonus is the system's earth-friendly design which eliminates the need for ozone-damaging CFC refrigerants.

Value also comes in the form of creative construction planning. When British Petroleum (BP) moved their central computer operation to Anchorage in 1986, they needed a larger air conditioning system in a big hurry. In addition to expanding the computer room by 1,000 square feet, the existing 5,000 square feet required nearly complete rearrangement. Computers are the life's blood of BP operations, and long shut downs were absolutely out of the question. Working with the BP project manager, AMC recommended a

Electrical Principal, David D. Adams and Mechanical Principal, Boyd Morgenthaler.

AMC Principal, Boyd Morgenthaler takes time from his job for community activities including coaching U12 soccer tournament champions, the Red Hoxt Chilly Peppers.

partnering approach with the mechanical contractor. With fire extinguisher in hand, AMC coordinated the work of pipefitters and computer operators as the final underfloor piping cut-in was made. The project was completed nearly $250,000 under budget, ahead of schedule, and with less than two hours of computer shut-down time. That's value added services.

"The beauty of our corporate design approach is that we offer innovation above and beyond the initial design requirements set forth by the client," explains Dave Adams, the firm's co-founder and president. "We like doing business that way — that's part of our corporate vision. In fact realizing the vision of being a 'value added engineering firm' is our most important accomplishment."

Adams, armed with Bachelor's and Master's degrees in electrical engineering from Stanford and six years of experience as a project engineer including significant work at the North Slope's Kuparuk oil field, and Morgenthaler, a mechanical engineering graduate of the University of Washington with experience on the construction administration of Seattle's Kingdome and design work on Anchorage's Sullivan Arena, founded their Anchorage based engineering firm in 1981 with seven employees. Longtime Alaskans will remember the early 80s as a time when government and private sector construction was booming in Alaska's largest city. The private construction market as well as public school buildings represented the bulk of AMC's engineering efforts by its workforce which had grown to 18. But with a downturn in world oil prices and a subsequent recession in the heavily oil dependent Alaskan economy, the firm in the mid 1980s saw the number of new construction projects in Alaska shrink.

"Diversification, a positive attitude, and an ability to adapt allowed us to thrive," says Adams. "We developed several industry-leading skills that set us apart from other mechanical/electrical engineering firms. We developed large scale energy management and control systems, very energy efficient buildings, custom computer aided design software, and were the first engineering firm in the region to put the latest indoor air quality guidelines into practice. We are also one of the state's leading consultants in data communications systems."

Each year since the bottoming of the Alaskan economy in 1987 AMC has enjoyed steady growth, reaching a peak of 35 employees. The firm had stabilized at 28 employees by the end of 1994.

Along the way, AMC and its staff garnered an impressive list of professional awards as

University of Alaska Anchorage Business Education Building, Award Winning Project "Good Lighting Practices," International Illumination Design Award presented by the Illuminating Engineering Society of North America for the University of Alaska Anchorage School of Business, 1993 and "Award of Excellence for Energy Efficiency," an International Illumination Design Award presented by the Illuminating Engineering Society of North America for the University of Alaska Anchorage School of Business, 1993.

Swimming pool in Nikiski, Alaska with 135 foot long water slide, the only water slide in the state. Other interesting features include: innovative, low glare lighting, containment under a geodesic dome.

well as national recognition for its mechanical and electrical engineering projects. For its work on the University of Alaska Anchorage School of Business building AMC was presented the "Good Lighting Practices" International Illumination Design Award by the Illuminating Engineering Society of North America in 1993. AMC received the same award for its work on Shemya (Air Force Base) Recreation Center in the Aleutian Islands, also in 1993. Again in 1993 AMC received the "Award of Excellence for Energy Efficiency," also for the University of Alaska Anchorage School of Business building. Notably, this building was one of just three projects to receive this recognition in the entire nation. In 1987 the "ASHRAE Energy Award," Outstanding Achievement in the Design of Energy Efficient Buildings was presented by the American Society of Heating, Refrigerating and Air Conditioning Engineers for the Kulis Air National Guard Base Operations and Training Facility in Anchorage. Work on that same Air National Guard facility earned Adams, Morgenthaler and Company a share in the coveted "Blue Seal Award" for Design Excellence presented by the Department of Defense in 1986. The Blue Seal Award is presented only every other year for the best designed Department of Defense facility worldwide. Most recently AMC received the 1994 Associate Of The Year award from the Associated General Contractors of Alaska.

The future looks bright for AMC. Associates Dave Crews and Pat Cusick bring the company expanded leadership and a solid core of mid-level engineering project managers provide depth which sets the company ahead of competing firms.

"We'll continue to thrive and diversify," says Dave Adams of his firm's future. "Let's face it, much of the engineering work of the future will be in international and emerging markets — and some of those, like the former Soviet Union, will be in northern and Arctic climates. The world wants what America has, and when it comes to engineering expertise, we have it."

Alaska Home Mortgage, Inc.

Alaska Home Mortgage, Inc. (AHM), a wholly-owned subsidiary of Alaska USA Federal Credit Union, was incorporated in March 1992 and began operations in May 1992. The primary focus of AHM is on providing comprehensive, cost-effective and professional mortgage service for the purchase or refinance of one-to four-family residential properties. A strong commitment to this focus, combined with close working relationships with realtors in the Anchorage area, provides borrowers with high quality and responsive mortgage lending services.

The home-buying consumer and realtor response to AHM's approach to mortgage lending has been significant. Within the first year of operation, AHM expanded both staff and offices at the 36th Avenue location in Anchorage.

By the end of the second year of operation, AHM had a total staff of 16, with seven full-time mortgage loan originators. At that time, annual financing and refinancing volumes exceeded $93 million.

AHM offers a wide variety of conventional, FHA, VA, AHFC, and Jumbo loans, with originators guiding the borrowers through the entire mortgage process from prequalifying through closing. While origination and process-

Lorran Skinner, President (right), Richard Mantyla, Senior Mortgage Loan Originator.

ing functions are handled in-house, AHM utilizes Alaska USA for underwriting, closing, secondary marketing, shipping, and various administrative and management requirements.

Virtually all of the mortgages originated by AHM are serviced by Alaska USA. Consequently, the servicing of the borrower's mortgage stays in Alaska with one of the largest mortgage loan servicers in the state. Availability of local servicing is considered an important benefit by most borrowers and a requirement by some secondary market investors, such as Alaska Housing Finance Corporation.

The Alaska real estate market closely reflects the Alaska economy and its dramatic swings in activity and growth. With the backing of its parent organization, AHM has made a long-term commitment to the Alaska real estate market and has the financial capacity to provide consistent service by maintaining a staff of highly experienced mortgage originators. These are important attributes to borrowers, realtors, and secondary market investors.

Alaska families will always have a need for quality housing, and AHM will continue to assist them in obtaining the right financing to acquire the homes of their dreams.

The quality of service provided by AHM originators and support staff has resulted in phenomenal growth for the company.

ABR, Inc. Environmental Research Services

Fairbanks is home to ABR, Inc., but this tight-knit cadre of environmental specialists roams the nation and the world. Their primary mission is providing the expertise to help both government and the private sector satisfy the often complex regulations established to safeguard environmental values.

A mature and progressive company highly ranked by analysts, ABR displays a remarkable level of responsibility to its clients, its employees and to the laws that govern the tricky interface between government and industry, and between industry and the land. The work performed by ABR in numerous natural settings ranges from relatively simple inventories and environmental assessments to complex applied research projects. Projects completed by ABR are as diverse as its experienced staff, many of whom received their scientific training in one or more of the renowned scientific programs of the University of Alaska at Fairbanks. Major services include but are not limited to:

- Wildlife and fish studies
- Vegetation and habitat analyses
- Environmental impact assessment
- Ecological restoration
- Permit consultation
- Bioremediation
- Wetland delineation
- Ecological risk assessment
- Resource inventories
- GIS applications

The firm has not been reluctant to venture into the more difficult areas of environmental concern, such as wetlands and endangered species. For example, ABR's mobile radar bird study program incorporates state-of-the-art technology into portable field units with far-ranging capabilities. Equipped with marine radars, night vision and video equipment, the units have given ABR an advantage in conducting highly accurate, cost-effective studies of bird movements and migration. Accurate data are critical in addressing environmental concerns and developing proactive strategies for mitigating environmental impact.

The company's work in wetlands runs the gamut from mapping and permit assistance to surveys, habitat enhancement, and restoration. ABR is also in the forefront of ecological restoration with projects that range from simple mine reclamation with native grasses to the development of complex aquatic and terrestrial communities that host micro-organisms, plants, insects, and vertebrate animals.

"We have been and will remain on the leading edge of practical and applied technology to fulfill the spirit and letter of our environmental laws, while providing industry with cost-effective strategies for mitigation and restoration," says Bob Ritchie, ABR presi-

The Horned Puffin is one of many species of wildlife that ABR has studied.

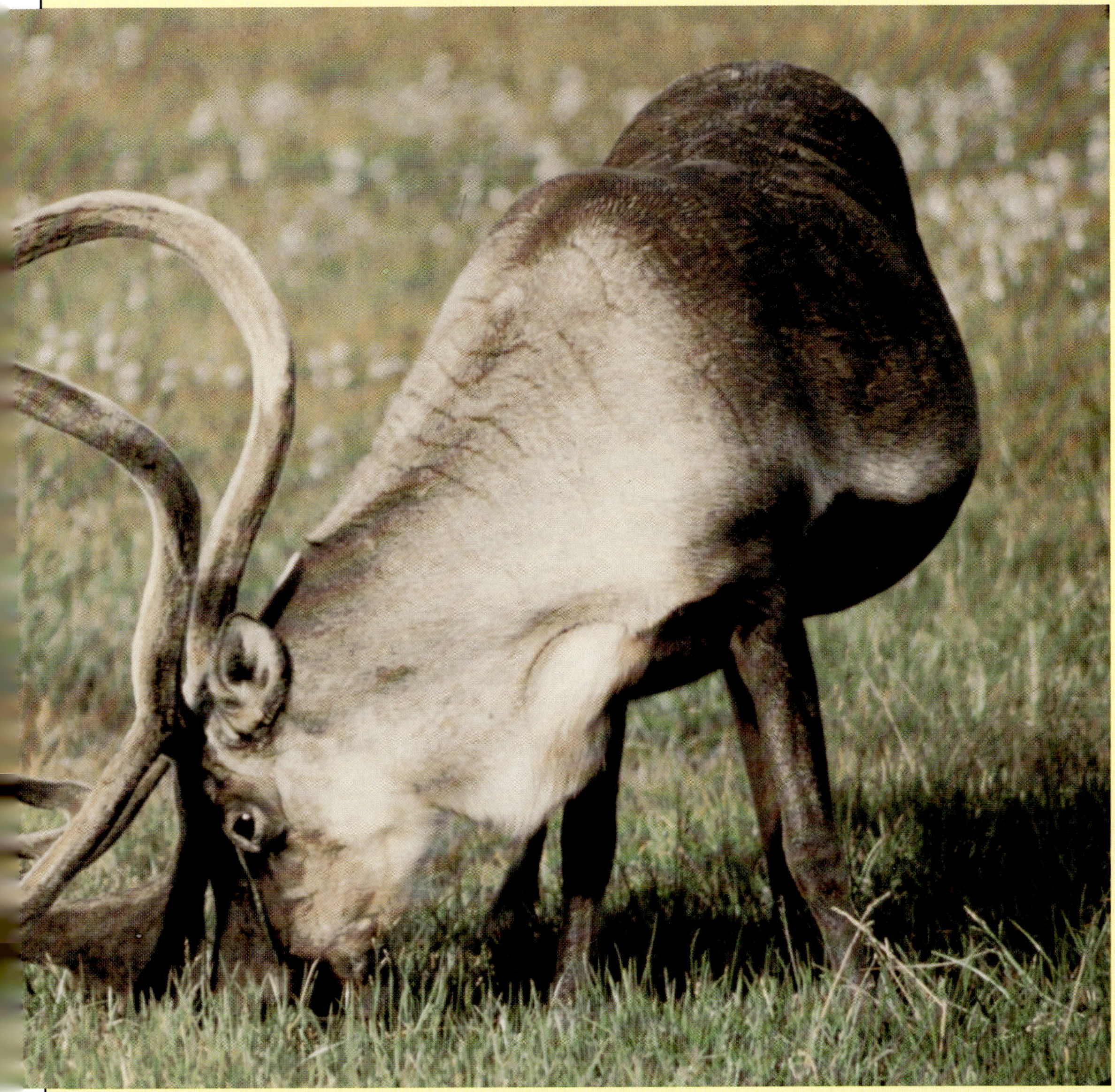

Betty Anderson, photographer.

LEFT: *A caribou bull feeds in an arctic meadow.*

Brian Cooper, photographer.

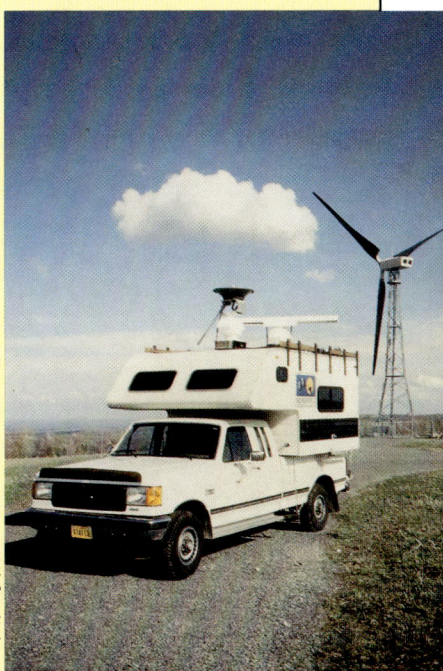

ABR's Radar Labs have been used for environmental assessments worldwide.

dent. "Our experience is the key here. We know industry, we know science, we know the law. There are numerous ways to meet environmental challenges within the budget range of today's business community, and our job is to find them."

ABR believes strongly in leading by example. It has been praised by government and industry for internal, environmentally friendly policies, including car pooling, socially responsible investing, compensating employees for volunteer time, and matching their charitable contributions. Employees have ranged as far as Belize and Israel, donating time to wildlife projects, and regularly visit local schools to promote interest in resource management issues and careers.

"The plain fact is, profit is not our only incentive. We love our work in the most basic way and we look for ways to improve our communities," says Ritchie. "From long experience we know that most companies and their employees typically want no less. This makes us natural partners."

Minch Ritter Voelckers Architects

By almost any measure — longevity, stability, client satisfaction, awards — the Juneau firm of Minch Ritter Voelckers Architects (MRV) ranks as one of Southeast Alaska's, and the state's, preeminent architectural firms.

The practice, now run by three principals, can trace its origins to 1952 when Linn A. Forrest, previously Alaska Regional Architect for the U.S. Forest Service, launched the firm. Its first major project: To design the Juneau-Douglas High School. Interestingly,

Juneau Empire Building — *This building is a combined office and printing plant. The precast exterior panels integrate with native carved panels.*

when the school district decided in 1982 to completely renovate and expand the building, they again called upon the organization, by this time known as MRV and headed by Robert Minch, Richard Ritter, and Paul Voelckers.

The choice was a natural. Throughout its history the firm has designed large numbers of educational facilities, with projects and locations as varied as elementary schools in Craig and Klukwan in Southeast Alaska and the Geophysical Institute at the University of Alaska Fairbanks.

MRV has also done extensive work in the fields of library, museum, office, commercial and housing design — in locales that vary from downtown Juneau (where the city's award-winning, nationally-acclaimed public library perches atop a four-story parking garage) to Unalaska on the Aleutian Chain. Housing projects range in scale from multiple (50 units of affordable housing for the Alaska Housing Finance Corporation) to individual units such as Paul Voelcker's own A.I.A. design-award waterfront residence.

If the firm's projects range widely both in location and in kind, at least one common thread weaves throughout them all: *the principals' passionate commitment to what they call a 'participatory process" with clients.*

The goal and role of an MRV architect, says Robert Minch, is to be constantly in touch with owners every step of the way, examining with them each project's often conflicting issues (special needs, finances, regulations, site limitations; the list goes on). "And then," says Minch, "we fashion a satisfying whole from the various pieces."

One reason the firm has been able to do so, says Richard Ritter, is the company's size. "We've stabilized at a staff of ten to twelve professionals and support personnel for a long time now. There's a dynamic that happens at that scale. The principals can be hands-on, involved in the process from start to finish." The result, he says, is a better product for the client.

Paul Voelckers agrees. "Even with a large project and intense workloads," he notes, "we opt to work longer hours

Juneau Public Library — *This view is toward the circulation area with public seating areas beyond.*

instead of temporarily expanding. There's a certain high quality we want to maintain, a certain degree of personal participation we want to achieve. Our present size allows us to accomplish both of these ends."

Proud of their past, enthusiastic about the present, confident of the future, all three look forward to maintaining this professional commitment for a long time to come.

Architects Alaska

Alaska is beautiful; encompassing at least five distinct climatic and environmental regions. It is also a rigorous place to live and build. Architects Alaska, and its predecessor firms, have been providing professional design services in the state for over 40 years. As the oldest firm in the state, their project experience can be counted in every region, including sites as remote as both the Arctic and the furthest of the Aleutian Islands.

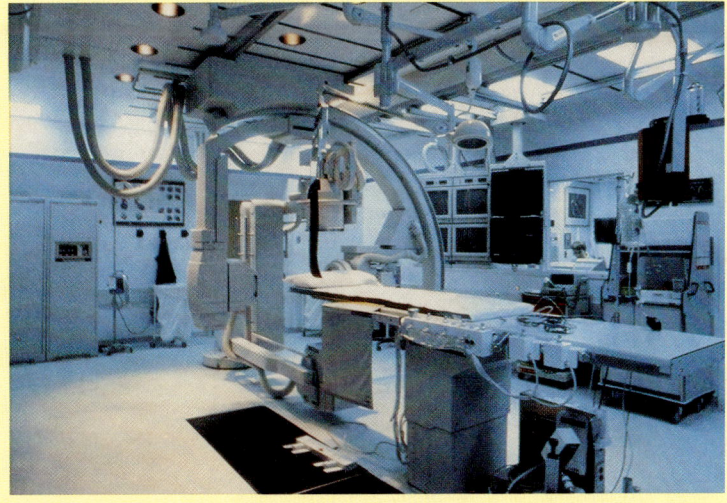

Providence Hospital, Cardiac Catheter Laboratory #2.

Today the firm has three Principals: Stuart F. Smith, AIA; Marvin G. Ungerecht, AIA; and Mark A Kneedler, AIA; who, says Smith, all feel that "Alaska is a very special place in which to practice architecture. Over the past four decades our Principals, from founder Edwin Crittenden to the three of us today, have had the rare opportunity and privilege to have been part of providing some of Alaska's significant infrastructure." They also emphasize that practicing architecture in Alaska requires much more than aesthetic solutions to design problems. Environmental forces impose great stresses on structures and also impose the need for particular consideration of the psychological and physical requirements of occupants. These factors require detail and design solutions found nowhere in the "lower 48," making architecture a very specialized practice in Alaska.

The firm's portfolio reflects established, long-term relationships with clients and a project list which includes civic centers, regional libraries, museums, recreation centers and educational facilities for the University of Alaska and school districts statewide. Private and corporate work is represented by hospitals, hotels, and headquarters buildings for oil companies and banks. Many of these have been recognized by both professional design organizations and the construction industry for excellence in design.

Architectural firms are different from one another. At Architects Alaska, the principals are committed to being "working architects" as well as administrators and managers. Mark Kneedler, who works with their clients in the health care industry, is convinced that this active involvement is what keeps them "tuned to the needs of our clients and to developments in the field. It's important to really listen and understand the people we are working for." Every project in the office is headed and actively managed by one of the principals. This dedication to quality focuses the firm and its personnel on service, continuity, timely performance and cost-effectiveness. Design and production is 100% computer automated which allows them to coordinate document production and quality control with both their local consultants and those located in other parts of the nation.

Alaska is young, as states and building go, and it experiences the swings of growth and development typical of its resource based economy. While many design firms have come and gone over the past several decades, Marvin Ungerecht emphasizes that "Alaska is our home, our clients know that Architects Alaska will be here tomorrow, we place our reputation on it."

University of Alaska Anchorage, Fine Arts Complex.

Quality of Life

Alaska Native Medical Center

A chapter of Alaskan history is about to close, marking the beginning of a new tradition. The new Alaska Native Medical Center, the work of literally hundreds of Alaskans, will be opening its doors in Anchorage in 1996, in partial fulfillment of the nation's sacred commitment to its indigenous peoples.

The state-of-the-art, 150-bed facility, as welcoming and comfortable as it is culturally sensitive and medically well-equipped, was a cooperative effort from the start, bringing together Alaska Native professionals in the spirit of true self-determination, with dedicated participation from government, industry and organized labor. Beginning with extensive design consultations and continuing with an impressive level of Native hire during construction, the U.S. Public Health Service sought the views and talents of those who rely on the center. In fact, the architects traveled to rural Alaska for a cold winter sojourn to elicit design ideas that would meet the functional needs and aesthetic values of patients.

The story of the Alaska Native Medical Center actually begins with a little-known historic anecdote. In the Treaty of Cession by which the United States assumed control of Alaska, Russian and American negotiators stipulated that Alaska Natives would be provided for in the same manner as Indians elsewhere in the country. Eventually, this meant the services provided by the federal Indian Health Service of the U.S. Public Health Service. Although small

This state-of-the-art, 150-bed facility was a cooperative effort from the start, bringing together Alaska Native professionals with government, industry and organized labor.

clinics and traveling practitioners were the rule for decades, by 1948 it was clear that a more substantive facility was needed to respond effectively to an increasing patient load, particularly given the high incidence of tuberculosis.

In November, 1953, the $4.6 million hospital opened its doors at Third and Gambell Street in Anchorage. Although it pales in comparison to the new $167.9 million structure, the hospital in its early days was a source of pride. Observers remarked on the attention paid to the "optimistic" color scheme, the innovative nurse call system and other features provided for the comfort and health of patients. Still, it was a frontier undertaking in a vast wilderness territory characterized by small isolated communities, most of which were not readily accessible. In the hospital itself, for example, medical calls were received by short-wave radio from schoolteachers, missionaries and village residents which were then patched into the telephone system at the hospital. The radios might be located in village schools, airline offices or canneries, and were not always reliable because of weather, disrepair and other complications.

More important than the physical structure, however, was

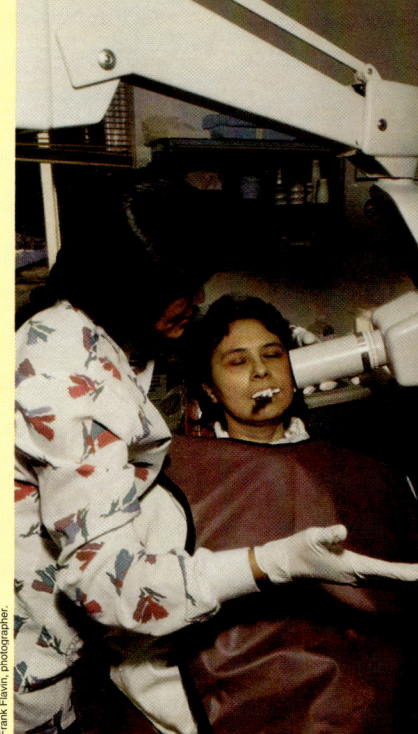

The compassionate human spirit that for so long characterized the old hospital will now reside in the Alaska Native Medical Center at its new location, where staff of the Indian Health Service will continue their commitment to the health and well-being of Alaska's indigenous peoples.

what transpired inside the walls of the venerable old Native hospital. When people are thrust together in crisis, whether overshadowed by tragedy or uplifted by the prospect of a joyous outcome, remarkable things begin to happen. How many beautiful children were brought into the world? How many revered elders and other loved ones passed on? How many family reunions and anxious vigils were held over those old beds? To the old hospital came those struggling against introduced diseases, as well as those injured in a thousand ways living as their forbears did in a beautiful but uncompromising land. Between patients and their doctors, nurses and orderlies, and between the patients themselves, a million bonds of friendship were tied.

The compassionate human spirit that for so long characterized the old hospital now resides in the Alaska Native Medical Center at its new location, where staff of the Indian Health Service continue their commitment to the health and well-being of Alaska's indigenous peoples. At 380,635 square feet, it is the largest project ever undertaken by the PHS and in addition to the 150 acute care beds, houses a 59-bed hostel and a Centers for Disease Control Arctic Investigations laboratory. With a breathtaking view of the Chugach mountains, the building is designed to allow daylight to flood the interior in a way that also reduces the apparent scale of the structure. A series of warm, friendly gathering spaces are located throughout the facility. The main lobby, decorated with traditional Native motifs and art, is designed to function in a manner similar to a community hall where people can meet and socialize with family and friends. Several one-story buildings with sloped roofs are located across the front of the facility to create a village-like group of buildings reminiscent of rural settings. In addition to building design, the facility also boasts new equipment critical to its health care mission, as well as provisions to retain its important functions as a referral hospital for other health care facilities in rural Alaska and as a much-needed training center for Indian Health Service Programs.

The new Alaska Native Medical Center is an impressive structure. But as with its predecessor, the new hospital will sustain the long tradition of competent health care begun at the old site not through beams and trusses alone, but through the beaming smiles of well-served customers and the bond of trust between staff, patients and families.

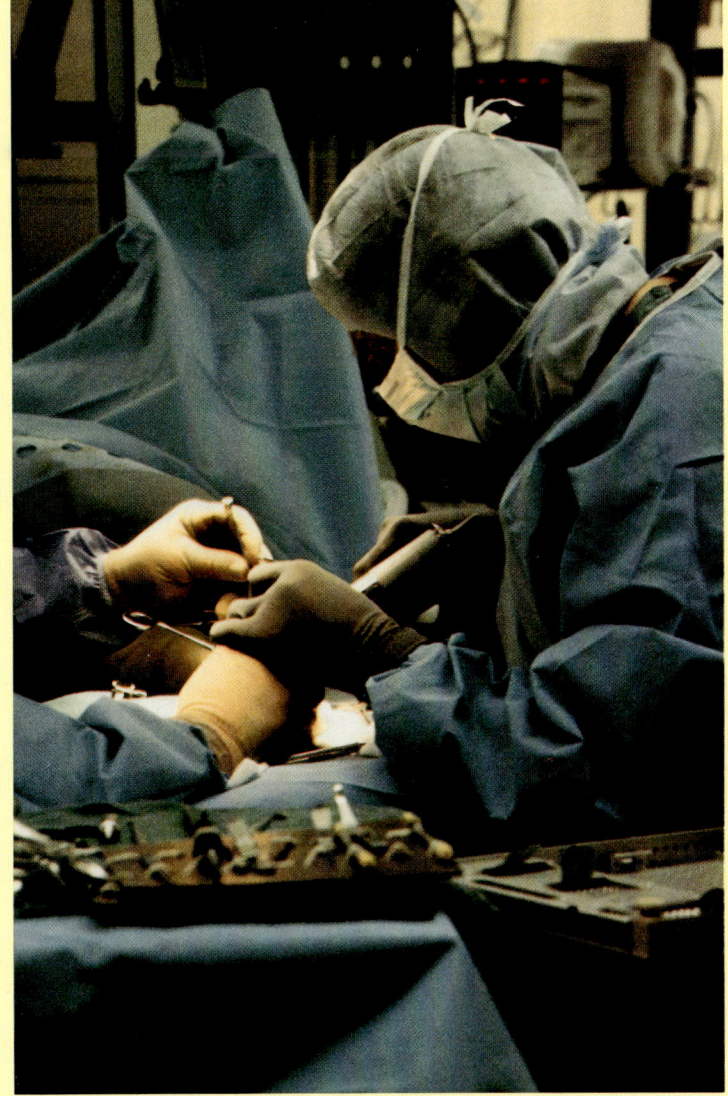

The Alaska Native Medical Center performs approximately five thousand surgical procedures annually.

With a breathtaking view of the Chugach mountains, the building is designed to allow daylight to flood the interior in a way that also reduces the apparent scale of the structure.

University of Alaska

Graduate, Kelly Strauss, proudly displays the diploma she received at the UA's Kenai Peninsula College.

The University of Alaska has come a long way since its humble beginning on September 22, 1922, when six students arrived for the first day of school.

Today, the University of Alaska has grown into a state-wide system of higher education with three multicampus universities, located in Anchorage, Fairbanks, and the Southeast, that meet the challenge of responding to local, regional and state needs of Alaska's diverse population. These main campuses and their extended satellite colleges and sites throughout Alaska, including over one hundred extension and research sites, serve more than 33,000 students.

An act of Congress on March 4, 1915, laid the foundation for the institution. The act set aside lands near Fairbanks for the Alaska Agricultural College and School of Mines. In 1917, the territorial legislature created a board of trustees and accepted the land grants. In 1935, the school was renamed the University of Alaska, and in 1959 when Alaska became the 49th state, it was established as the state university in the Alaska State Constitution.

The University of Alaska Fairbanks (UAF) sits atop scenic College Hill near Fairbanks. It is a comprehensive, four-year, doctoral degree-granting institution with five professional schools and three colleges that offer bachelor's degrees in more than sixty-five major areas, recognized master's degrees in professional disciplines, and doctorates in the sciences and mathematics. The three colleges are liberal arts, natural sciences, and the rural college, which has branch campuses and centers throughout the state. The five professional schools consist of agriculture and land resources management, engineering, fisheries and ocean sciences, management, and mineral engineering. These colleges and schools offer certificate, associate, and baccalaureate degrees as well as a wide range of technical/vocational programs. Master's degrees are offered in over fifty fields, and

The John family — Jolene, Theresa, Agatha and Mark — lead the University of Alaska Fairbanks commencement processional with a traditional Yup'ik entrance song as they drum their way past the class of 1993.

doctoral programs are offered in the areas of anthropology, atmospheric sciences, biology, geology, geophysics, mathematics, oceanography, physics, space physics, and wildlife management.

UAF has branch campuses in Bethel, Kotzebue, and Nome, and rural centers in Unalaska, Dillingham, Fort Yukon, McGrath, Nenana, and Tok. Strong in physical and natural sciences studies, UAF places particular emphasis on northern environments. The 2,250-acre campus includes two lakes and twenty kilometers of ski trails. The library and museum house the state's major information resources and cultural collections.

Research facilities include the Agricultural and Forestry Experiment Station; Alaska Native Language Center; Center for Cross-Cultural Studies; Fishery Industrial Technology Center in Kodiak; Juneau Center for Fisheries and Ocean Sciences; Mineral Industry Research and Petroleum Development laboratories; institutes of Arctic Biology, Marine Science, and Northern Engineering; the world renowned Geophysical Institute, with studies of the aurora borealis and its Poker Flat Rocket Research Range north of Fairbanks; and the Arctic Region Supercomputing Center, with its Cray supercomputer utilized by scientists worldwide via the global information highway known as the Internet.

The University of Alaska Anchorage (UAA) offers baccalaureate and associate degrees, as well as certificate programs, through its colleges of arts and sciences, career and vocational education, and nursing and health sciences, as well as the schools of business, education, engineering, and public affairs. In addition, master's degrees are offered in nine programs from the campus' colleges and schools. It also provides adult and continuing education programs. Medical science is provided through a joint agreement with the University of Washington. Research programs are emphasized, primarily in biological and health sciences, public policy, and social and economic studies. The college of community and continuing education provides both credit and non-credit instruction to the greater Anchorage area and to all military bases in the state.

Beyond Anchorage, UAA serves Alaskans through four colleges: Kenai Peninsula, with campuses in Soldotna and Homer; Matanuska-Susitna, located between Palmer and Wasilla; Kodiak, working closely with the fishing industry and Coast Guard to fill the community's specific needs; and Prince William Sound Community College, serving Valdez, Cordova, and the Copper River Basin. Local financial support earns community college status for this school.

The University of Alaska Southeast (UAS) is a comprehensive regional university with the primary purpose of providing post-secondary education in Southeast Alaska. The University of Alaska Southeast has campuses in Juneau, Ketchikan, and Sitka, and outreach locations throughout its region. It offers certificate programs and associate of applied science degrees in vocational-technical and business-related areas; an associate of arts degree and baccalaureate degrees in the liberal arts, sciences, education, business, and public administration; and master's degrees in selected professional fields. In the statewide system, this institution shares responsibility for programs in public administration, early childhood education, and educational technology.

The Juneau campus of UAS integrates the political activity of the state capital into its programs, offering government, business, and public administration students insight into state government. The needs of private industry, commercial fishing, boat building, welding, diesel repair, office occupations, and other areas are met through various programs.

At both UAF and UAA there are strong athletic programs, and student activity facilities include sports and recreation centers. Student housing is available at each of the three major campuses.

Over the years, the University has steadfastly adhered to its mission: "providing for the public post-secondary educational needs of the citizens of Alaska -- to make higher education of the highest quality accessible to all who have the interest, dedication and ability to learn."

The Elmer Rasmuson Library, located on the University of Alaska Fairbanks campus, is the largest in the state with more than 1.5 million volumes. Collections contained in the library include the world-class Alaska and Polar Regions Collection, covering books, periodicals, archives, manuscripts, historical photographs, oral histories, and maps.

The flashes, identified by University of Alaska Fairbanks Geophysical Institute professors Sentman and Westcott are called "red sprites" and "blue jets." This summer the flashes were captured in color for the first time with special low-light-level cameras designed by project engineer Dan Osborne.

Building Alaska

Seals relax on glacier ice.
R.J. Hayes, photographer.

Veco Corporation

From humble beginnings in Alaskan oilfields, VECO Corporation has risen to global pre-eminence as an EPC contractor with numerous projects to its credit throughout the world. With its diversity of talent, managerial flexibility and financial stability, VECO has the ability to take any industrial or resource project from concept and design stages all the way through construction and operation.

VECO is a well-established and growing firm which has always stood for sensible, environmentally-sound economic development in all of its theaters of operations. As a corporation with a conscience, VECO takes great pride in the dedication and professionalism of its employees who are committed to the communities where they live and work.

VECO Corporation is not only a leader in exporting ingenuity from the last frontier, it is a pioneer. The firm has played a major role in building Alaska's industrial, commercial and transportation infrastructure. From oil drilling, production and refining facilities to mining projects, roads, bridges and hotels, the firm has parlayed its vast experience into a firm known worldwide for its expertise in extreme environments and its esprit de corps in rising to stiff challenges. VECO is perennially one of Alaska's top employers and revenue generators.

VECO performs maintenance on a large variety of oil and gas production facilities, refineries, process plants and pipeline facilities.

Major infrastructure projects are typified by VECO's experience in developing roads and pads in the Arctic, to building highways, bridges and power generation facilities.

While the majority of VECO's business is in engineering and construction associated with the development of Alaska's resources, the firm also generates substantial revenues in general construction. From the windswept tundra of Alaska to the howling North Sea and the glaring deserts of the Middle East, VECO has dispatched its teams to take on not only complex development projects, but urgent, complex environmental crises as well. In such arenas, success is measured in equal parts of high-tech know-how, an ability to think on your feet, and raw corporate nerve. In a nutshell, these are the key ingredients of the company's success, its resilience and its excellent prospects for the future.

Change is the rule rather than the exception in the development of Alaska's oil industry—sometimes driven by economics, sometimes technological or political developments. With a strong commitment to excellence in all its endeavors, VECO has survived numerous shifts in the fortunes of the oil industry in Alaska and abroad. In fact it prospers today through the closely coordinated effort of five independent divisions providing a wide range of services. Here is just a glimpse of the family album:

The International Division, headquartered in Houston, Texas, includes a wide array of worldwide companies specializing in program management and execution in support of infrastructure and resource development throughout the world, including Pakistan, India, the Caspian Sea, the Middle East and the Russian Federation, as well as prospects in other regions. Services include program management, engineering, construction, oil and gas drilling and production, and operations and maintenance;

The Engineering Division is headquartered in Bellingham, Washington and offers multi-disciplined engineering and design. It is noted for designing new and modified resource processing plants and refineries as well as power plants. The division provides program management services to the domestic and international energy industry, ranging from procurement, planning and logistics to design construction and risk management;

The Construction Division is headquartered in Anchorage, Alaska and is made up of three companies which provide services ranging from major civil construction to module fabrication and installation to power generation facilities. These companies have provided project and construction management for billion dollar developments for major industry. Their broad experience in construction covers the oil and gas industry, heavy industrial construction, power generation and major civil construction.

The Drilling and Production Division is headquartered in Denver, Colorado and owns and operates rigs and producing properties in the western U.S. and enjoys an excellent reputation for its experience in complex drilling projects and the ability to field diverse state-of-the-art equipment. VECO Drilling specializes in oil and gas production, but has also completed numerous geothermal projects;

The Operations Division is headquartered in Anchorage and offers operation and maintenance management and execution in support of industry, ranging from long-term operations and maintenance projects to casual labor and equipment, from general maintenance to specialized electrical, mechanical, instrumentation and civil work and managing client inventories of support supplies and equipment. This division, like all other members of the VECO family, provides equally good service on small tasks and large ones, such as the Alaskan oil spill in 1989, which required immediate mobilization of 12,000 people and 6,000 pieces of equipment.

Another division manages a unique publishing venture committed to preserving the voice of reasonable development in Alaska. Taking many by surprise, VECO bought the ailing *Anchorage Times* as much to provide a community benefit

VECO provided design, construction, installation and commissioning for the quarters on this offshore platform in Cook Inlet. Besides engineering and construction, they provide operations and maintenance and drilling and workover operations worldwide.

This 100,000 barrels per day Lisburne Production Facility on Alaska's North Slope illustrates VECO's experience in construction planning and controls, operation support, logistics and procurement.

as to initiate a business venture. The move was made in the hopes of maintaining a healthy, competitive journalistic atmosphere in Alaska. VECO and the newspaper earned considerable praise for objectivity, service orientation and close attention to stories of local concern. In a unique precedent-setting arrangement, the venture was eventually purchased by the rival Anchorage newspaper, which agreed to continue publishing Voice of the Times, a half page of commentary and analysis prepared by three professional journalists underwritten by VECO as a public service.

VECO has actually earned its reputation for industrial savvy several times over. An impressive list of projects in progress throughout the world only begins to tell the story. Previous credits, including all the nuts and bolts of planning and building development facilities for the Endicott, Lisburne and Milne Point oil fields near Prudhoe Bay, and the firm's extensive work on the Red Dog Mine near Kotzebue, add more to the picture of VECO's record of leadership on complex industrial projects, projects which have contributed significantly to building Alaska's economy.

Perhaps no call to action has tested the mettle of VECO more than recent environmental crises. The company is proud that its unprecedented mobilization kept the 1989 Alaskan oil spill from being even worse than it was. Within hours of the initial tanker spill, VECO personnel were on-scene, taking charge of spill cleanup, shoreline remediation, construction and operations support, logistics and procurement, engineering and design. It was a $2 billion, six-month fast track effort involving 17 million work hours, with peak manpower of 16,000, more than 100 subcontractors and 2,000 vessels. In all, 1,000 miles of beaches in a 2,000-square mile remote area were successfully cleaned. VECO has responded to spill disasters from Huntington Beach, California to the Persian Gulf. In the aftermath of the Gulf War, VECO responded and provided planning and clean-up for the Saudi Arabian beaches that were impacted by that war.

Beyond its reputation at work, VECO has for years been a good neighbor to Alaskans. VECO has contributed extensively to charity, from United Way to public broadcasting. This quality of dedication to the communities where VECO operates has not only marked the company's successes, but also helped define its future.

Where *does* a company as large and successful as VECO go in the twenty-first century? With a characteristic sense of mission, VECO has identified a number of areas throughout the world where developing countries are struggling with the new challenges and opportunities of nurturing free market economies and safely extracting and processing their natural resources to do so. Though these prospects require time and patience, VECO's strategic planners foresee working on projects in nations of the former Soviet Union and nations of the Pacific Rim, including the free enterprise frontiers of China and Vietnam. Projects will likely include ventures in the energy, mining, and timber industries, as well as transportation and other civil infrastructure. In addition, VECO's commitment to Alaska remains strong. Noting that increased resource extraction is vital to the state's economy, VECO officials cite the firm's expertise in developing marginal oil fields as just one area where VECO can continue to contribute significantly to Alaska's well-being and

A single VECO Project Team conducted multiple projects of construction, engineering, logistics and procurement, and commissioning and start-up for the world's largest and most remote zinc and lead mine . . . Red Dog Mine and the Delong Port development.

As part of a multiple Project Management Alliance with ARCO, VECO installed and commissioned 20 units such as this 5,127 ton gas compression module for the Prudhoe Bay Field Gas Handling Expansion Phase 2 Program.

its world leadership position as a responsible developer of diverse natural resources.

In addition, to develop growth potential on the basis of geography, all of VECO's divisions continue to improve and expand upon their capabilities and performance according to priorities identified in ongoing strategic planning efforts. For example, VECO Engineering has set specific targets for enhancing its technical base in response to customer needs and new trends emerging in the market. Engineering is one of the most active and exciting areas for future company growth, not only because so many areas are in need of this kind of fundamental expertise, but because aggressively cultivating engineering projects often leads to additional work for other VECO divisions. VECO Construction is taking steps to more aggressively pursue mining and power projects and wastewater treatment facilities, both in Alaska and overseas. Economic realities and recent developments in the marketplace suggest new opportunities for VECO Operations to provide more extensive services in programming, preventive maintenance and control systems for major industrial facilities.

All the internal planning and the external performance harken back to VECO's commitment to being simply the best Engineering, Procurement and Construction contractor in the business. While all divisions must in essence be able to stand on their own, they must be equally

The VECO Alliance concept is a client/contractor partnership that results in cost efficiencies and flexibility in personnel utilization. As with Alyeska Pipeline Service Company, they provide increased response options for both short term and long term needs.

prepared to function as a tight-knit team — ready, able and willing to perform to exacting standards anywhere in the world, sometimes on very short notice. Helping to hold the VECO family together is a mission statement which sets forth the values by which the company operates wherever it is needed. It is a mission statement that unequivocally puts VECO clients first. The mission statements says in part:

Recognizing that each client is unique and has different needs, we shall:
• Provide our services to the highest standards of safety;
• Provide high quality and environmentally correct services;
• Align ourselves with our clients' goals;
• Identify their specific requirements and accomplish them;
• Supply correct professional services that meet all codes, standards and regulatory requirements;

Program Management for this Gas Utilization Project in the Caspian Sea included design, fabrication, transportation, installation, hook-up and commissioning for the 150 MMSCFD offshore pipeline system.

• Fairly estimate the services required and meet or beat the budget that we set;
• Accurately forecast the time required to complete the work and meet all milestones; and
• Be a positive influence by being proactive on those issues which may impact our industry and community.

That same mission statement has also placed a high premium on company employees and on continuing to be the best possible corporate neighbor, a progressive attitude that has always been VECO's hallmark. Building on this kind of commitment, as well as its excellent record of competent, timely performance, the VECO family is not only getting bigger, it is getting better.

Linder Construction

Linder Construction has make a name for itself by performing superbly where many of its competitors are reluctant to tread.

Linder Construction, Inc. is the creation of a very special couple — Al and Linda Henrikson. With Linda's dynamism and passion for business and customer relations and Al's genius for managing construction in Alaska's often remote locations and harsh climates, the firm has always done well in general construction. However, sensitive to changes in the industry, they made a strategic move in a new direction — environmental construction projects.

Linder breaks ground for the Veterans Domiciliary project in Anchorage.

It was a classic case of building on your strengths to leverage entry into a new growth market. With numerous government projects in its portfolio, Linder was very familiar with federal contracting complexities, procedures and agencies. In fact, a bulging file of reference letters attests to Linder's constant attention to detail, both in business and operational construction performance.

"Ms. Henrikson exhibits a high degree of professionalism and the ability to work with owners, contracting officers, engineers and inspectors," wrote Susan Roggenkamp of the Small Business Administration. "This begins with the exemplary way the firm's proposal packages are assembled and continues through project completion of all objectives on time or ahead of schedule and within budget. As a result, the firm receives superior ratings on performance."

The secret of winning competitive bids and still delivering quality that exceeds customers' expectations lies with Al's shrewd construction acumen. The centerpiece of his strategy has been the building of a fine team of extensively trained environmental construction professionals equipped with the best construction equipment available. Linder's decision to own equipment and retain their employees job after job has translated into the ability to react to changing customer needs and created a pervasive sense of "Linder Pride" throughout the company.

The result is satisfied

Linda and Al Henrikson with Senator Stevens in his Washington D.C. office.

clients time after time. Lieutenant Colonel Michael A. Cravens, Director of Contracting, Elmendorf AFB, U.S. Air Force, noted. "Linder's timeliness and effectiveness are outstanding."

"Once we moved into environmental construction, we did it right," says Linda. "We invested thousands of dollars into training our team and acquiring the necessary certifications. This is critical to protect our work force and an absolute must for regulatory compliance." Fundamental to the company's success, however, is their basic construction doctrine of completing a quality job ahead of schedule for a fair price.

The Henrikson's proven approach to positive negotiation and project management and a well-deserved reputation for commitment to quality, gives Linder a distinct advantage in the often challenging environmental construction market. Now, environmental construction comprises fully seventy-five percent of Linder's work.

Since making this move, Linder has attained an enviable market share in a remarkably short time. Projects have included a wide range of

Linder crew removing a 10,000 gallon underground storage.

technical requirements and geographical sites throughout Alaska. Examples include:

• **Underground Storage Tank Removal, U.S. Navy, Adak**
This project called for the removal of abandoned fuel lines, tanks, and contaminated soil on a remote Aleutian island. Linder completed the two-year contract in less than one season, winning additional work and a follow-on contract.

• **U.S. Army Corps of Engineers Remedial Action Contract**
This innovative contracting method allows the Corps to issue delivery orders for immediate action by Linder for the fundamental work of the actual site cleanup. These design-build contracts bypass the exhaustive scientific studies which were the norm of the past. Three delivery orders have been issued to date, saving the customer hundreds of thousands of dollars.

• **Veteran Center Addition, Alteration, and Upgrade, Anchorage**
Work includes abating lead and asbestos, correcting safety deficiencies, renovating the existing building into a domiciliary for homeless and disabled veterans, and constructing a work therapy addition. Linder performed much of the work at cost and even donated resources to ensure success of the vital project for Anchorage's veterans.

Citations from relieved and satisfied clients continue to pour in. Military contract specialist Genevieve E. Boguslawski monitored a Linder project involving soil remediation and underground storage tank removal. "We have found (Linder's) prices to be more reasonable than other . . . firms for identical projects. (Their) original prices are within reason; therefore, extensive negotiations to reach fair and reasonable prices are not required," she says. "Mrs. Henrikson is amiable when negotiating, which results in win-win, rather than win-lose negotiations." According to Karen Weidenbaugh, a contracting officer for the Alaska Air National Guard who has overseen several of the company's environmental projects in Anchorage, "Linder Construction excels in this type of work."

Linder long ago committed itself to total quality management on every project. Now, working in the environmental arena gives the whole Linder team an even stronger sense of mission. Dedication to clients is further strengthened by the positive impact of their work experience to restore contaminated areas and reducing environmental hazards. More than ever before, Linder goes the extra mile!

"Linder Pride" shown brightly in Washington D.C. recently when the company was presented with U.S. Coast Guard's 1994 Outstanding Contractor Award for *Women Business Enterprise*. "Our challenge now," says Linda "is to reach new heights in customer satisfaction!"

"We do nasty stuff!" John Klempke of Linder Construction cleaning out a waste oil crib.

NC Machinery

After 218 years in Alaska, NC Machinery is going home—to Russia. Although entry into the newly opened far east market is a long term prospect and the firm will continue to generate the bulk of its revenues in the U.S., NC Machinery does indeed trace a long and honorable history to beginnings in Mother Russia. Today's successful purveyor of heavy equipment to industry began in 1776 as a fur-trading business founded by two wealthy merchants, Gregor Shelikof and Ivan Golikof. The company has also figured prominently in the Gold Rush era and throughout Alaska's colorful history, by supplying miners with goods and transport. It eventually became the Northern Commercial, Co., known to locals as simply "NC." When NC was named Caterpillar dealer for Alaska and the Yukon in 1926, the company's modern era began.

Now owned by Tractor and Equipment Co. of Montana, NC Machinery is one of the largest Caterpillar dealers in the U.S., with over twenty branch operations throughout Alaska, Washington and Montana. William L. Hopper, Vice President of NC's Alaska division, is proud of his firm's deep roots in Alaska. With a high degree of autonomy, key management and marketing decisions are made in Hopper's Anchorage office, a significant factor in being able to respond to the changing needs of the Alaskan market.

"We have 200 resident employees, paying their taxes

NC Machinery has made an important long-range investment in the markets of the Russian Far East, where industries in a fledgling free-market system look increasingly to Alaska for inventory and expertise to modernize their economy.

NC's Vice President Bill Hopper & Fairbanks Branch Manager Dave Graham donated a Caterpillar engine to the students of the Diesel/Heavy Equipment Program at the University of Alaska Fairbanks Tanana Valley Campus. Accepting on behalf of the University were two program coordinators & Ruth Lister, Director of Tanana Valley Campus.

here and serving their neighbors with the highest degree of personal commitment and professional dedication," says Hopper. "Their efforts make it possible for our customers to add value to their operations. For us to be successful, our customers must also be successful. We're always striving to that end."

No less important to NC's customers than its extensive inventory of equipment are the highly-trained service force and a top-notch, computer-driven parts department. Service is a key ingredient of the association with Caterpillar, involving a joint commitment to excellence and a continuous process of factory training and certification. With their state-of-the art network, NC's parts technicians are capable of swiftly dispatching everything from nuts and bolts, to tires and drive shafts to the remote mining and construction job locations that are so common in the state of Alaska.

Hopper expects Russian sales to grow, but he's also optimistic about Alaska, where mineral exploration opportunities are improving and the potential is fabulous.

Throughout Alaska, the Pacific Northwest, and more recently the Russian Far East, equipment sold and serviced by NC Machinery is in the forefront of Alaska's resource and economic development, providing the mechanical muscle for mining, oil and gas, timber and infrastructure projects.

NC Machinery's long association with Caterpillar gives customers a wide range of high quality products designed for rugged and long-lasting use in heavy applications.

Big Three Lincoln Alaska, Inc.

There are those companies that keep a low profile but perform the yeoman work vital to any vigorous economy. Big Three Lincoln Alaska, Inc., a leading provider of industrial gas and welding equipment, is one of these. Although their efforts are usually not noted in the headlines of the day, the cheerful, highly-trained employees of Big Three service a universe of complex, specialized and sometimes hazardous industrial activities with a high level of competence and experience.

"It would be hard to point out a machine, a building, a bridge or other structure that involves welding or fabrication, or any oilfield or manufacturing project in Alaska that is not employing our tools, supplies or services," says Thomas Labno, Sr., company president. "We're especially proud of the role we've played in the development of a mature, world-class oil industry in Alaska's arctic and sub-arctic areas."

Although a diverse range of high-quality products is important to Big Three's customers both large and small, key to the company's enviable reputation is a long-standing commitment to

Big Three's central warehouse and corporate offices are located at the foot of the Chugach Mountains in Anchorage.

service. "It's really the service that sets us apart," declares Labno. "Our staff cheerfully hand out their phone numbers to customers and often come down to open the store after hours to walk people through unexpected situations."

He notes that the company's growth as well as direct feedback from customers make it clear that service orientation is key to Big Three's success. "A growing number of customers have come to rely on us to put them first. They know we'll do whatever is needed to get the job done, to back our products, to make their work easier and more profitable."

Labno foresees that service will be a cornerstone of future growth. In addition, diversification of products and services will result in greater selection and convenience for long-time customers and increased market share in new market segments.

As a wholly owned subsidiary of the renowned Lincoln Electric Company, Big Three provides a comprehensive product line for its customers. Product lines include all mixed and specialty gases; all medical, industrial and liquefied gases; welding systems and filler metals for gas, stick, mig, tig, innershield and sub arc welding processes; abrasives for all metal removal applications; and Harris and Victor gas cutting and welding equipment. Complementing these products are a wide range of customer services including in-house and field demonstrations of welding equipment and processes and equipment rental, repair and maintenance, to name a few. A fleet of custom transportation rigs insures prompt and safe delivery of gas products.

"Our association with Lincoln is one of our most important strategic advantages," states Labno. "We have this worldwide asset at our disposal, 24 hours every day at a moment's notice. It is no exaggeration to say that Lincoln is the dominant name in the U.S. arc welding industry. We work closely with them, not just to back up the products we sell, but to devise custom products or adaptations to customer needs."

Relying on the resources of the Lincoln Electric Company, Big Three places a high priority on training its staff in the uses and applications of new products and technologies. In a move to more aggressively respond to customer needs, Big Three has set its sights on an ambitious new venture: construction of a $2 million Oxygen-Nitrogen Production Plant on the Kenai Peninsula, the heart of Southcentral Alaska's petroleum refining industry.

"This is very exciting for us, a great example of a win-win situation for Alaska's economy. The market for these products is strong, since they are vital to the

Medical and industrial customers are reliant upon Big Three's bulk cryogenic delivery systems.

Big Three operates an extensive industrial/medical gas cylinder filling and maintenance plant in Palmer, Alaska.

Flange rebuild for Alaska oil and gas industry utilizing a fully automatic Lincoln Electric submerged arc welder.

refining process. Producing oxygen and nitrogen at the doorstep of the customer improves their margins and is profitable for us, too," says Labno.

Traditionally, oxygen and nitrogen have been shipped from the Lower 48 and trucked to the Peninsula. With the new plant on-line, Big Three offers price stability and reliability of supply in one strategic move.

"If the refineries lose product stream, or if the flow of nitrogen is inhibited in any way, it can be very costly for them," explains Labno. "Nitrogen is used for pressure testing, purging and inerting pipes and pipelines and vessels prior to maintenance. Oxygen is used for functions related to cutting.

"With this new state-of-the-art production plant, we remove the vagaries of transportation and provide consistent and sufficient supply. In essence, we've created a utility-type environment with the reliability that the customer can take to the bank."

While the new plant is a great way to herald the beginning of a new century of service to Alaska, it is by no means the only strategic move planned by the company. "It's critical that we serve the markets in Southeast Alaska and the Aleutian Islands," remarks Labno. "We feel the fishing, mining and construction industries in those areas offer potential for very healthy growth."

Wherever they go, Big Three will continue to offer a comprehensive array of goods and services, the leading "cutting edge" innovations needed by Alaskan industry. "We view ourselves as a total solution company because we understand how the gases and equipment affect the welding process, and how best to apply these sophisticated processes in diverse industrial environments," states Labno. "Anybody can sell the hard goods. We want to get our customers to the best end result. If that means meeting them more than half way, we're happy to do it."

Waukesha Alaska

"We have designed and installed generators sets to power oil fields and villages in the harshest Arctic environments," says John E. Haxby, vice president.

Knowing Alaska is the largest state in the Union scarcely prepares a person for the magnitude of tundra, forest and mountain. In many ways still a frontier region, with youthful ambitions matched by great prospects, many parts of Alaska lack the customary civil, transportation and commercial infrastructure. Yet Alaskans have found a multitude of ways to trade, to work, to market resources, to thrive in even the most rigorous and remote corners of the land. Waukesha Alaska Corp., distributors of generators, pumps and compressors since 1972, has made this possible in very key ways.

"We have designed and installed generators sets to power oil fields and villages in the harshest Arctic environments," says John E. Haxby, vice president. "We have built and maintained the electrical systems for many Alaskan cities and villages, and solved some of the most complex pump, air compressor, gas compression and process challenges confronting industry."

The firm has not limited its activities to Alaska, either. Waukesha engineers have been routinely traveling to Russia, China, Eastern Europe and South America to provide their expertise to those emerging economies.

With their decades of Alaskan experience and many years of accumulated technical know-how, Waukesha has assembled an inventory of equipment to sell and service that is unequaled in the state. With performance and durability as the chief criteria, they have assembled some of the most respected names in the world, including Waukesha's own gas and diesel engines, Hatz air-cooled diesel engines, Atlas Copco compressors, and Kato, Marathon and Generac generators. There are many more, but in Alaska, customers have come to realize they need to know only one name—Waukesha—to access a huge network of power generation solutions. In fact, new clientele are sometimes pleasantly surprised when they learn the company isn't just a sell-it-off-the-shelf kind of an outfit.

"Sometimes manufacturers just don't make what you need," says Haxby. "In those cases, we customize equipment to suit needs. We even design and build from the ground up."

Waukesha also offers equipment rental and lease options.

"The key point is, we're in business to provide the most cost-effective way to get our customers up and running. We'll do whatever it takes to create and service a system, so all the customer has to do it turn it on and let it run."

Through the years, Waukesha Alaska has garnered a long list of satisfied clients, many of them repeat customers. The projects tackled by the firm are as varied as they are diverse in technical complexity and global reach.

"We handle really large-scale jobs, such as designing and building all kinds of equipment for mines, oil fields and large municipal operations, and we've had to work in extremes of weather ranging from minus 70 degrees at Prudhoe Bay to the wilting heat and humidity of the Philippines," Haxby says, noting that the firm is equally expert in designing, building and servicing small projects.

With performance and durability as the chief criteria, Waukesha has assembled some of the most respected names in the world, including Waukesha's own gas and diesel engines, Hatz air-cooled diesel engines, Atlas Copco compressors, and Kato, Marathon and Generac generators.

With their decades of Alaskan experience and many years of accumulated technical know-how, Waukesha has assembled an inventory of equipment to sell and service that is unequaled in the state.

"Sometimes the little jobs are the hardest. Everything has to be scaled down, except the quality and reliability, of course.

In fact, quality is the foundation of Waukesha's commitment to industry. According to Haxby, the firm is guided every day and at every level of policy and operation by a mission statement that focuses specifically on quality:

• We strive to create long term relationships with our customers, and to meet their needs and exceed their expectations at all times;
• We will continuously improve our products and services to industry through innovation, design and engineering;
• We will strive for technical excellence by innovation and research;
• We are dedicated to the quality of our personnel through training and teamwork.

This philosophy—and the talents of its 18-member team of professionals—has been a winning formula.

"We at Waukesha have maintained a consistent growth pattern by improving our product mix and service areas to meet the ever changing Alaska and worldwide market requirements," says Haxby. "Sales volume has continued to grow in recent years. The expansion of the company has surpassed local industry standards simply because of our mission and commitment to the industry. This has been the impetus for our overseas growth, with excellent results. For example, our Eastern European business is projected to grow 20-30 percent over the next several years."

A strong sense of commitment and competence was clearly evident during one notable project overseas: design and manufacture of several specialty power generation packages utilized during the Gulf War in Iraq.

Waukesha has built and maintained the electrical systems for many Alaskan cities and villages, and solved some of the most complex pump, air compressor, gas compression and process challenges confronting industry.

"These were specialty packages designed to operate for months without maintenance in a desert warfare situation," says Haxby. "The system provided power to an unmanned drone which flew in enemy airspace. Using infrared and other top secret technology, the drones would map out enemy locations and encampments and send this information via satellite to the fire control batteries of ships and artillery for automatic targeting. The system worked flawlessly, and for us it was a strong affirmation that we really can go anywhere, anytime and meet the challenge."

Of course, not all projects are so exotic, but Haxby predicts that exporting Waukesha's merchandise and know-how will be key to the company's future.

"Future growth in Alaska will come from the maintenance and support side of the business. Alaska is a maturing market, and production in the oilfields is declining. As oil production declines, maintenance and support of the existing machinery will increase," Haxby says. "Future growth for engineered products and projects will come from overseas markets. We have three people in Eastern Europe who are pursuing projects there. We have an additional three people in Russia and one in China. We also have a team working in Venezuela. We're finding that it's both exciting and profitable to export our Alaskan experience to new frontier areas, and we're looking forward to new challenges."

Udelhoven Oilfield System Services Incorporated

The Arctic is an uncompromising place for any human enterprise, leaving little room for error. Udelhoven Oilfield Services Incorporated, specializing in electrical and mechanical engineering, construction, maintenance and technical systems for oil field structures, has successfully overcome both the natural elements and the adversity of stiff business competition through the consistent application of a set of core values. These values, spelled out in the company's mission statement, embody the personality and philosophy of founder and CEO, James Udelhoven. The seven principles are:

1. To build a company that provides a service or builds a project to the complete satisfaction of our customer.
2. We shall strive to be number one in reputation with our customers and our employees.
3. We must provide quality performance.
4. We must perform safely.
5. We must make a profit.
6. We shall share our success and profits with our employees.
7. Work can be taken from us in many ways, but our reputation is ours to lose. Our reputation is the key that will open doors to new business in the future.

Udelhoven Oilfield System Services' Anchorage office.

The multiple references to a close relationship with employees are no accident. They now own more than 20 percent of the company, thanks to Udelhoven's progressive views on cultivating loyal and highly-motivated workers.

When Jim Udelhoven founded the firm in 1970, he was the only employee, a man with vision of providing dependable service to what was then a relatively new oil industry. Now, with offices in Anchorage, Prudhoe Bay, Soldotna and Bellingham, scores of employees, $22 million in sales annually and a superb reputation, much of that vision has been fulfilled.

"I feel quite proud of what we've accomplished. And quite proud of my people. They've made this company," says Udelhoven. He reflects for a moment on the arduous transitions brought on by Alaska's mid-1980s recession when the oil patch sharply contracted. "It was truly the people that made the difference."

Difficult as those days were, they also provided some vindication for Udelhoven's meticulous approach to business. When recession-driven bank failures effectively tied up the company's assets, jeopardizing payroll and other obligations, it was Udelhoven's history of reliable, competent service that prompted oil industry clients to accelerate payments, allowing Udelhoven to continue focusing on projects. Customers also benefit from another Udelhoven tenet: don't let the lure of rapid company growth compromise the job at hand.

"I started out with no money, essentially," Udelhoven recalls. "Since then, we have tried to maintain controlled growth. It just seemed more comfortable. What it does is give us more time, more attention for the current client. We sell the next job by our performance on the last one. If there's a problem, we'll make it right."

One of the biggest and most recent projects on which Udelhoven has done right by its customers is the GHX-2 gas injection facility for a consortium of North Slope oil producers. To the company fell the job of monitoring the construction and installation of the huge, multi-module structure, and conducting its functional check out. "In short, we became the start-up team, charged with overseeing a lot of details and troubleshooting any problems that might arise."

Udelhoven's superlative performance earned a heartfelt citation from Arco, one of the primary customers for the project. Robert Schacht, Arco's North Slope construction manager, notes that Udelhoven's role as a bridge between the builders and the operators of the facility was vital for timely start-up, requiring extensive and current technical expertise in industrial electrical systems and their computerized nerve centers, and equal parts of attention to detail and a vision of the overall project. "It was a very critical piece of work performed with complete competence. Jim Udelhoven consistently treats his people very well. With that kind of reputation, he attracts the kind of talent vital to the success of a project like this," he says.

Changes in the fortunes of the oil patch have brought the need to diversify. Udelhoven has accomplished this with a two-pronged strategy; successfully seeking new markets within and outside Alaska, and doing so with a broadening array of services. In 1980, Udelhoven added general contracting to its list of mechanical and electrical subcontracting qualifications. The Bellingham, Washington office opened in 1991 to take advantage of new refinery opportunities. More recently, the firm has been cultivating overseas prospects.

"The things we're capable of doing are vast," says Udelhoven. Add to that the underlying persistence and integrity that have become synonymous with the company's name and you have a sure-fire formula for the future. "We don't lose sight of our goals. We don't lose sight of where we came from and what we stand for."

GHX-2 Sealift Project, Louisiana to Prudhoe, 1993-94.

Superior Plumbing and Heating, Incorporated

It's one thing for a building to look great, to sparkle and shine on the outside. But if it does not *function* well *inside*, the brightest exterior can take on a rather shabby aspect. It takes a highly trained and experienced crew to design, build and install the complex heating, cooling, ventilation and water/sewer systems that enable northern buildings to function properly.

That is where Superior Plumbing and Heating Incorporated comes in. The company fields an all-pro team with extensive credentials. The team is headed by Jan Van Den Top, an engineer who found his way to Alaska from the Netherlands via Kenya. Founded in 1964 by Marion Fox and Bob Pope, this unassuming, no-nonsense company has simply put its head down and pursued the yeoman work of building the young state from the inside out with unparalleled competence and cost-effectiveness.

Though its competitors have come and gone, Superior has adapted to Alaska's changing market and continued to provide dependable service to industrial, commercial and residential clients. For their efforts, the company has consistently ranked among Alaska's top five construction subcontractors.

"What's important to us is that the design fits the project, that it works, and that it lasts," says Jan. "If your work doesn't last, you won't be around long, either."

Superior applies that philosophy equally to work performed in the state's urban areas and projects located in rural communities, where logistics and other factors vary widely from region to region and add significantly to the challenges of performing on schedule and on budget. But so consistent is Superior's performance that once they complete a project in one town, they are often invited to undertake several others. The top-rated fishing port of Unalaska provides a good example. In a small industrial town with growing pains and burgeoning opportunities, the infrastructure was lagging behind the needs of a growing population. Over a period of several years, Superior played a key role in designing and building high-quality systems for a hotel, post office, retail store, fish processing plant and office building.

The Bartlett Pool. It feels as good inside as it looks from outside.

Alyeska Prince Hotel. The outside is for looks, the inside is for comfort.

"In Alaska, you have to be flexible," Van Den Top says. "We pride ourselves on being able to ascertain the needs of a project and working closely with the whole design and construction team to insure that all aspects of the project function according to specifications. Flexibility also means going the extra mile for the customer when unforeseen problems arise. It is a team effort. All employees of the corporation pull together to make things happen." This is the kind of dedication that makes Superior Plumbing and Heating one of Alaska's premier mechanical contractors.

Marketplace, Tours, Journeys and Accommodations

Cattle grazing in Kodiak.
Ernst Schneider, photographer; Alaska Division of Tourism.

Princess Cruises and Tours

AN EXCITING QUARTER-CENTURY OF EXPLORING ALASKA

In the 18 years since its founding in 1972, Princess Tours® has taken a leadership role in the development and promotion of Alaska tourism — and, in doing so, has become a vital part of the 49th state's economy and way of life. And the future looks even brighter, as the company continues to formulate plans for growth and improvement.

These plans include construction of three new ships for Princess Cruises® — the 77,000-ton, 1,950 passenger supership Sun Princess, scheduled to debut in early 1996, along with its as-yet-unnamed sister vessel, to be launched in the Spring of 1997. The third ship, because of its 100,000-ton size and 2,500-passenger capacity, will be unable to pass through the Panama Canal, and will therefore be restricted to the Caribbean. These new ships, which represent an investment of approximately $1 billion, will increase the overall capacity of Princess Cruises by some 70 percent, making Princess® the second-largest cruise line in the world.

"These new ship orders not only demonstrate our commitment to growth, but also to those destinations we believe are particular areas of ongoing expansion, namely the Caribbean and Alaska," says Peter Ratcliffe, President of Princess Cruises. But the future of Princess in Alaska isn't entirely at sea. Negotiations have recently been concluded between Princess Tours and the Chugach Alaska Native Corporation for the construction of a 100-room hotel adjacent to Child's Glacier on the Copper River near Cordova, in Southcentral Alaska. This property will join three other Princess Cruises® Hotels in this state. In addition to the amenities offered by all of these facilities is the favorable economic impact they will continue to have on their respective communities.

According to Chugach Alaska Corporation Michael E. Brown, "The potential for business and employment opportunities for Chugach Alaska shareholders and other local residents in the Cordova area" was an important consideration in striking the agreement.

This continuing commitment to Alaska is, and almost always has been, a big part of

The 1,590-passenger Regal Princess in Glacier Bay.

The Midnight Sun Express crosses Hurricane Gulch on the journey to Denali National Park.

the Princess picture. In fact, programs first designed for the Alaska market have also been successfully applied in other Princess destinations, such as Mexico, the Caribbean, Europe and the South Pacific. But the success of this innovative packaged-tour company has been largely based on the earlier achievements of one of the world's largest cruiselines — Princess Cruises, which started out more than 25 years ago as a one-ship, Seattle-based company founded by Stan McDonald in 1965.

While the popular TV series The Love Boat deserves some credit for helping Princess become a household word in the mid-70s, the company's real turning point came in 1974, when it was acquired by Peninsular & Oriental Steam Navigation Company, Inc. (P&O), the world's oldest and largest shipping company, based in London. New ships were purchased, and in 1979, Princess Tours in turn acquired Johansen Royal Tours, which had pioneered escorted motorcoach tours in the Canadian Rockies. During the 1980s, the company expanded

This waiter at Denali is one of over 850 Princess employees in Alaska.

In 1993, 136,000 Princess passengers enjoyed such spectacular Alaska sights as College Fjord.

in several exciting new directions: new ships were commissioned (including the Royal Princess, one of the industry's first "superships"); Tour Alaska and Royal Hyway Tours were purchased, allowing new tour packages to be designed for the Alaska market — packages which included a variety of shore excursions and other visitor amenities, such as Midnight Sun Express® rail services, featuring private full-dome luxury cars traveling on The Alaska Railroad between Anchorage, Denali National Park, and Fairbanks. In 1988, Princess introduced the ULTRA DOME® rail cars, the largest coaches ever built for rail. These comfortable double-deck coaches offer not only an unparalleled panoramic view of Alaska's scenic splendor, but an amazing amount of headroom and aisle space as well.

In the late 80s, Princess' new specialization in Alaska travel was reinforced by the opening of the company's first hotel, Harper Lodge Princess (later expanded and renamed Denali Princess Lodge) in 1987; and by the purchase of Sitmar Cruises in 1988, which added four more ships to the fleet.

Since then, the company has opened several new facilities, including the Kenai Princess Lodge (recently expanded) and the Fairbanks Princess Hotel. Given the company's strong ties to Alaska, as well as its outstanding record of success, future development projects can be confidently expected. The current cruise schedule features a total of six ships operating out of San

The Fairbanks Princess Hotel opened in May 1993 on the banks of the Chena River.

The 60-room Kenai Princess Lodge offers spectacular views of the Kenai River and surrounding mountains.

Francisco and Vancouver, B.C., on the ever-popular "Inside Passage" tours of Southeastern Alaska, together with "Voyage of the Glaciers" cruises to Seward. During the 1993 summer season, more than 136,000 Princess passengers traveled on cruises and cruisetours to and within Alaska, increasing the company's capacity by 27 percent, and setting the new industry record in the process.

With the preeminence of Princess Tours and Princess Cruises in the northern market so firmly established, the Princess presence in Alaska is amply demonstrated by the fact that the company boasts more than 850 employees within the state. The ULTRA DOME® rail cars and various Princess hotel and tour facilities are as accessible to residents as they are to visitors — just one more example of the many ways in which Princess Tours and Princess Cruises continue to contribute both to the prosperity and to the quality of life in the Great Land.

The upper-level lounge on the Midnight Sun Express affords 360 degree views from reserved seating.

Princess offers tours throughout the Great Land—Southeast, Kenai, Denali, Prudhoe Bay, the Arctic, and Canada's Yukon.

NANA Regional Corporation

There are few places in the world that still look like they did when the vanguard of European exploration touched their shores. Even rarer are those places where visitors are greeted by indigenous peoples who still honor the values of a traditional culture that predates the European arrival by thousands of years. However, the large expanse of pristine Arctic coastline, tundra and riparian forests of Northwest Alaska is such a place. The Inupiat who have roamed the 36,000 square-mile area for millennia have made it their business, literally, to share their unique culture with visitors from around the world. Indeed, the area may be one of the first visited in North America. Many believe that the Indigenous people of the Americas first came by crossing the Bering Sea into Alaska, into a Region sometimes called "Berengia."

Together, the Inupiat own NANA Corp., a diverse business venture capitalized by proceeds from the Alaska Native Claims Settlement Act of 1971.

In Kotzebue, Alaska, 26 miles above the Arctic Circle, a young Eskimo girl displays the traditional arts of skin sewing and beadwork to an interested visitor. Personal interchange between visitors and local Eskimo people is a highlight of an Arctic Tour. The local sightseeing company, Tour Arctic, is a subsidiary of NANA Regional Corporation, one of thirteen regional native corporations.

That act also confirmed Native title to lands the people had traditionally used for hunting, fishing and gathering.

From the outset, NANA placed a high premium on protecting traditional values and uses of the land. With expertise gained in oil, gas and mineral development, NANA has gained a secure foothold in Alaska's resource industries. Shareholders have also long recognized that tourism might also represent job and revenue potential. Consequently, the corporation developed the high-quality Nullagvik Hotel as well as a unique cultural museum in Kotzebue, the commercial and transportation hub of the region.

Even in their modest beginnings, NANA's tourism ventures set a new standard for cultural attractions. NANA's Tour Arctic conducts a six-hour excursion which includes the NANA Museum of the Arctic; a Culture Camp, where Inupiat Elders pass along their traditions to youngsters; and a walk on the tundra. Research conducted by both industry wholesalers and NANA indicate visitors are highly satisfied with this experience. Building on this success, NANA added tours to the Prudhoe Bay oilfields, which supplies about twenty percent of the nation's oil supply, and more recently ecotourism to the more remote parts of the Region.

A number of events have steadily boosted Alaska's appeal as a visitor destination. As a result, NANA Corporation has seized the opportunity to study the feasibility of adding substantial new experiences to its tour offerings, this time in smaller communities in the region, bringing visitors much closer to the land and its people.

An increasing number of visitors to Alaska are willing to depart the beaten path to explore more remote areas of the state. Many are seeking a unique experience that blends travel in a pristine environment with an intimate look at the traditional culture of the area. Recently, summer visitors to

Visitors enjoy a tundra walk near Kotzebue, sampling wild berries and photographing tundra colors. Tundra tours are featured on Kotzebue excursions.

The Alyeska Prince Hotel has 307 well-appointed guest rooms including three townhouse style suites and a Royal Suite, 1000 square feet of living space excluding the two bedrooms.

from the northern hospitality and professionalism of members of the staff who are trained to anticipate and meet the needs of guests quickly and unobtrusively. Whether it is an inquiry about room service, dinner entrees, ski conditions or activities in the surrounding area, they are ready and willing to serve.

Many visitors are intrigued by the area's gold rush past; the old Iditarod Trail passes nearby and the few remains of a bygone era rust away as the forest reclaims the present. However, the beauty of the Alyeska Prince experience is in the way it points the traveler gently to riches far greater than the gold extracted from the ground: to the clean and fragrant air, to the songs of rushing streams, to the undisturbed comings and goings of lynx, bear, beaver and Dall sheep, to scenery that opens the mind to new possibilities and to good fun with good friends.

of runs like Trapline, Mighty Mite, Mambo, Dogleg, Gear Jammer, Silvertip, Main Street, Ptarmigan Gully, Ego Flats and Von Imhoff Drive. A short walk from the lodge is Chair 7 which conveys visitors both to lower slopes and alternate lifts to the steeper runs, including the covered chairs of the Spirit Quad. With more than 560 inches of snow each year, the resort encompasses 470 acres of skiing heaven, 60 trails and nine lifts with a capacity of nearly 10,000 skiers per hour.

Although Alyeska Prince Hotel was born of the robust fun of an Alaskan winter, the chateau is a home base for adventure all year round. Nearby, visitors can find gold panning, hiking, flightseeing, windsurfing, fishing and much more.

Regardless of the season or the favored pursuits of guests, the amenities of Alyeska Prince Hotel ensure a luxurious visit. More than 300 rooms and four suites are complemented by exercise facilities, an indoor pool and a 18-person whirlpool located in a bay window overlooking the fish pond and the north face of Mt. Alyeska. In an effort to cater to every need, the hotel offers a sundry shop and a logo boutique. There are also meeting and reception facilities for 200 or more people. Airport shuttles are available as well.

While these offerings are impressive and the scenery unforgettable, the warmth of the Alyeska Prince experience flows

Guests enter the Alyeska Prince Hotel through double bronze and glass doors into a lobby that is three stories high. The ceiling is reminiscent of the Alaskan winter sky with twinkling lights resembling stars and lighted effects similar to the Aurora Borealis. An Alaskan scene including a polar bear is represented in the diorama that is also visible from the third floor balcony. Rich cherry wood paneling, granite floors with carpet insets, and Alaskan stone columns create a warm, inviting first impression.

Alaska Sales and Service

"Now." Alaska Sales and Service Dealership today, located on East 5th Avenue.

There is a good reason why Alaska Sales and Service sells more vehicles than all other Anchorage dealers. The reason is service and lots of it. It actually begins before each sale with the informative, respectful and unhurried rapport between staff and prospective customers, and extends long after each sale to insure total satisfaction, both with vehicles and their maintenance.

For more than 50 years, long before it entered the lexicon of today's business gurus, customer service has been the foundation on which the company has built its reputation as a forward-looking, rock-solid firm which stands behind every transaction. Leonard Bryant, president and general manager, notes wryly that even if service falls out of favor with pundits of profitability, he expects it will remain key to the future growth of Alaska Sales and Service as long as it produces results for customer and company.

"When you've been around as long as we have, you can really see trends in your performance, in the cause and effect relationship between how you treat your customers and how often they return," Bryant says. "Return business has been key to our lasting success, and repeat customers flow directly from our high level of integrity, honesty and service. That's not guesswork—that's reflected in 50 years of hard data."

A half century of statewide service also gives the firm a distinct advantage as a northern operation. A long list of satisfied fleet and individual customers attests to the company's ability to put customers into the right rigs for the job, regardless of season, terrain or remote location. A large specialized fleet department not only knows Alaska but maintains an excellent

Leonard Bryant, General Manager/President of Alaska Sales and Service.

rapport with manufacturers to ensure that orders are filled promptly according to specifications.

Alaska Sales and Service stands out as one of the state's most prominent entrepreneurial success stories largely because it has made the concept of service a guiding principle in all arenas, not just the maintenance department with which it is often most associated. It is a full-blooded notion applied with goodwill and professionalism by a highly-trained staff. It has enabled the company to diversify and respond with flexibility to a market that is vastly different than it was when the firm began.

Always Alaskan-owned, Alaska Sales and Service opened in 1944 as a franchise-holder for Chevrolet, Oldsmobile, Pontiac, Cadillac and GMC trucks. The Buick and GEO passenger cars, and both Chevrolet medium duty and GMC medium duty truck lines were added later. The world is a far different place, several times over, than it was in 1944, or even in 1965 when Bryant was a mechanic just starting out with the company. The firm had just opened a new 600,000 square foot location that was literally the talk of the town. In a 28-page, ten cent edition of the Anchorage Times, the facility and its grand opening consumed five pages, three articles and two photos, to

"Then." Alaska Sales and Service Dealership during the late '50s and early '60s, located on the corner of 3rd Avenue and E Street.

say nothing of twenty large congratulatory ads. Most of these were from contractors or vendors extolling the extreme honor of being involved in such a significant project, including one placed by Alaska Aggregate Corporation which conveyed the celebratory mood:

"A dream for the future, interpreted by modern science into a thing of stunning beauty and great functional utility. Built to serve the needs of man for a century to come!"

It sounds grandiose today, but those who were there recall that the agency, where the firm is still headquartered, was truly an eye-opener for a town of only 35,000.

"To have a dealership of that magnitude was something at the time. Every mechanic had three stalls and there was an acre of parking on the roof," Bryant says, his recollections underscoring the working man's appreciation for having a nice place to practice his craft. "It was a facility that could easily handle a heavy workload. This was the premier place to work. It was a big deal, it was enormous. They were building for the future." Bryant feels now that Anchorage has grown to a quarter of a million residents, Alaska Sales & Service continues to build for the future and remains a great place to work.

Alaska Sales and Service has always succeeded where many others have faltered or compromised: being an Alaskan-owned and operated firm with a performance record and reputation that match or exceed the best that big-city agencies the rest of the nation has to offer. Through reliable application of its customer service philosophy, it remains both one of the largest Alaskan-owned companies in the state, and a firm that is consistently top-ranked by industry analysts.

"With more than $100 million in sales annually, and well over 100,000 vehicles sold since we opened, there's nobody in Alaska that comes close," says Bryant. "And not a lot of car dealerships can boast being around for 50 years. You can bet we'll be here another 50 after that."

Alaska Sales and Service employees, all wearing company jackets, at the "500 Sale" kick-off breakfast.

The Captain Bartlett Inn

Years ago, when newcomers arrived in the north, they found a harsh and forbidding land. But they also found something else: a warm, welcoming hospitality that has become renowned throughout the world. This is exactly the spirit offered by The Captain Bartlett Inn in Fairbanks, where the rustic lodge atmosphere invites visitors to relax as the staff delivers warm, friendly, first-class service.

The atmosphere is unique among the hotels available in Alaska's Golden Heart City. From the lobby built of gorgeous Rosy Creek spruce logs to the dining room where a crackling birch log fire glows all winter in the Interior's largest fireplace, The Captain Bartlett Inn provides a cozy, congenial setting where business travelers, tourists and Fairbanksans mingle with the ease of old friends.

"The Captain Bartlett Inn is a place travelers can expect to be greeted by name when they return, and where the staff, in complete confidence, ask, 'How was your stay?'" says general manager Randy Kincaid. "Our entire staff is genuinely friendly. We're really proud of that."

The Captain Bartlett Inn just completed a major renovation of its guest rooms and corridors, utilizing rich hardwood trim and warm textured fabrics designed especially to enhance your senses. Adding to the experience is the unrivaled service provided by The Captain Bartlett Inn. For example, guests are offered complimentary transportation to and from the airport and around the local Fairbanks area. The Captain Bartlett Inn provides facilities and services tailored especially with the corporate traveler in mind. The corporate upgrade extends a free local newspaper and complimentary continental breakfast each morning. On the concierge level, the business suite offers big-screen television and video games, as well as a washer and dryer, vending machine, telephone, modem, and other services that the business traveler hopes for in a lodging facility.

Female executives will also appreciate the consideration of their needs that has gone into the recent design of service improvements. In addition to thoughtful security measures; hair dryers, make-up mirrors and floor length mirrors have been added for that extra touch of comfort and convenience.

"At the end of the day, travelers need to feel like they can really let go. Whether they are tourists who have been taking in the sights all day long, or business people who have been negotiating sales, their relaxation is our specialty," says Kincaid. "The Dog Sled Saloon's rustic decor, nightly honky-tonk piano, and Sourdough bartender "Baldy", bring to life a small town camaraderie. "Slough" Foot Sue's serves an all you can eat seafood buffet that has become famous with locals and tourists. It's a fabulous dining experience and, like the guest rooms, it's a great value, too."

"When it's time to check out, you'll feel like you're leaving home to go home." So, the next time you are in Fairbanks, be sure to bask in the warmth and luxury of The Captain Bartlett Inn... Now that's hospitality!!

"Slough" Foot Sue's serves an all you can eat seafood buffet that has become famous with locals and tourists.

The rustic lodge atmosphere at The Captain Bartlett Inn is unique among the hotels available in Alaska's Golden Heart City.

Santa Clause House

The year was 1949. The city was Fairbanks, in the territory of Alaska. In the back room of a newly established trading post, a young couple found a Santa Claus suit. All summer Con Miller had trekked into Interior Alaska trading for furs. Now, on his first Christmas trip, he donned the suit and brought the spirit of St. Nick to many village children for the first time.

The trading post venture was short lived. As competition in Fairbanks grew, the Millers found themselves quite broke. The newly settled area of North Pole, fourteen miles south, beckoned. In 1952, they bulldozed a place large enough to erect a cache and a tent and began hewing spruce logs.

As Miller and his sons struggled to erect the building, a truck load of village children drove by and called, "Hello, Santa Claus! Are you building a new house?" The Millers looked no futher for a name for their new business. It became "Santa Claus House."

With its unique decor, Alaskan gifts, soda fountain, and groceries, Santa Claus House became a community store and well-known tourist stop. For several years it also housed the North Pole Post Office with Nellie Miller, Con's wife, as postmaster. Con helped launch North Pole as an incorporated city in 1953, and served as its mayor for seventeen years. Two sons, the late Terry Miller, and Mike Miller, both had records of public service in local and state government, with Mike currently serving in the Alaska Senate.

In 1970, the state rerouted the highway leading into Fairbanks, passing by the city and Santa Claus House. Faced again with financial ruin, the Miller family rebuilt on the four-lane highway.

Santa Claus House founders Con and Nellie Miller represented the characters of Mr. & Mrs. Santa to the community for forty years.

After ten years in the new location, growth in the tourist industry led to expansion, with the store being enlarged to more than four times its original size. The larger building brought departmentalizing and the addition of a complete toy shop, Christmas shop, coffee counter, two museum windows, and expansion of the collectibles and gift area. Some twenty-five local people are employed at the peak of the summer season. Winter business emphasizes mail order and the original "Letter from Santa." Santa Claus House is open from March through December. Head salespersons are AlaskaHost trained and customer service is a hallmark. As always, however, the staple of the business has remained the original Alaskan gifts and jewelry section so popular with visitors and Alaskans alike.

Nestled among tall spruce, Santa Claus House's brightly decorated exterior is a frequent photo subject for visitors to the area.

Alaska Marine Highway System

A VERY ALASKAN WAY TO VISIT THE NORTH COUNTRY

The trim blue and white vessel, 418 feet long with hundreds of passengers aboard, glides slowly toward the dock in Ketchikan. Scads of excited visitors, anxious for a first close look at Alaska, crowd the rails. Behind the dock, the city spreads north and south for miles in a long, thin urban crescent, and climbs the lower slopes of otherwise green forested hills and snow-capped mountains.

Shortly, the ship is secure. Passengers stream ashore — on foot, in cars and RV's, in motorcoaches.

These aren't cruiseship tourists. These visitors have come here by ferry, the *Columbia*, from Bellingham, Washington. During the course of a week, others will arrive aboard the *Malaspina*, *Matanuska*, and *Taku* from Prince Rupert, British Columbia. Mostly, they are independent travelers. The economic impact they have on large and little communities is substantial.

They fill local hotels and spill over into Bed and Breakfasts everywhere. They take totem viewing tours in Ketchikan, visit National Historical Park sites in Sitka and Skagway, book glacier-landing helicopter rides in Juneau, see world-class concentrations of bald eagles in Haines, eat their fill at Norwegian smorgasbords in Petersburg, and cruise the wilderness of the Stikine River out of Wrangell. Utilizing the smaller ferries *Aurora* and *LeConte*, they sample Tlingit Indian village and small community life as well.

In Southcentral Alaska, the story is the same. There, the ferries *Tustumena* and *Bartlett* connect the Kenai Peninsula with Prince William Sound, Kodiak Island, and even the misty, mysterious westerly-stretching Aleutian Islands.

The Alaska Marine Highway System (that's what Alaskans call their waterborne network, a *highway*) had its start with the arrival in Southeast Alaska of the *Malaspina* in 1963. The small ferry *Chilkat* operated between Juneau and Haines before then, but had limited impact on the region. Until 1963, most coastal Alaskans relied almost entirely upon air travel; visitors could choose between airliners and cruiseships. Now, more than three decades and eight ferryliners later, travelers can "drive" Alaska's marine highway routes easily, safely, economically, and year-round — stopping off at any of 32 ports for a day or more, then reboarding the system to explore other destinations.

These ships, incidentally, share many of the amenities of their more costly cruiseliner cousins. They include staterooms and convenience shops aboard the largest vessels and passengers on all ships can enjoy spacious viewing lounges, dining facilities, heated solarium decks, and vehicle space. On selected sailings, passengers can hear informative talks by forest and wildlife naturalists and can enjoy art, Native culture, and musical

Kathleen Brezina and Pete, Rachel and Harry Johnson give a traditional Tlingit performance aboard an Alaska Marine Highway vessel. The Arts on Board program brings a variety of artists, dancers, musicians, weavers, carvers and storytellers on sailings to share their talents with ferry passengers.

presentations. No question about it, the ferryliners of the Alaska State Marine Highway offer a unique and very Alaskan way to travel the coastal waterways of the North Country.

Alaska Marine Highway vessels, from the 193-foot M/V Bartlett to the 418-foot M/V Columbia, are large enough to carry passengers and vehicles, be it a bicycle, motorcycle, car or large recreational vehicle.

Sheraton Anchorage Hotel

The Sheraton Anchorage Hotel features extensive Native art displays in the culture of Alaska's Eskimo, Haida, Tlingit, Athabascan and Aleut people.

Alaska is a ruggedly beautiful land with sights, moods and activities to match every imagination. It is a treasure trove of natural resources of global significance, as well as world-class recreational opportunities for all four seasons. It is a place whose rich history, pristine forests, mountains and rivers and unique Native cultures summon adventurers of every stripe from every continent.

Each year more and more business travelers, as well as those exploring Alaska for the fun of it, rely on Anchorage as the hub of their northern trip. With growing frequency, they choose the affordable elegance of the Sheraton Anchorage Hotel as their headquarters for sojourns, sales calls, conventions, or an extra day of skiing or fishing in season added onto their business itinerary.

Operating under the umbrella of Korean Air, the Sheraton's stature continues to grow among international travelers, whether they are visiting Alaska for work, pleasure or both. Situated in a superb downtown location with stunning views of the Chugach Mountains and Cook Inlet, the hotel offers an equally appealing atmosphere in its spacious, warmly lit atrium lobby. Native art murals in Italian marble provide a striking and beautiful complement to the hotel's 378 comfortably appointed rooms.

Although the list of amenities offered at the hotel is a long one, it is interesting to note the features that draw comments from the Sheraton's cosmopolitan clientele. Chief among them are the superb sushi bar in Legends, the hotel's highly-regarded nightclub. Also greatly appreciated are the coffee brewers available in each of the guest rooms. The Sheraton's many repeat customers likewise appreciate convenient access from downtown to the international airport.

Additional features which distinguish the hotel from others in Anchorage include ample parking, and a rate structure that considers the budget of its visitors without sacrificing their comfort and convenience. The Sheraton also boasts the state's largest hotel grand ballroom and a complete menu of convention services.

Perhaps the Sheraton's greatest asset is its welcoming staff. These friendly, professional, service-oriented people understand the needs and desires of the hotel's diverse customers. They know how much the comfort and convenience of guests depends on their prompt, reliable satisfaction of high expectations and they are grateful for the chance to serve.

With these kinds of attributes, in a setting like Alaska, it is no wonder that a major international player in the transportation and tourism industry such as Korean Air would welcome a chance to be part of ITT Sheraton's tradition of Alaskan hospitality.

The 16-story Sheraton Anchorage Hotel, one of Anchorage's most prominent landmarks, is in the heart of downtown, close to business and shopping.

Bibliography

ALYESKA—THE GREAT LAND

Alaska Blue Book 1993-94, Alaska Department of Education, Division of State Libraries, Archives & Museums.

Alaska Official State Guide and Vacation Planner, 1994.

Alaska Official State Map.

Facts About Alaska, the Alaska Almanac®, Alaska Northwest Books.

On Board, passenger publication of the Alaska Railroad, 1993.

Travels in Alaska, John Muir, Houghton Mifflin.

THE GOLDEN PAST

Castner, Lt. Joseph C., Lt. *Castner's Alaskan Exploration*, 1898, Cook Inlet Historical Society, Anchorage, AK, 1984.

Cole Dermot, *Frank Barr: Bush Pilot in Alaska and the Yukon*, Alaska Northwest Publishing Co., Edmonds, WA, 1986.

Cole, Terrence, *E.T. Barnette: The Strange Story of the Man Who Founded Fairbanks*, Alaska Northwest Publishing Co., Anchorage, AK, 1981.

Garfield, Brian, *the Thousand Mile War: World War II in Alaska and the Aleutians*, Doubleday and Co., New York, NY, 1969.

Griffin, John V., *Icy Cape*, Quail Roost Press, Sterling, MA, 1980.

Harkey, Ira, *Pioneer Bush Pilot: The Story of Noel Wien*, University of Washington Press, Seattle, WA, 1974.

Heller, Herbert (ed.), *Sourdough Sagas*, Comstock Editions Inc., Sausalito, CA, 1967.

Herron, Edward A., *Wings Over Alaska: The Story of Carl Ben Eielson*, Simon and Schuster, New York, NY, 1967.

Naske, Claus-M. and Herman E. Slotnick, *Alaska: A History of the 49th State* (2nd Edition), University of Oklahoma Press, Norman/London, 1987.

Potter, Jean, *The Flying North*, Ballantine Books, New York, NY, 1972.

Stuck, Hudson, *Ten Thousand Miles with a Dog Sled*, University of Nebraska Press, Lincoln, NE, 1988.

GETTING FROM HERE TO THERE

Alaska Blue Book 1993-94, Alaska Department of Education, Division of State Libraries, Archives & Museums.

Alaska Intermodal Plan, Survey of the Alaska Transportation Network, 1994, HDR Engineering, Inc., for the Alaska Department of Transportation.

Alaska Official State Guide and Vacation Planner, 1994.

Alaska Railroad 1994 Passenger Services.

The Milepost®, Vernon Publications Inc.

Senior Voice, March 1991.

HOST TO THE WORLD

Jacobin, Lou, *Lou Jacobin's Guide to Alaska and the Yukon*, Alaska Centennial Edition, Guide to Alaska Inc., Anchorage, AK, 1967.

McDonald, Lucille Saunders and Jean Chapman (ed.), *Alaska Steam: A Pictorial History of the Alaska Steamship Co.*, Alaska Geographic Society, anchorage, AK, 1967.

McDowell Group, *Alaska Visitor Statistics Program, Alaska Visitor Expenditures, Summer, 1993*, Alaska Division of Tourism, Juneau, AK, 1984.

McDowell Group, *Alaska Visitor Statistics Program, Alaska Visitor Arrivals, Summer, 1993*, Alaska Division of Tourism, Juneau, AK, 1994.

McDowell Group, *Alaska Visitor Statistics Program, Alaska Visitor Patterns, Opinions and Planning, Summer, 1993*, Alaska Division of Tourism, Juneau, AK, 1994.

Satterfield, Archie, *The Alaska Airlines Story*, Alaska Northwest Publishing Co., Anchorage, AK, 1981.

COMMUNICATION NETWORKS

Alaska Blue Book 1993-94, Alaska Department of Education, Division of State Libraries, Archives & Museums.

ENTREPRENEURIAL SPIRIT

Report to the Legislature, University of Alaska, 1992-93.

CHALLENGES IN THE GREAT OUTDOORS

Alaska - The Inside Passage 1994, Southeast Alaska Tourism Council.

Alaska Wilderness Recreation and Tourism Association Directory of Members.

Chugach National Forest Alaska, U.S. Dept. of Agriculture, Forest Service.

Tongass National Forest, U.S. Dept. of Agriculture, Forest Service.

BRIGHT MINDS AND STRONG IDEAS

Anchorage Daily News 9-4-94, *Summary of Alaska's Public School Districts: Report Card to the Public 1992-93*, Alaska Dept. of Education.

Report to the Legislature, University of Alaska, 1992-93.

Alaska 2000, Alaska Dept. of Education, Summer, 1994.

HARVESTING THE OCEAN

Alaska Seafood Industry, Alaska Department of Economic Development.

Alaska Seafood Industry Study, the McDowell Group for the Alaska Seafood Industry Study Commission.

Alaska Seafood Industry Sector Report, Institute of Social and Economic Research, University of Alaska Anchorage.

Alaska Seafood, 1993 Annual Report, Alaska Seafood Marketing Institute.

Alaska's Wildlife, March-April 1992, Alaska Department of Fishand Game.

Discover Southeast Alaska - Petersburg, brochure, Petersburg Chamber of Commerce.

Fisheries of the United States 1992, published May 1993, U.S.Department of Commerce, National Marine Fisheries Service, National Oceanic and Atmospheric Administration.

ALYESKA—ITS GREAT PEOPLE

Alaska Blue Book 1993-94, Alaska Department of Education, Division of State Libraries, Archives & Museums.

THE RICH FUTURE

Arnold, Robert D., et. al., *Alaska Native Land Claims* (2nd Edition), Alaska Native Foundation, Anchorage, AK, 1978.

McBeath, Gerald A. and Thomas A. Morehouse, *Alaska Politics and Government*, University of Nebraska Press, Lincoln/London, 1994.

Metcalfe, Peter, *Alaska Blue Book, 1993-94*, Alaska Dept, of Education, Juneau, AK 1993.

Naske, Claus-M., *An Interpretive History of Alaskan Statehood*, Alaska Northwest Publishing Co., Anchorage, AK 1973.

Saunders, Dan, *Alaska: Memoir of a Vanishing Frontier*, Avon Books, New York, NY, 1975.

Thompson, Laurie K. and Carolyn Smith (ed.), *Facts About Alaska: The Alaska Almanac* (15th Edition), Alaska Northwest Books, Bothell, WA, 1991.

Partners in Alaska

Companies and organizations dedicated to making Alaska a better place to live, work and do business.

ABR, Inc.
Environmental Research & Services
P.O. Box 80410
Fairbanks, Alaska 99708
Phone: (907) 455-6777
Fax: (907) 455-6781
Page: 268

ASCG Incorporated
301 Arctic Slope Avenue, Suite 100
Anchorage, AK 99518-3035
Phone: (907) 349-5148
Fax: (907) 349-4213
Page: 258

Adams, Morgenthaler and Company, Inc.
3333 Denali Street, Suite 100
Anchorage, Alaska 99503
Phone: (907) 279-0431
Fax: (907) 272-5593
Page: 264

Alaska Credit Union League
4000 Credit Union Drive, Suite 650
Anchorage, Alaska 99503-6647
Phone: (907) 562-1255
Fax: (907) 563-7676
Page: 182

Alaska Division of Economic Development
P.O. Box 110804
Juneau, Alaska 99811-0804
Phone: (907) 465-2017
Fax: (907) 465-3767
Page: 187

Alaska Division of Tourism
P.O. Box 110801
Juneau, Alaska 99811-0801
Phone: (907) 465-2012
Fax: (907) 465-2287
Page: 185

Alaska Forest Association
111 Stedman Street, Suite 200
Ketchikan, Alaska 99901
Phone: (907) 225-6114
Fax: (907) 225 5920
Page: 189

Alaska Home Mortgage, Inc.
P.O. Box 196850
Anchorage, AK 99519-6850
Phone: (907) 563-3033 in Anchorage
Fax: (907) 261-6401
Page: 267

Alaska Humanities Forum
421 West First Avenue, Suite 210
Anchorage, Alaska 99501
Phone: (907) 272-5341
Fax: (907) 272-3979
Page: 188

Alaska Marine Highway System
P.O. Box 25535
Juneau, Alaska 99802-5535
Phone: (907) 465-3946
Fax: (907) 465-2476
Page: 215, 310

Alaska Native Medical Center
Alaska Area Native Health Service
250 Gambell Street
Anchorage, Alaska 99501
Phone: (907) 279-6661
Fax: (907) 257-1168
Page: 274

Alaska Option Services Corporation
P.O. Box 196233
Anchorage, Alaska 99519-6233
Phone: (907) 786-2951
Fax: (907) 276-6398
Page: 256

Alaska Public Radio Network
810 East Ninth Avenue
Anchorage, Alaska 99501-3826
Phone: (907) 277-2776
Fax: (907) 263-7450
Page: 184

Alaska Sales and Service
1300 E. 5th Avenue
Anchorage, Alaska 99501
Phone: (907) 279-9641
Fax: (907) 276-5167
Page: 306

Alaska Seafood Marketing Institute
1111 W. 8th Street, Suite 100
Juneau, Alaska 99801-1895
Phone: (907) 465-5560
Fax: (907) 465-5572
Page: 242

Alaska USA Federal Credit Union
P.O. Box 196613
Anchorage, Alaska 99519-6613
Phone: (907) 277-5577 in Anchorage
Fax: (907) 561-4857
Page: 252

Alyeska Resort
P.O. Box 249
Girdwood, Alaska 99587
Phone: (907) 783-2222
Fax: (907) 783-1090
Page: 304

Architects Alaska
411 W. 4th Avenue, Suite 200
Anchorage, Alaska 99501
Phone: (907) 272-3567
Fax: (907) 277-1732
Page: 271

Arctic Slope Regional Corporation
301 Arctic Slope Avenue, Suite 300
Anchorage, Alaska 99518-3035
Phone: (907) 349-2369
Fax: (907) 349-5476
Page: 226

AVIS Rent a Car
P.O. Box 190028
Anchorage, Alaska 99519-0028
Phone: (907) 243-4300
Fax: (907) 243-2294
Page: 202

Big Three Lincoln Alaska, Inc.
6415 Arctic Blvd.
Anchorage, Alaska 99518-1533
Phone: (907) 563-3133
Fax: (907) 564-9743
Page: 288

The Captain Bartlett Inn
1411 Airport Way
Fairbanks, Alaska 99701
Phone: (907) 452-1888
Fax: (907) 452-7674
Page: 308

Carlile Enterprises, Inc.
1524 Ship Avenue
Anchorage, Alaska 99501
Phone: (907) 276-7797
Fax: (907) 278-7301
Page: 210

Coffman Engineers
550 W. 7th Avenue, Suite 700
Anchorage, Alaska 99501
Phone: (907) 276-6664
Fax: (907) 276-5042
Page: 260

Echo Bay Mines
3100 Channel Drive, Suite 2
Juneau, Alaska 99801
Phone: (907) 586-4161
Fax: (907) 463-5740
Page: 230

GCI
2550 Denali Street, Suite 1000
Anchorage, Alaska 99503-2781
Phone: (907) 265-5600
Fax: (907) 265-5525
Page: 192

Goldbelt, Incorporated
9097 Glacier Highway, Suite 200
Juneau, Alaska 99801
Phone: (907) 790-4990
Fax: (907) 790-4999
Page: 239

Golden Valley Electric Association, Inc.
P.O. Box 71249
Fairbanks, Alaska 99707-1249
Phone: (907) 452-1151
Fax: (907) 451-5633
Page: 211

Ketchikan Pulp Company
7559 North Tongass Highway
P.O. Box 6600
Ketchikan, Alaska 99901
Phone: (907) 225-2151
Fax: (907) 225-8260
Page: 218

Linder Construction
8220 Petersburg Street
Anchorage, Alaska 99507
Phone: (907) 349-6222
Fax: (907) 349-8303
Page: 284

MACtel Cellular System
3900 Denali Street, Suite 100
Anchorage, Alaska 99503-6091
Phone: (907) 563-8000
Fax: (907) 561-5510
Page: 208

Markair
P.O. Box 196769
Anchorage, Alaska 99519-6769
Phone: (907) 266-3609
Fax: (907) 266-3698
Page: 113

Maserculiq Incorporated
P.O. Box 90
Marshall, Alaska 99516
Phone: (907) 679-6512
Fax: (907) 679-6740
Page: 248

Matanuska Telephone Association, Inc.
1740 S. Chugach Street
Palmer, Alaska 99645
Phone: (907) 745-3211
Fax: (907) 746-9676
Page: 204

Minch Ritter Voelckers Architects
800 Glacier Avenue
Juneau, Alaska 99801
Phone: (907) 586-1371
Fax: (907) 463-5544
Page: 270

Municipal Light & Power
1200 East First Avenue
Anchorage, Alaska 99501-1685
Phone: (907) 279-7671
Fax: (907) 263-5804
Page: 206

NC Machinery Company
6450 Arctic Blvd.
Anchorage, Alaska 99519
Phone: (907) 561-1766
Fax: (907) 786-7580
Page: 286

NANA Regional Corporation
1001 E. Benson Boulevard
Anchorage, Alaska 99508
Phone: (907) 265-4100
Fax: (907) 265-4123
Page: 234

NANA Regional Corporation
Tour Arctic Manager
P.O. Box 49
Kotzebue, Alaska 99752
Phone: (907) 442-3301
Fax: (907) 442-2866
Page: 302

National Bank of Alaska
P.O. Box 100600
Anchorage, Alaska 99510
Phone: (907) 265-2963
Fax: (907) 265-2879
Page: 262

Northern Television
A.G. Hiebert, Chairman/CEO
1007 W. 32nd Avenue
Anchorage, AK 99503
Phone: (907) 562-3456
Fax: (907) 562-0953
Page: 198

Ocean Beauty Seafoods Inc.
P.O. Box 70739
Seattle, Washington 98107
Phone: (206) 285-6800
Fax: (206) 281-5897
Page: 244

PTI Communications
3940 Arctic Blvd.
Anchorage, Alaska 99503
Phone: (907) 562-1231
Fax: (907) 561-1325
Page: 214

Petro Marine Services
Harbor Enterprises, Inc.
P.O. Box 389
Seward, Alaska 99664
Phone: (907) 224-3190
Fax: (907) 224-3937
Page: 222

Petro Star Inc.
201 Arctic Slope Avenue, Suite 200
Anchorage, Alaska U.S.A. 99518-3030
Phone: (907) 344-2661
Fax: (907) 267-6429
Page: 228

Princess Cruises and Tours
2815 Second Avenue, Suite 400
Seattle, Washington 98121
Phone: (206) 728-4202
Fax: (206) 443-1979
Page: 298

Santa Claus House
Santa Land
North Pole, Alaska 99705
Phone: (907) 488-2200
Fax: (907) 488-5601
Page: 309

Sea-Land Service, Inc.
2550 Denali Street, Suite 1604
Anchorage, Alaska 99503
Phone: (907) 263-5600
Fax: (907) 274-0430
Page: 200

Sealaska Corporation
One Sealaska Plaza, Suite 400
Juneau, Alaska 99801
Phone: (907) 586-1512
Fax: (907) 586-9223
Page: 236

Sealaska Timber Corporation
2030 Sealevel Drive
Ketchikan, Alaska 99901
Phone: (907) 225-9444
Fax: (907) 225-5736
Page: 238

Sheraton Anchorage Hotel
401 East 6th Avenue
Anchorage, Alaska 99501
Phone: (907) 276-8700
Fax: (907) 279-9142
Page: 311

Superior Plumbing & Heating, Inc.
8861 Elim Street
Anchorage, Alaska 99507
Phone: (907) 349-6572
Fax: (907) 349-4480
Page: 294

Taku Smokeries
550 South Franklin St.
Juneau, Alaska 99801
Phone: (907) 463-4617
Fax: (907) 463-5312
Page: 246

Tesoro Alaska Petroleum Company
3230 "C" Street
Anchorage, Alaska 99503
Phone: (907) 561-5521
Fax: (907) 561-8218
Page: 232

Tundra Times
P.O. Box 92247
Anchorage, Alaska 99509-2247
Phone: (907) 274-2512
Fax: (907) 277-7217
Page: 212

Udelhoven Oilfield Systems Services, Inc.
11401 Olive Lane
Anchorage, Alaska 99515
Phone: (907) 344-1577
Fax: (907) 522-2541
Page: 292

University of Alaska
P.O. Box 755340
Fairbanks, Alaska 99775-5340
Phone: (907) 474-7272
Fax: (907) 474-7273
Page: 276

VECO Corporation
813 W. Northern Lights Blvd.
Anchorage, Alaska 99503
Phone: (907) 277-5309
Fax: (907) 264-8130
Page: 280

Waukesha Alaska Corporation
P.O. Box 111098
Anchorage, Alaska 99511-1098
Phone: (907) 345-6800
Fax: (907) 345-0311
Page: 290

Weaver Bros. Inc.
1611 E. First Street
Anchorage, Alaska 99501
Phone: (907) 278-4526
Fax: (907) 276-4316
Page: 196

World Trade Center
421 West First Avenue,
Suite 300
Anchorage, Alaska 99591
Phone: (907) 278-7233
Fax: (907) 278-2982
Page: 186

Index

A
Adak, 74, 80
Adventure Travel Society (ATS), 108
Aerial Photography, 96
AeroMap U.S., 96
Air Travel, 42
A-J Mine, 92-93
Alaska 2000 Education Initiative, 132
Alaska Aerospace Development Corporation (AADC), 100
Alaska Agriculture College and School of Mines, 124
Alaska Department of Education, 132
Alaska Department of Health and Social Services, 127
Alaska Department of Revenue, 94
Alaska Distance Education Services, 80
Alaska Division of Economic Development, 150
Alaska Division of Tourism, 64, 85
Alaska Earthquake Information Center, 123
Alaska Highway, 45, 47, 49, 74
Alaska Inventors & Entrepreneurs Association, 100
Alaskaland, 38-39
Alaska Lumber and Pulp Company, 93
Alaska Magazine, 85
Alaska Marine Highway System, 10, 12, 22, 44, 47, 48, 71
Alaska National Interest Lands Conservation Act, 39
Alaska Native Claims Settlement Act of 1971, 39
Alaskan Beer Brewery, 99
Alaskan Highways, 47
Alaska Peninsula, 21
"Alaska Seafood Industry," 150
Alaska Seafood Marketing Institute (ASMI), 143-144
Alaska Space Academies, 130
Alaska State Board of Education, 132
Alaska Wilderness Recreation and Tourism Association, 108
Alaska Public Broadcasting Commission, 78
Alaska Public Radio Network, 81
Alaska Purchase, 12
Alaska Railroad, 13, 15, 50, 53, 55, 70
Alaska Range, 18, 67, 74
Alaska's First City, 12
Alaska Science and Technology Foundation (ASTF), 93, 94, 99, 175-176
Alaska Steamship Company, 63
Alaska Telecom Incorporated, 86
Alaska Volcano Observatory, 123
Alcan Highway, 47
Aleut, 26
Aleutian Chain, 80
Aleutian Islands, 10, 13, 21, 22, 28, 33, 36, 79, 126, 136
Alexander Archipelago, 12
Alutiiq Dancers, 68
Alyeska, 10, 30
Alyeska Central School, 131
Alyeska Resort, 116
Amatignak Island, 21
Anchorage, 13, 15, 18, 22, 42, 47, 49, 50, 55, 61, 63, 65, 66, 67, 74, 81, 86, 90, 92, 100, 105, 109, 110, 116, 117, 124, 129, 131, 139, 151, 154, 159, 164
Anchorage Daily News, 81
Anchorage Fur Rendezvous, 15, 17, 106, 117, 161
Anchorage International Airport, 13
Anchorage Visitor Information Center, 64
Angoon, 12
Anthropology, 123
ARCO, 92
Arctic 18, 63, 68, 109
Arctic Circle, 18, 20, 26, 42, 163
Arctic Ocean, 10, 18
Arctic Pak Development, 94
Arctic Region Supercomputing Center (ARSC), 120, 122, 124
Arctic Sounder, 163
Attu Island, 21
Asia, 13, 26
Athabascan, 17, 18, 26, 28, 68, 165
Auke Lake, 55
Aurora Borealis, 85, 96, 117, 123, 158, 168-169
Australia, 146

B
Baranof, 28
Baranof Island, 74
Barrow, 20, 33, 42, 74, 85
Basic Education, 131
Bear, 18, 110; Brown, 22, 116; Polar, 133
Bellingham, Washington, 10, 12, 44
Bergman, Ingrid, 26, 33
Bering Glacier, 10, 51
Bering Land Bridge, 120, 154, 163
Bering Sea, 13, 18, 21, 26, 77, 118-119, 134-135, 144-145, 170, 171
Bering Straits, 18, 26
Bering, Vitus, 28, 44
Bethel, 42, 81, 160
Bethel Flats, 154
Bidarkas, 44
Big Diomede, 18
Big Lake, 15
Bodega y Quadra, 30
Bradley Lake Dam, 120-121
Bristol Bay, 30
British Columbia, 10, 12

Brooks Range, 20
Bull Caribou, 63
Bull Walrus, 15
Bush Flying, 33, 42
Buschmann, Peter, 136, 150

C
Calving, 106
Camping, 110, 161
Canada, 146
Canoe, 44, 110
Cape Spencer, 74
Caribou, 18, 110, 116
Carter, Jimmy, 39
Celebration, 162-163
Char, 115
Chatanika, 27
Chesapeake, 136
Chilkat Dancers, 157
Chilkat Oil Company, 92
Chilkoot Pass, 31
Chilkoot Trail, 60
Chistochina, 32
Chitina, 49, 70
Chugach National Forest, 115
Chugach State Park, 15
Chukchi Seas, 26
Chocolate Lily, 127
Circumpolar Regions, 126
Clam Gulch, 15
Clams, 147, 164
Coal, 18, 44
Coastline, 10
Cod, 141, 148, 171
Cold-Region Engineering, 168
Colville River, 63
Communication Infrastructure, 76
Computer, 99, 120
Construction, 93
Contact Creek, 47
Cook Inlet, 15, 30, 53, 90-91, 92, 115
Cook, Captain James, 30
Copper, 90

Copper Mines, 64
Copper River, 92
Cordova, 30, 92, 136
Crab, 22, 134-135, 136, 144-145, 147, 149, 170
Crackerjack Mine, 97, 171
Cray Y-MP M98 (Cray Supercomputer), 120, 122
Crosson, Joe, 42
Crow creek Mine, 30
Cruiseships, 22, 44

D
Dall Sheep, 29, 116
Dalton Highway, 20, 50
DAT/EM Systems International, 96, 97
Dawson Creek, B.C., 49
Dead Horse Gulch, 55
Delta Junction, 49, 74
Denali, 10, 67
Denali National Park and Preserve, 15, 16, 18, 49, 53, 61, 110, 117
Dillingham, 164
Dixon Entrance, 12
Dredge, 37
Ducks: Shovellers, 97
Dutch Harbor, 21, 36, 42, 79, 136

E
Eagles, 177
Eagle River, 15, 63
Earp, Wyatt, 26, 32
Earth Stations, 80
Eco-Tourism, 68
Educational Network, 127
Egan Convention Center, 61
Egegik, 50, 136
Eielson, Colonel Carl Ben, 42
Eisenhower, Dwight, 37
Electrical Power Generation, 94
Ellis, Bob, 42
Eskimo, 18, 20, 37, 92, 101, 122, 152-153, 154, 159, 161

Europe, 13, 77
Eyak, 26
Exit Glacier, 65
Experimental Farm, 129

F
Factory Ships, 148
Fairbanks, 10, 13, 15, 18, 20, 27, 31, 32, 37, 39, 42, 49, 50, 53, 55, 58, 71, 81, 85, 86, 97, 100, 116, 117, 120, 131, 154, 159, 163, 164, 172
Far North, 10, 18, 20, 42, 96
Ferry, 44
Film Production, 82, 85
Finite Technologies of Anchorage, 99
Fisheries, 64
Fishing: Commercial, 22, 34, 44 90, 93, 164, 171; Pleasure, 15, 65, 108, 109, 115, 136-151, 160; Processing, 143
Fish Traps, 34, 37, 140
Fjords, 64
Flight Seeing, 65
Floatplanes, 49, 55, 109, 115
Float Trip, 63
Fort Ross, California, 29
Fur Trade, 28, 90, 164, 171

G
Galaup, Jean-Francois de, 30
Galena, 132
Gates of the Arctic, 110, 117
Geology, 124-125
Geophysical Institute, 122, 123, 124, 133, 168-169, 173
GeoSpace Environmental Data Display Center, 123
George Parks Highway, 49
Gillnet, 147
Girdwood, 110, 114, 116, 156
Glacier Bay, 67, 93, 161
Glacier Bay National Park, 52-53, 154
Glacier Route, 47

Glaciers, 10, 12, 52, 60, 64, 65, 67, 76
Great Land, 10, 22, 58, 157
Gold, 18, 31, 32, 33, 61, 63, 90, 92-92, 102, 136, 156, 164, 172
Golden Heart City, 71
Gold Mines, 27, 64
Gold Rush, 20, 70
Golf, 109
Grayling, 115
Groundfish, 141, 146, 148
Gulf of Alaska, 10, 47, 92, 171
Gustavus, 154, 156

H
Haida, 12, 26
Haines, 10, 12, 48, 50
Haines Highway, 50
Haines Junction, 50
Halibut, 115, 136, 140, 141, 144, 146, 150, 161, 164, 171
Hawaii, 13, 21, 136
Healy, 55
Helicopters, 45
Herring, 139, 144, 147, 163, 171
Hiking, 110, 160
Hockey, 124
Hollywood, 33
Homer, 13, 15, 20, 92, 120-121
Homestead Agriculture, 18
Honolulu, 13, 15
Hoonah, 12, 74
Hope, 70
Horned Puffins, 71
Houston, 13, 15
Hudson's Bay Company, 92, 101
Hughes, Howard, 25
Hunting, 18, 108, 116, 160, 161
Hurricane Gulch, 53
Huskies, 49, 154
Hydro Alaska, 94
Hyperbolic Paraboloid, 131

I
Ice Climber, 69
Ice Fields, 67, 76
Ice Sculpture, 17
Icy Straits Packing Company, 136
Iditarod, 32
Iditarod Sled Dog Race, 15, 17, 22, 52, 55, 70, 81, 108, 154
Illiamna Village, 32-33
Immaculate Conception Church, 15
Independence, 70
Independence Mine, 110
Indian, Alaska, 46
Institute for Circumpolar Studies (ICHS), 126-7
Inside Passage, 47, 49, 154, 175
Inspiration Point, 55
International Pacific Halibut Commission, 146
Intrastate Communication, 85
Intercontinental Cable, 77
Interior Alaska, 10, 15, 17, 18, 49, 96
Inupiaq, 26
Inupiat, 68

J
Jackson, Nathan, 160
Japan, 21, 117
"Journeys to Alaska", 60, 61
Juneau, 12, 13, 32, 42, 47, 55, 65, 74, 78, 80, 81, 85, 92-93, 99, 106, 109, 116, 124, 131, 151, 154, 156, 159, 161, 163, 164
Juneau Empire, 81

K
Kalifonsky, 15
Kake, 12
Kaktovik, 163
Kalamazoo, 78
Katalla, 92
Katmai National Park and Preserve, 19, 21

Kayaking, 110, 161
Kenai, 15, 29, 70, 131
Kenai Peninsula, 15, 31, 90, 92, 117
Kennecott Glacier, 34
Kennecott Mine, 34
Ketchikan, 12, 42, 47, 70-71, 74, 78, 92, 93, 124, 136
Ketchikan Pulp and Timbermill, 94
King, Jeff, 55
Kitch Kawk, 35
Klondike, 31, 44, 90, 136
Klondike Gold Rush of 1898, 12, 31
Klawock, 12, 163
Kobuk River, 109, 110
Kobuk Valley National Park, 110
Kodiak, 21, 22, 29, 50, 68, 70, 100, 101, 136, 154, 164
Kodiak Bear, 21
Kodiak Island, 21, 100
Kotzebue, 20, 44, 58, 78, 85, 161
Kotzebue Sound, 20
Kuskokwin 300, 160

L

Lake Bennett, B.C., 55
Lakes, 76
Last Great Race on Earth, 15
LeConte Glacier
Legislative Information Offices, 85
Legislative Teleconference Network, 86
Legislature, 132
Lena Point, 74
Lend Lease, 33
Little Diomede Island, 18
Little Norway, 12
Living Culture, 67
LLR Technologies of Anchorage, 94
Long Distance Education, 127-129
Los Angeles, 74
Low Bush Cranberries, 68

M

Magazines, 77, 83
Malaspina Glacier, 10
Marshall, 32
Matanuska Glacier, 65
Matanuska-Susitna, 131
Matanuska Telephone Association, 83
Matanuska Valley, 15, 116
McCarthy, 49
McCarthy Road, 49
McNeil River, 22
Media, 81
Mega Liners, 44
Mendenhall Glacier, 65, 106
Mendenhall Lake, 106, 161
Mendenhall River, 106
Merrill Field, 96
Metlakatla, 12
Mica, 90
Microwave Station, 72-73
Mid-Atlantic, 136
Midnight Sun, 64
Military, 78, 93, 164
Mining, 18, 26, 34, 70, 90, 93, 172
Misty Fjords, 49
Monkey Flowers, 47
Montgomery Lab, 99, 127
Moose, 42, 110, 116
Moosing, 50
Mountain Goats, 116
Mt. Edgecumbe Residential School, 131
Mt. Fairweather, 124-125
Mt. Marathon, 161
Mt. McKinley, 8-9, 10, 16, 56-57, 58, 67, 74, 104-105, 110, 162, 166-167
Muir, John, 10, 12
Murre, 65
Mushing, 17, 55, 61, 116, 117, 157, 160, 161

N

NASA, 123
Naknek, 136
National Marine Fisheries Service, 146
Native Land Rights, 37
Newspapers, 77
New Stuyahok, 30
New York, 74
Ninilchik, 15
Nixon, Richard, 26, 37
Nome, 15, 20, 22, 31, 32, 42, 58, 63, 71, 85
Northern Lights, 85, 96, 117, 158, 168-169
North Slope, 22, 50, 53, 163
Norton Sound, 20
Nulato, 29

O

Oil, 15, 18, 37, 44, 86, 90, 92, 93, 164, 168, 170, 171, 172, 175
Oil Rig, 28-29
Old Crow Creek Mine, 114, 156
Oomiak, 44
Oregon, 74
Oregon Steamship Company, 60
Otter, 29, 44
Otter Sound, 151
Otto Geist Museum, 124
Oysters, 151

P

Pacific Northwest, 42, 44
Pacific Coast Steamship Company, 60
Palmer, 15, 55, 110
Pan American, 42, 44
Pedro Creek, 26
Perez, Juan, 29
Permanent Fund, 170, 171
Petersburg, 12, 42, 136
Petersburg Harbor, 17
Petersburg's Little Norway Festival, 162
Pike, 115

Placer Mining, 102
Pochnoi Point, 21
Poker Flat Optical Observatory, 123
Poker Flat Research Range, 123, 173
Population, 76
Portage Glacier, 65, 66
Portage Lake, 66
Port Hardy, B.C., 161
Portland, Oregon, 34, 60
Post, Wiley, 26, 31, 32, 42
Potlatch Dancing Costumes, 33
Pribilof Islands, 13, 21
Prince of Wales Island, 30, 90, 97, 99, 151, 171
Prince Rupert, B.C., 10, 12, 44, 55
Prince William Sound, 15, 20, 26, 30, 47, 67, 115, 139
Promyshlenniki, 29
Prospectors, 31, 32
Prudhoe Bay, 13, 18, 20, 37, 50, 88-89, 92, 101, 163, 169, 171, 172, 177
Pt. Adolphus, 74
Pt. Barrow 18, 20, 21, 31
Public Radio, 81
Public Television, 81
Pulp, 93, 100

Q

Queen Charlotte Islands, B.C., 29

R

Radio, 77, 83
Rafting, 106
Rail Belt, 55
Rain Forest, 68
RangeMapper, 99
RATNET, 81
Red Dog Mine, 172
Red Fox, 58
Resurrection Bay, 15, 115
Resurrection Creek, 32

Retail, 93
Revillagigedo Island, 30
Richfield Oil Corporation, 92
Rivers, 76
Rockets, 101, 123, 173
Rogers, Will, 26, 31, 32, 42
Round Island, 15
Ruby, 32
Rural Alaska Television Network, 81
Russia, 18, 21, 22, 28, 29, 31, 33, 44, 58, 139
Russian Academy of Sciences, 127
Russian America, 12
Russian America Company, 90, 92
Russian Fur Hunters, 28, 70
Russian Magadan Region Ministry of Health, 127
Russian Orthodox Church, 29, 31, 159
Russian Ferry Pilots, 32

S

Salmon, 22, 32, 34, 110, 115, 136, 138, 139, 140, 142-145, 161, 164, 171
Salmon Canneries, 64
Salt Chuck Mine, 99
San Francisco, 60, 90, 151
Satellite, 78, 80, 101
Satellite Delivery Television, 81
Satellite Revolution, 78, 80
Saxman, 12
Scallops, 147
Scidmore, Eliza Ruhamah, 61
Seafood Processing, 136, 143
Seafood Safety, 144
Seal: 29, 44, 164; Fur, 90; Harbor, 93
Sea Lions, 29, 168
Seattle, Washington, 34, 44, 47, 55, 151, 156
Seiner, 147, 148
Semisopochnoi Island, 21
Seward, 13, 15, 47, 55, 65, 71, 74, 136

Seward, William H., 31
Seward's Folly, 90
Shaktoolik, 81
Shelikof, 28
Shellfish, 147
Shields, Mary, 17
Shrimp, 136, 147
Shriners Hospital, Galveston, Texas, 127
Siberia, 44, 77
Silver Bay, 32
Simmons, Shell, 42
Sitka, 12, 29, 30, 32, 35, 59, 61, 70, 93, 124, 131
Sitka Christmas Boat Parade, 161
Skagway, 10, 12, 50, 55, 60, 67, 70, 90, 151
Ski: 160; Cross-country, 110, 116, 161; Downhill, 108, 116; Nordic, 116; Resorts, 108
Snow Machines, 116, 160
South-Atlantic, 136
Southcentral Alaska, 10, 13, 15, 20, 26, 34, 49, 66, 71, 172
Southeast Alaska, 10, 12, 17, 26, 42, 47, 52, 60, 67, 68, 71, 100, 115, 172
Southwest Alaska, 10, 21, 22, 42, 132
Soviet Union, 127
Space Technology, 168
Spitsbergen, Norway, 42
Statehood, 34
Statehood Act, 37
Sternwheeler, 18
St. Petersburg, 28
Sub-Arctic, 68
Sub-Arctic Tundra, 10, 18
Subsistence Lifestyle, 18, 164
Sullivan Arena, 67
Sunrise, 32
Sunshine, 70
Surimi, 146, 148
Swanson River, 92

T

Taku Glacier, 61
Talkeetna, 15, 110
Tanana River, 18
Telecommunications, 74, 76, 86, 93, 168
TeleClass, 129
Telecourses, 129
Telephone, 77
Television, 77
Tesoro, 92, 96
Timber, 44, 90, 92, 93, 100, 164, 172-173, 175
Tlingit, 12, 26, 33, 35, 163
Tok, 74
Tongass National Forest, 93, 100, 115
Totems, 64, 68, 70, 160
Tourism, 58-71, 93, 106-117, 164, 168, 175
Trans-Alaska Pipeline, 15, 37, 39, 96, 170, 177
Travels in Alaska, 10
Trawls, 147
Treaty of Cession, 31
Trout, 115
Tsimshian, 12, 26
Tundra, 18, 22, 110
Tundra Trucks, 53
Tundra Vole Software, 97
Turnagain Arm, 30

U

Umiak, 12, 152-153
Unakwik Inlet, 139
Unalaska,. 21
United Kingdom, 146
United States, 31
Unocal, 92
University of Alaska, 18, 59, 78, 83, 120, 122, 123, 124, 129, 130, 131, 132, 133, 168-169, 173
U.S. Department of Defense, 78, 120
U.S. Forest Service, 115

V

Valdez, 13, 15, 20, 30, 50, 53
Valdez Creek, 32
Valdez Mountains, 154
Valley of 10,000 Smokes, 19
Vancouver, B.C., 44, 47
Virginia, 74
VSAT Uplinks, 76

W

Walrus, 44
Washington State, 10
Wasilla, 15
Waterborne Commerce, 44
Wave Energy Corporation, 94
West, Chuck, 58
Western Arctic Herd, 110
Western Union, 77
Whale: Bowhead, 44
Whalers, 31
Whale Hunt, 161, 163
White Birch, 86
Whitehorse, Canada, 74
White Pass & Yukon Route, 54, 55, 63, 71
White Pass Summit, 55
Whittier, 15, 53, 55
Wien, Noel, 42
Wildlife Magazine, 136
World Championship Open Sled Dog Race, 15
World War II, 33, 37, 47
Wrangell, 12, 14, 42, 77, 164
Wrangell Narrows, 136

Y

Yakataga, 92
Yakutat, 12
Yukon, 10, 26, 44, 50, 90, 136
Yukon River, 18, 29, 132
Yukon Territory, 18
Yupik, 26, 68
Yupiit School District, 132, 133